La Pérouse

Pacific Explorer

Pacific Explorer

The Life of Jean-François de La Pérouse
1741-1788

John Dunmore

Naval Institute Press

© J. Dunmore Ltd

First published in 1985
by
The Dunmore Press Limited
P.O. Box 5115
Palmerston North
New Zealand.

Published and distributed in
the United States of America and Canada
by
the Naval Institute Press
Annapolis, Maryland 21402

Library of Congress Catalog Card No. 85-60578
ISBN 0-87021-519-1

Previous pages: La Pérouse's ship anchored at Maui, Hawaii.

This edition is authorized for sale only
in the United States and its
territories and possessions and Canada.

Printed by Kerslake, Billens & Humphrey Ltd, and bound by L.D. Hanratty Ltd.

Contents

Allegorical frontispiece to the Atlas of the Voyage *published in 1797. The traditional element of apotheosis is muted by the expressions of sorrow of the various figures.*

(Courtesy Alexander Turnbull Library)

ATLAS
DU
VOYAGE
DE
LA PÉROUSE

Albi and the river Tarn.

1
The Young Jean-François

ALBI is a gentle town, somnolent under the warm sun of south-west France, nestling in a curve of the river Tarn. Local pride and devotion have saved its medieval heart from destruction: the narrow streets wind their way as they did five hundred years ago, the soft pink of the old brick buildings aglow in their own shade.

A survey of Languedocian towns in the mid-eighteenth century estimated its population at '1936 hearths' or approximately 10,000 souls. Albi's population today is five times greater, spilling out from the old centre towards new anonymous suburbs, and even reaching out to the Go where Jean-François de Galaup was born on 23 August 1741.

His birthplace still stands today, scarcely changed after more than two hundred years. It is an austere square building, double-storied, with an inner courtyard defended by high stone walls and a blank-faced gate. The windows are few and narrow, giving an impression more of a fortress than of the summer residence it was once. The river runs past, a couple of hundred yards away, barely concealed by a tangle of trees and bushes, and rich meadows on all sides beckon children to play or the grown-ups to organize a country fête.

The Galaups had taken to spending an increasing portion of their time at the Go, which lay a mere five kilometres from town. The summer months saw them there, from May until the leaves began to turn yellow and fall into the waters of the Tarn in late September. The Galaups were well-to-do, owning two houses in Albi and two vineyards in addition to the Go property and a small farm — the *métairie* of La Pérouse which was to provide a new patronymic for Jean-François and, through him, to become immortalized. Of these properties the Go manor was the most valuable: when La Pérouse's estate was divided after his death, the Go was estimated at 70,300 francs out of a net worth of 126,300 francs; during the years 1783-

85, prior to his departure for the Pacific, it had brought him in an income of 1900 *livres*. The *métairie* of La Pérouse was worth less than half, being valued at just under 27,000 francs for probate purposes.

The stern aspect of the Go house was less a consequence of unimaginative architectural design than a reflection of local history. The austere manor was the heart of an extensive farm unit — much more extensive than at present — stretching out on three sides to the banks of the Tarn. Enclosed in a loop of the river, it had its own strategic value and dominated, albeit in a modest way, an ancient river crossing to the nearby settlement of Lescure; the word *guo* in southern French means 'a ford'.

By the time the Go was built, the troubled history of the Albigeois district was receding into the past, but it had left its imprint on the minds of the people, the most impressive evidence of this being Albi Cathedral, which rises like a stark crucifix-shaped medieval dungeon standing 150 metres high, with, at its side, an even more fortress-like bishop's palace complete with ramparts and guard towers, the human element happily retained by the use of the typical small flat bricks and by quiet formal gardens and courtyards. Even in the town, watchtowers still remain, staring out at the horizon as if at any time the dust of an advancing enemy column might still appear, rising up from the shimmering haze.

They had all come here in their day — Roman legions, barbarian tribes, warring barons, English troops, and in the thirteenth century an entire crusade bent on eradicating the strange Manichean religion which had spread all through the region, to Toulouse, Castres and a host of lesser towns, becoming known as the Albigensian heresy and now to be totally destroyed by blood and fire with all the stark cruelty that marks military campaigns in which greed is mixed with intolerance. Albi itself had emerged comparatively unscathed out of the Albigensian crusade; it became a loyalist stronghold, run by the bishop, collecting royal grants and privileges, and fortunate because of its location and its defences, to resist all attempts by the English to capture it during the Hundred Years War.

When the worst of the troubled times ended (the main dangers then lying further to the south where the Spanish still occasionally threatened) Albi settled down to quiet prosperity. The vineyards provided a good if unspectacular wine, the crops had seldom to contend with excessive storms or droughts, and the river was navigable enough for some profitable trade. The fortunes of the Galaups rose with the town's. At first merchants, they moved towards the law, occasionally venturing into medicine. Typical burghers, they kept their contacts with every area of profit, be it land, trade or the professions.

The first Galaup to appear in extant town records was Huc who became a member of the Albi town council — a *consul* in 1478 and again in 1487. A family tradition was beginning — his sons Jehan and Pierre were both *consuls*, in 1503 and in 1520 and 1527 respectively. Prior to his consulship, Pierre, who is listed as a merchant, had been appointed 'captain of the health service' in the plague years of 1507 and 1517. It is probable that Jehan died during one of these plague epidemics, as no further mention occurs.

Pierre Galaup probably died around 1530. His son Ramon served as *consul* in 1552, but it is Jean, Ramon's brother, or possibly his first cousin, who provides us with more tangible evidence of the family's rising fortunes. In 1558 this Jean de Galaup signed a contract for the purchase of an estate at Orban from the Cardinal de Clermont. He was named as 'Seigneur et Baron de Brens et de Saint-Félix' and his claim to nobility on grounds of the ownership of land was recognized by a document dated 18 August 1558.

At this point, therefore, the Galaups acquire the yearned-for-nobiliary particle. His descendants, including Jean-François, would be known as 'de Galaup'. Typically, however, the *de* was more prized by the bourgeoisie than by the hereditary nobility. In 1579 the Ordonnance de Blois stated that the purchase of a fief with associated rights and privileges did not *ipso facto* confer the status of noble to the purchaser. Clearly, the king was becoming concerned about unwarranted assumptions of nobility which tended to erode his own powers, since ennoblement was a prerogative he found useful as a bargaining counter and as a means of rewarding a loyal servant. What had in fact begun was a trend which continued to gather strength in subsequent years and became almost uncontrollable in the eighteenth century. The middle class, anxious to share the social and economic advantages of the aristocracy, tried by every means to assume an appearance of patronymic nobility. We shall see later how Jean-François' father followed the general trend.

Jean de Galaup's entry into the provincial nobility could hardly be fairly challenged: the family had held office over three generations, and magistrates were entitled to become 'anoblis par leurs fonctions' after an equal period of service. He apparently made no claim to the more pretentious title of Baron de Brens, which oddly enough reappears years later in a notarial document of 1780 relating to La Pérouse's house in Albi, where he is referred to as 'Messire Jean-François de La Peyrouze de Galaup, baron de Brens'.

The rise of the Galaups becomes more evident in the next generation. Jean's son Claude was *consul* in 1585, 1590 and 1599, and first consul — or mayor — in 1611; he married Catherine de Ciron, the daughter of a magistrate, and bought the Go property. Claude's younger sister, Lavezonne, married Clement de la Jonquière in 1605, thereby establishing a clear link with the landed and more ancient nobility. By then the family had its coat-of-arms — 'gules with a galloping horse argent above a *terrasse de sinople'*.[1]

His own son Jean was elected first consul in 1628 and again in 1643; his wife Jeanne Le Brun was herself the daughter of a first consul, François Le Brun, who had held the office in 1604, 1616 and 1625. In the next generation Pierre de Galaup, a 'doctor and lawyer', was to marry Catherine-Isabeau de Carrière, the daughter of a captain in the Ventadour regiment and a man whose links with the nobility were stronger, for if the Galaups belonged to the 'gown nobility' — the *noblesse de robe* — the Carrières belonged to the more highly regarded 'sword nobility' — the *noblesse d'épée*.

The link was strengthened in the next generation when Jean-Antoine de Galaup, La Pérouse's grandfather, married Claire de Metge in 1704: her father was a captain in the cavalry. When his wife died, Jean-Antoine moved over to the Church: taking holy orders he became Canon of St Salvy, a thirteenth century church with quiet elegant cloisters made for rest and meditation, and close to the more

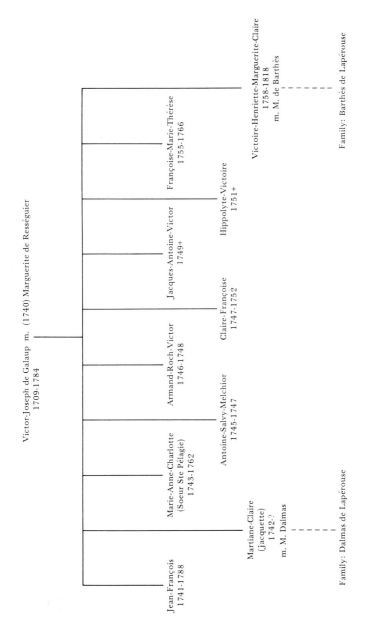

Victor-Joseph de Galaup m. (1740) Marguerite de Rességuier
1709-1784

Jean-François
1741-1788

Martiane-Claire
(Jacquette)
1742-?
m. M. Dalmas

Family: Dalmas de Lapérouse

Marie-Anne-Charlotte
(Soeur Ste Pélagie)
1743-1762

Antoine-Salvy-Melchior
1745-1747

Armand-Roch-Victor
1746-1748

Claire-Françoise
1747-1752

Jacques-Antoine-Victor
1749+

Hippolyte-Victoire
1751+

Françoise-Marie-Thérèse
1755-1766

Victoire-Henriette-Marguerite-Claire
1758-1818
m. M. de Barthès

Family: Barthès de Lapérouse

The Galaup Family

Marguerite de Resseguier, mother of La Pérouse.

The Go, La Pérouse's birthplace.

imperious cathedral. The Galaup family had by now moved away from direct involvement in trade. They had money, property, connections. They could not be termed wealthy in an age when the rich were overwhelmingly so, but in the setting of their own town and district they were well-to-do, influential in local matters and local administration. But they were still members of the bourgeoisie for fiscal purposes: Victor-Joseph, father of La Pérouse, was one of the most highly taxed citizens of Albi, an unsought honour which he shared with his father and grandfather. There were ways and means of reducing the burden or avoiding taxes altogether, such as entering the ranks of the 'true' nobility or joining the king's service. The irresistible ascension of the Galaups was bringing them closer to that goal, generation by generation. It was Victor-Joseph's great hope that his son would reach it. He was often disappointed by a son who seemed to set little store by it; he was fortunate to die before the outbreak of the great Revolution which, by abolishing the age-old privileges of the aristocracy, destroyed the *bourgeois gentil-hommes*' dreams with it.

Jean-Antoine and his own father had married the daughters of army captains. Victor-Joseph went one better: he married Marguerite de Rességuier, daughter of the colonel commanding the famed regiment de Condé. Jean-François de Galaup was their first-born.

There was some fear at first that the baby might not survive. It was a time when child mortality was high: the Galaups were to have ten children in all; only three of them were to reach adulthood. Jean-François was provisionally baptised — *ondoyé* — soon after his birth. It was a lay ceremony, the very basic admission of a child into the Church, as there was no chapel near the Go. The formal christening was held nearly two months later, on 6 October 1741, when the family moved back into town from their summertime residency. The godfather was old Fr Jean-Antoine, the boy's grandfather, although the ceremony was not held at his own church of St Salvy but in the parish church of St Julien. The somewhat elaborate baptismal font of St Salvy still exists today, but nothing is left of St Julien's church which was razed during the Revolution of 1789.

Jean-François spent his first fifteen years in Albi or at the Go.

His earliest education may have been the work of his mother, in between her numerous confinements, for she had a daughter born in 1742, another in 1743, a son in 1745 and another in 1746, followed by a daughter in 1747 and a further son in 1749. He probably attended a small school near his home in the Rue de l'Ecole-Mage. In 1750 he entered the Jesuit College in Albi, which today is the large State-run Lycée Lapérouse. He remained there for six years.

We know little of his school years: the Jesuits were to be expelled in 1764 and the Revolution helped to scatter what records were kept. We can assume that he was an average pupil, more gifted in mathematics, since he found his later studies of the science of navigation fairly easy to master, than in French — his spelling is endearingly erratic and his syntax uneven. We can visualize him roaming through the narrow streets of Albi, getting into scrapes with his friends — one of whom was Pascal de Rochegude, also born in 1741, who would end his life as an admiral and local benefactor — and inviting them to the Go for the summer months. They talked of the Austrian War which had recently ended, re-enacted distant victories and defeats, daydreamed of future battles in the West Indies or the East. They were boys from important local families, but boys first and foremost, boasting, planning, arguing about the world with the soft singing accent of south-west France, which we may assume, toned down though it was by his upper middle-class environment, La Pérouse never lost.

Only one anecdote remains from his schooldays, probably apocryphal at that, but it fits the image of a strong-willed, quick-witted youth. Discipline at the College was maintained by one Musson whose energetic floggings had earned him the nickname of *Bras-de-fer* — 'arm of iron'. Young Galaup, when a teacher threatened to send him to Musson to be punished, for some misdemeanour, replied: 'I will meet this arm with a backside of brass'.

In December 1756, having just turned fifteen, Jean-François de Galaup left his native town to join the Navy.

At first sight, the decision was a strange one. Albi is a typical

A street in Albi

inland town, 300 kilometres from the Atlantic and 150 from the Mediterranean. The Tarn was only navigable to small riverboats and young Galaup would have seen nothing larger. There was no tradition of seagoing in his family and although the Albigeois district can boast of being the birthplace of several admirals, none of them preceded La Pérouse. This is not to say that the district had given no recruits to the French navy, whether the royal or the merchant, although one does not have to go as far as did Emile Ripert to seek a motivation, who in a speech given for the bicentennial of La Pérouse's birth spoke of the Albigensians as 'mystics since the eleventh century . . . for whom the sea presents the attraction of the infinite.'[2] The people of the region are essentially men of the land and the Galaups were men of their town above all else.

The first point to bear in mind is the limited range of opportunities available to Jean-François and acceptable to his socially-conscious father. Trade was to avoided: it was no longer necessary for the family fortunes and it was too much of a middle-class activity. The law, superior at that time to medicine which was generally so incompetently practised as to be socially ill-considered, required greater scholarly application than the boy had displayed at the Jesuit college. It was moreover a sedentary occupation, even more narrowing to the mind in the context of a small country town, and it would not have suited his character. The Church was equally unsuitable from the family's point of view: Jean-François was not just the Galaup's eldest son — and eldest sons were seldom encouraged into the Church — he was their only surviving boy. Antoine had died in 1747 at the age of two, Armand in 1748 at the same age; Jacques born in 1749 had survived for a mere twelve days. If Jean-François entered the Church, clerical celibacy would ensure that the proud family name would die with him. There was the added and not inconsiderable factor that he had no vocation: later evidence shows him to have been a lukewarm Christian, rather more interested in the arguments of the *philosophes* of his day than in theology. It was left to his younger sister Marie-Anne-Charlotte to represent her family in the Church: she entered a convent at Albi, taking the name of Sister Pélagie, although she did not survive beyond her novitiate, dying at the *hospice* not long after her eighteenth birthday.

This left the army or the navy. There were numerous precedents for the former. The Galaups had married into military families for three generations. One can sense his mother urging him gently towards the career which had been her father's. There were, it is true, certain problems: the very fact that an army career was highly considered, that the foreign polices of Louis XIV and Louis XV had been based on military strength, that service in the army was expected of the nobility, and that it was in fact the basis of the feudal structure, meant that advancement came more easily to the highly born that to the aspiring minor nobleman. The transition from *noblesse de robe* to *noblesse d'épée* was not so easily achieved, especially at a time when the aristocracy was determined to hold on to its remaining privileges. How far Jean-François could progress in the army was uncertain. In addition, an army career, especially in the earlier years, would be expensive to foster, because so many young officers came from wealthy aristocratic backgrounds and viewed army life as a mere extension of court life.

Had Jean-François opted for the army, Victor-Joseph would have agreed because of the social progression it implied, although his bourgeois background would have rued the heavy cost. The navy, which Jean-François and his young friend Rochegude both picked, was socially desirable, since the general rule was that only those who could give evidence of noble birth were allowed in the officer corps, and it would entail lesser expenses. There was, moreover, a family link with the service, which may have been the crucial factor in Jean-François' choice of a career.

In 1605, it will be remembered, Clement de la Jonquière had married Lavezonne de Galaup. Their descendant Clément Taffanel de la Jonquière, born in 1706, was a prominent naval officer who had commanded several frigates, including the *Emeraude* at the battle of Cape Ortegal in 1747. Even better known was his uncle Pierre-Jacques, born in 1680, who rose to the rank of commodore and ended his life as Governor of French Canada.

The careers of the La Jonquière were a matter of pride. Jean-François would have boasted about his cousin's deeds to his school-fellows. The period he spent at the Jesuit college coincided with one of the rare moments of European peace — the interval between the end of the War of the Austrian Succession in 1748 and the formal outbreak of the Seven Years War in 1756. Periods that follow a major war are often glamorized by those too young to have been involved; La Jonquière brought tales of the sea into the humdrum atmosphere of the quiet inland town. Glamour was magnified by distance and isolation. In fact, Clément de la Jonquière may have met the boy only twice before the latter's decision to enter the navy. It is of the essence of naval life that a great deal of time is spent at sea: it was a disadvantage of a region such as the Albigensis that a sailor could travel back home only infrequently, especially in the eighteenth century when roads, although improved from the impassable quagmires they had once been, were still unreliable and tiresome. La Pérouse himself was not to make the journey very often. La Jonquière was home in 1749 when Jean-François was only eight years old. His influence on the boy may have been on this occasion little more than marginal, although stories of the recent war may have left their mark. More important was a visit made to the Galaups when Jean-François was twelve, an age when careers would have been a subject of frequent and serious discussion within the family. By that time, his three brothers had died, and only two sisters survived, one the future Sister Pélagie. His father, aged forty-four, was anxious to settle the family's future which depended entirely on Jean-François.

Accompanying La Jonquière was the Chevalier de Ternay, a younger man who was also in the navy and had recently returned from a three-year novitiate with the Knights of Malta. Both men stayed overnight at the Galaups, both had adventures to relate and, what was more important, precise information for the boy and his father on what a naval career implied and required. Both eventually became the boy's protectors, La Jonquière acting as his banker, probably by arrangement with Victor-Joseph who, with proper bourgeois caution, was anxious that his son should not have access to his allowance without the supervision of a trustworthy adult. La Jonquière's careful account of his disbursements will give us a valuable insight into the young La Pérouse.

The practice of senior officers — and thus of noblemen — of taking cadets under their tutelage was part of a far wider and older tradition in French society. The term used to describe this protector-client relationship was *fidélité*, a bond of mutual service and dependence between a *maître* and his *fidèle*, which descended from the apex of the social pyramid, in which the king numbered the nobles among his *fidèles*, to the nobility itself and to every aspect of government administration. Thus Jean-François would become the *fidèle* of La Jonquière and then of Ternay, each of them assuming responsibilities towards him. When he had acquired seniority, Jean-François would in turn, with equal informality, move into a position in which he would become responsible for young *fidèles*.[3]

Many years later, La Pérouse would cite La Jonquière's marriage in an attempt to wrest his father's approval for his own marriage to Eléonore Broudou. La Jonquière had married a girl from the Ile de France, where Eléonore lived, and had taken her back to his château at Lasgraisses near Albi without incurring the least social stigma. The point was that the creole came from a wealthy family, old Galaup would reply, forbearing to add that the Jonquières were secure members of the nobility and as such could do things which the Galaups could not risk.

Once Jean-François had decided on a naval career, his father was prepared to support him to the full. The danger of a constant drain on his funds to maintain the standard of aristocratic camp life was averted, but Victor-Joseph was determined that his son would have every chance of success — and the first step towards this was a change of name. Galaup, even with its nobiliary 'de', sounded inadequate beside such names as Taffanel de la Jonquière and d'Arsac de Ternay. La Jonquière no doubt warned Victor-Joseph of the tensions that existed in wartime between the aristocratic officers of the royal navy — the Reds, as they were known from the dominant colour of their uniforms — and the 'temporary gentlemen' who were commissioned from the merchant service or allowed in through some exceptional arrangement, and known as the Blues. It is likely that he advised him to ensure that his own son would not be subjected to

LA CAMPAGNE commencée le 11 Juillet 1785

OFFICIERS-MAJORS.

M. De La Peyrouze Capne. de Vau. Commandt.

A lui supplément, comme commandant 120 et y 16 mpi, 2

De Clonard Lt. de Vau.

Descurrer idem.

De Boutin Lusigned

Pierre Vert Enseigne

Colinet Lt. de la Frigte.

Muster-book of the Boussole, showing one of the various spellings of the commander's name.

petty innuendoes from his fellow cadets, and that a good way to do this was to add a landed title to his name.

It was by then a widely adopted practice. A century earlier, Molière had ridiculed the trend by making it the basis of the intrigue of his *L'Ecole des Femmes*, but nothing could stop it. Those whose family names, indicating a local origin or being merely descriptive, began with *De* or *Du* eagerly split the article from the noun and dubbed themselves Du Bois or Du Pont. Others bought a property and added its name to their own which, if it sounded too plebeian, they could eventually eliminate:

> The substitution of a landed name for the patronymic name was without doubt the most elegant [manner of acquiring a noble name.] Then one might drop the patronymic after a generation or two, or keep both as patronymics. The retention was more logical: it is also easier to surmise the existence of a title in front of such a name, be it no more than 'Lord of'. This aspect of the procedure ensured its success.[4]

The Galaups owned a tenanted farm – a *métairie* – along the Chemin de Fauch close to Albi. Later – and indeed possibly then – it was known as Le Pigné, roughly the equivalent of Pine Tree Farm, after a large pine tree that grew near the farm buildings. More generally it was referred to as the 'Métairie de La Peyrouse' or the 'Domaine de La Peyrouse', this name being that of the district or *quartier* in which the property was situated. It had belonged to the Cirons, cousins of the family, but whether Victor-Joseph already owned it or bought it in 1756 specifically to provide a second name for his son is unclear.

Certainly, La Peyrouse (or La Pérouse, as it was spelt thenceforth) was a better-sounding name than that of the other property, Le Go, which would have placed a 'Galaup de Go' in the ambiguous and challengeable category of those who wore a descriptive geographical name, the de l'Isle, the Du Pont, the De la Rivière. There are numerous places called La Peyrouse or La Pérouse in south-west France; the original La Peyrouse family can trace its ancestry back to St Louis and the Crusades, and were lords of extensive lands in Périgord and Languedoc. The Galaup property, although quite small, had a suitably aristocratic sound, but such a thought would have been more in his father's mind than in his own, because Jean-François was no snob. His passion was the sea and navigation; he was to drive his father to the edge of distraction over the question of his marriage — and whatever official documents might say, he invariably signed letters and reports with the single word: Lapérouse.

The intention was also to provide the young man with his own income, although for years his father acted as trustee and handled the money. No actual transfer of the La Peyrouse property occurred until 1782, when two notaried transactions are recorded, on 10 September and on 28 December, possibly in anticipation of his marriage — to the highly suitable Mademoiselle de Vésian, not to the unacceptable Mademoiselle Broudou — or because Victor-Joseph who was to die in 1784 at the age of 75 felt the need to settle his affairs.

Eventually Jean-François became known as the Comte de la Pérouse, a title which by the late eighteenth century had lost much of its significance. In the *Almanach Royal*, the official Year Book of the French court, La Pérouse makes his appearance for the first time in 1788, following his promotion to *Chef d'Escadre*, as Monsieur de la Pérouse; others, such as the Comte d'Estaing, appear with their title: in 1789 the situation remained unchanged, but the following year Jean-François is listed as Monsieur le Comte de La Pérouse. In the 1791 edition all titles disappear. There is no record of his elevation to what Anglo-Saxons all too often equate with an earldom: the compiler of the *Almanach* had his attention drawn to the fact that La Pérouse had been referred to as a Count for several years, and he amended the list accordingly. Nevertheless, one should see in it nothing more than a customary title of courtesy, consequent upon his entry at court and his meetings with Louis XVI.

> Etiquette still required, prior to 1789, that one should be admitted to the honours of the Court only with a title; that one should seek the King's signature at the foot of an appointment or a commission to the higher ranks or to a major post only for a titled gentleman. The title which might thus be given for reasons of courtly etiquette remained in the family, since it was a courtly maxim that a king can do no wrong.[5]

This does not lessen in any way the high regard which surrounded

La Pérouse in his later years, nor his family's claims to a place among the provincial nobility. Indeed, without a valid claim of this nature, Jean-François could not have entered the navy as a *garde de la marine*, or royal cadet.

It was Louis XIV's great adminstration under Colbert which set up the first *gardes* in 1670 at the ports of Brest, where Jean-François was being sent, Rochefort and Toulon. They were reorganized in 1683 in the form which La Pérouse was to know, each corps consisting of 49 cadets in the charge of officers and a few specialist teachers. Their status was equal to that of the royal *Gardes du corps* or Bodyguards, an élite group, so that evidence of nobility covering four generations was a prerequisite to admission. La Pérouse had to provide in addition to his own certificate of baptism copies of the marriage certificates of his father, grandfather and greatgrandfather. In this way, the rank of the Galaup family was officially confirmed; indeed Victor-Joseph also had to obtain confirmation of their rank in the same year, as he was to attend meetings of the Estates of the Albigeois, a gathering of local *notables*. Thus, from two different authorities, came the acceptance of their *preuves de noblesse* — a status which was to be swept away in little more than thirty years, with the Abolition of Privileges during the Revolution, the *gardes de la marine* disappearing even earlier, in 1786, when the sheer need for more recruits forced the French government to suppress the exclusive corps.

Now unchallenged and equipped with new clothes and money, Jean-François de Galaup de La Pérouse set out from Albi to begin his career on a sea he had as yet never seen. It was December 1756.

Notes

1. *Livre des consuls de la ville d'Albi: XVIIe siècle.*
2. *Revue du Tarn*, December 1941, p. 295.
3. See R. Mousnier, 'Les concepts d'ordre, d'états, de fidélité et de monarchie absolue en France de la fin du XVe siècle à la fin du XVIIIe, in *Revue historique*, 247 (1972), pp. 289-312.
4. Breuil, *De la Particule dite nobiliaire*, p. 86.
5. La Roque, *Armoirial de la noblesse du Languedoc*, p. xxxii. No mention of the Galaups or of La Pérouse occurs in this armorial, published in 1860.

2
The Garde de la Marine

THE JOURNEY to Brest took over a week. The mild Languedoc winter was left behind, giving way to damp and sleet, to occasional flurries of snow and winds that swept inland from the Atlantic, and finally to the cold misty rains of Brittany. Jean-François was introduced to the diversity and complexities of France under the Old Régime. There were toll gates near towns, fees to be paid at river crossings, internal customs guards checking for smuggled goods, especially salt, which represented an important and hated form of taxation. Accustomed to the speech patterns of the Albigeois, he now met the burr of Poitou, the dialects or patois of country districts, and in Brittany, villages where only the innkeeper understood French. There were new sights to be seen, new food to be sampled, the hurly-burly of the fairs, the distant prospect of an elegant castle by the banks of a river, the first sea-going ships, preludes to the forests of swaying masts in the great ports, and his first sight of the sea, a long grey line softly drawn across the distant horizon, and inshore thundering waves foaming around the rocks, a foretaste of storms he would soon encounter and a warning of the death that awaited him.

There was the dirt and the smells of towns where he spent the night in an uncomfortable inn, the slush of the country roads where the coach sometimes sank down to its axles, the poverty-stricken peasants sheltering in the doorways of their hovels, and the beggars. But the merchants he met at mealtimes, the laden drays creaking their way to the market place, the road works and new buildings, reminded him that France was also a prosperous country, whatever evidence of social inequalities met his eyes. The great disasters of the Seven Years War lay ahead; the cost of the Austrian war had been countered by seven years of peace during which France had succeeded in restoring much of her shattered fortunes.

During the eighteenth century, France would be at war for a total of over 40 years, mostly in a struggle to retain her position against the rise of English power and the encroachments of more distant Prussia. The first years of the reign of Louis XV had been peaceful, largely thanks to the efforts of the elderly Chief Minister, Cardinal Fleury. But even he had been unable to halt the slide towards war in 1741. Although the French had won enough victories to satisfy any national ego — the capture of Prague in 1741, Dupleix's capture of Madras in 1746, and in Flanders victories at Courtrai, Ménin, Yvres and Furnes as well as the spectacular battle of Fontenoy, the war had been costly and its eventual outcome of little significance. At sea, for instance, France and Spain had lost some 3,500 ships, and it was little consolation to know that England and her allies had lost 3,000. Nevertheless, France recovered quickly, with a determination made all the greater by the knowledge that the Treaty of Aachen in 1748 was less a document of peace than a truce signed by war-weary powers.

When La Pérouse reached the port of Brest on 19 November 1756, he found evidence both of France's growing prosperity and of her determination to organize for the next phase of the continuing struggle against England. Mignot de Montigny who visited it not long before La Pérouse's arrival, reported:

> The spectacle provided by the port of Brest makes one truly feel the greatness of the French monarchy: the channel is crowded by ships of all descriptions, a crowd of workmen are busily occupied in all the workshops that line the port. Four mighty vessels and two frigates being built on the slipways, two great ships and a frigate ready in the port, a ship of 84 guns in the repairs dock, numerous workshops set up for two new docks; six hundred convicts breaking stones to widen the quays along the harbour — all these great undertakings embraced in the one glance give one an impressive sense of the power which infuses them with life. Vast stores solidly built and plainly decorated and two immense rope works laid out as an amphitheatre complete, with the convict settlement and the hospital, the precinct where these works are carried out.[1]

All this was part of an effort to develop a strong French navy. It would double the population of Brest from 15,000 at the beginning of the century to over 30,000 at the outbreak of the Revolution.

Maurepas, who had held the post of Minister of Marine from 1723 to 1749, had written in his *Réflexions sur le commerce et la marine* (1745), 'I think it worth pointing out that one must fight a naval power mainly on the seas'. It reads like a platitude, but French kings had always planned their campaigns on the European continent. In 1759 one of Maurepas' successors, Machault, would lose his job when France, signing a treaty with Austria, turned her main attention to land campaigns and rejected his ambitious plans for further naval operations. Maurepas' proposals were for a fleet of 60 ships to provide the core for a coalition against England 'who is arrogating the pompous title of mistress of the sea'.

In spite of the shortage of money and of France's traditional neglect of the navy, especially in time of peace, Maurepas was able to achieve a great deal. His aims were to develop and fortify Toulon on which the Mediterranean fleet, blocked by the English in Gibraltar and Minorca, depended; to re-establish Dunkirk as a base which could threaten the English Channel and the Thames estuary; and give added protection to French settlements in Canada and India by strengthening the ports of Brest and Lorient and maintaining a long-range fleet.

Maurepas fell in 1749, not because of his activities at the Navy Ministry, but as a result of his role as Secretary of State responsible for the police, the smooth running of Versailles and the control of Paris. Attacks on the King's favourite, Madame de Pompadour, were growing in step with her influence. The jealousy and snobbery of the courtiers expressed itself in lampoons and cutting witticisms. French humour is often expressed through puns and word play. In the case of Madame de Pompadour, her family name – Poisson (fish) – provided ample opportunities, ranging from the witty to the scurrilous. Maurepas, whose functions included that of court censor – difficult enough task at the best of times – was reported to be the author of a number of these doubtful witticisms about the Favourite. Louis XV, a king who was usually more shy than weak, was reluctant to act, but when he did he was brutal and to the point. In April 1749, he sent Maurepas a brief note: 'Your services no longer suit me. You will hand in your resignation to Monsieur de

Florentin[2] and go to Bourges. You will see only your family. No acknowledgement is required'.

It was the end of an era. Maurepas was the nephew of Pontchartrain who had been Minister of Marine for many years before him. The immediate cause of his downfall might well have been the king's exasperation at the lampoons of the courtiers and gossip-writers, but he may also have felt it necessary to close a chapter that went back to the previous century. Maurepas' successor was Rouillé, a man drawn not from the nobility but from the administrative sector. Rouillé was a member of the Council of the French India Company and a career administrator; his deputy was Le Normant de Mézy, *intendant* or civil administrator of the naval forces. Together they pursued Maurepas' policy within the financial limits set by post-war needs. One result of their work was the setting up in 1752 of the Brest Academy of Marine.

Rouillé moved to Foreign Affairs in 1754, and was replaced by Machault, who, sensing the approach of war, set about organizing five squadrons based on the ports of Brest, Rochefort and Toulon. He was to fall in 1759 to be replaced in quick succession by Moras, Massiac and Berryer who in 1761 would be only too glad to make way for Choiseul. Nevertheless, the period 1748 to 1756 was one of wise planning and of a determined policy of expansion of which Brest provided ample evidence.

Brest was to be La Pérouse's *port d'attache* for the rest of his life. Only the island of Mauritius would rival the Breton naval base in his affections. He would spend some time in Paris later in his career and go home to Albi on occasions, but unlike many of his fellow officers who came from Brittany and could return relatively easily to their families, he had to contend with the problem of distance which made it possible for him to go home only when he was granted special long leave.

It was a town almost entirely dominated by its function as a naval base. It had been fought over in the fourteenth century and had actually been held by the English between 1342 and 1397, but it had only achieved its naval standing under Cardinal Richelieu who set up the *Marine du Ponant*, with Brouage, Brest and Le Havre as official naval ports, each with its *chef d'escadre*, general commissary and port captain.

Its geographical position set it well ahead of the other ports: it is protected by a long narrow entrance — Le Goulet, literally 'the Bottleneck' — defended by fearsome granite rocks and islets. The town itself had grown on both banks of the steepsided Penfeld; the north shore was known as the *Recouvrance*, the more populated south bank being defended by the Château, a near-impregnable structure of ramparts and barracks which is one of the few features of Brest to have survived the devastating attacks of 1944.

Past the Château, one could see the *Mâture* — the masting yards built in 1681; the Troulan repair shops built from 1683 to 1687 and brought up to date at intervals; the new general stores built in 1744 to replace the old buildings destroyed by fire; the prison built in 1750 and large enough to accommodate 3,000 convicts; the rope factory; the sheds where sulphur, hemp and tar were stored. On the north shore were the food stores, the carpenters' shops, and six repair docks built between 1692 and 1705.

La Pérouse would have entered the town from the land side, past one of the outlying guard posts — for the French government, always aware that the port was vulnerable to land-based assaults, maintained defensive posts around the town — and through the main gate. The streets were mostly narrow and twisty, especially as one neared the centre. A motley of shopkeepers' houses, artisans' yards, officers' lodgings, churches and convents crowded inside the city walls. There were private houses for noble families or for merchants growing wealthy on government contracts. Although these stood apart, with a cobblestone entrance for the coaches and a discreet formal garden, sometimes even the luxury of a small walled-in park, their staid grey stonework, their stolid architecture had none of the warmth of the old houses of Albi, with the gentle patina that time and the Languedoc sun had given them. These were residences rather than homes — and so they would remain for Jean-François.

The *gardes de la Marine* lived and studied at the Hotel Saint-Pierre, which backed on the Rue de Siam, close by the arsenal and near the administrative offices of the *Intendance*. It was a street where people of some status lived, quiet and dignified, but Brest was only a small town, and it led quickly into the Grande Rue, which had little that was grand about it beyond its name; it was a commonplace thoroughfare, a street of inns and taverns, gradually making way for grog shops and brothels as it neared the quayside. There the tang of the sea permeated the air, mixed with the smell of fresh tar, the scents of yesterday's fish, the first droplets of the rain that would soon sweep in from the Atlantic. And the streets were filled with the activities of a hundred trades, quickened into life by the knowledge that war was imminent — indeed had already unofficially begun.

The *gardes* had only recently moved to the Hotel Saint-Pierre. Previously they had been lodged in an old converted store built under Francis I and, not surprisingly, after nearly 200 years, in a state of chronic disrepair. It had belonged to the late Marquis de Crèvecoeur:

> In August 1752 the Hotel Saint-Pierre was bought from the Marquis' heirs and the gardes transferred to it. M. de Rouillé was concerned about their education; he ordered that nine sloops should be allocated and sent out at frequent intervals so that those who had already gone to sea could continue to take part in naval operations. He wanted them to learn theory on land, and for this purpose he had another wing . . . added to the building, to provide classrooms for tactical studies, and in 1756 a plot of land was purchased to increase the area of the yard they used for their training.[3]

The building was a substantial one, even without the addition of the Rouillé wing. It had an elegant façade, with a ground floor of extensive reception rooms, two upper stories and an attic with mansard windows. Within the dominant element of symmetry were accommodated the usual outbuildings — kitchens, stables, storerooms, implement sheds. There was a terraced garden on the south side and an extensive vegetable garden adequate for the needs of a noble establishment.

It was there that young La Pérouse reported in November 1756 to the commanding officer, Captain de Chézac, who had been appointed in 1752 when the *gardes* took over the Hotel Saint-Pierre and would remain in charge until 1764. He was assisted by one lieutenant — at the time the Comte de Lusseignet — and one ensign, Tournefort. There were also several petty officers and at least one civilian mathematics teacher.

The timetable was planned to turn young men into effective officers in a matter of months. Roll call was at 7 a.m. in summer and 8 a.m. in the winter, followed by Mass, breakfast and classwork until 11 a.m. The afternoon was set aside for practical work: weapon handling, drill, and visits to ships in port. The core of the training was the study of mathematics, which embraced astronomy, hydrography and the science of navigation. There was a weekly test on Saturdays, and eventually learning by heart the *Cours de Mathématiques* written by the teacher Bezout became a prerequisite for promotion. La Pérouse had no problems in this respect: he had a gift for mathematics and a strong sense of vocation.

Practical training continued on board ship, although when La Pérouse first sailed, a mere four months after his arrival at Brest, war had broken out and captains had other things to do than to follow to the letter the instructions laid down in 1716 for the education of youthful cadets:

> Every captain received orders to have all the *gardes* serving in his ship assembled at 6.30 a.m. to be instructed by the pilot in the art of navigation and the manner of drawing a plan of the roadsteads while at anchor and to show the rocks and underwater shoals. At midday the *gardes* were brought together on the quarter-deck to learn the use of the instruments. At 3 p.m. the master taught them the manoeuvres, the manner of dealing with accidents . . . and gave them a correct idea of the ship's layout. Twice a week the master gunner took them for gun practice. Once a week the master carpenter taught them how to carry out repairs, the master caulker the use of pumps.[4]

The education of the young aspirants was thus becoming increasingly professional. Men like Chézac had the full support of successive ministers in Versailles — indeed a professional naval corps had been planned by Colbert a century earlier and in spite of every difficulty this remained the official policy. The prime obstacle was the nobility which clung with a determination akin to desperation to its privilege of exclusive admission. One cannot doubt that La

Pérouse's fellows at the Hotel Saint-Pierre would have questioned him with consummate tact, but quite insistently, to satisfy themselves that he met the central criterion — almost the only one in their eyes — of adequate noble birth.

This attitude was a source of irritation to the administration, which consisted of the professional classes rather than the aristocracy and all of whom had to deal with the need to find enough able men for the ships France was building to send against the less fastidious English. Had there been a surplus of applicants of unchallengeable social standing and adequate potential, the middle-class element would easily have been eliminated. But there was not, so that at any one time up to one third of the *gardes* were of middle-class or arguable noble background. There might have been many noble youths who were attracted by the glamour of the naval service — the red and gold uniforms, the great ships straining under full sails, the company of others of equal rank — but the reality deterred them: the long absences, the filth, the promiscuity, the discomfort of heaving decks and damp quarters. The army, where dash and bravery were usually all one needed to add to the skill with weapons one had already acquired, was more attractive. One could always find good lodgings, bring one's servant, attend receptions and ride back to Versailles between campaigns. The social life in distant ports like Brest or Toulon was drab enough; in a ship on the high seas it was non-existent and made even less attractive by testy and domineering captains who, however aristocratic their own background might be, had little patience with ill-trained popinjays and seldom hesitated to say so in public.

When hostilities threatened, sheer necessity forced the authorities to accept recruits of promise but modest background, as well as officers from the merchant service, but protests arose promptly — to be rejected with no little impatience. Thus, Moras who replaced Machault as Minister of Marine soon after Jean-François' arrival at Brest, wrote in June to Du Guay, the Brest port commandant:

> I must admit that I have read with some surprise your letter of the 20th instant . . . Should not your desire to see naval officers recruited every time from the nobility of the kingdom, after those who wish to follow this

career have gathered the first elements of their profession in the class-rooms that have been set up in the ports and by a few voyages, give way to the needs of the service . . . ?I shall not conceal from you that, while keeping most carefully to the established rule under which *gardes de la marine* are only to be drawn from the nobility of this kingdom, I will seize every occasion to associate with the service members of another Estate who have deserved it through acts of valour or recognised talents.[5]

In fact, Du Guay's anxiety was well justified: Moras was determined to appoint 'blue' officers from the merchant navy to serve on royal ships alongside the 'reds'. The war left him and his successors no alternative, but Choiseul who took over in 1761 so favoured experience and ability over birthright that he took the first steps towards the total abolition of the *gardes de la marine* system — until the outraged nobility stopped him.

⚙

Now established and equipped, Jean-François could sample the pleasure of Brest. He cut an attractive figure in his uniform — a fifteen-year-old in breeches and silk stockings, blue coat cut away to reveal the scarlet waistcoat, gold-braid epaulettes, brass buttons down to the waist and on sleeves and pockets, cocked hat, black shoes with gold buckles.

Brest offered a few opportunities for the young man to display this finery: the salons of senior officers; the public garden originally attached to the hospital, but now unofficially available to local residents; the theatre, such as it was, at first frowned upon because 'it would distract the *gardes de la marine* from their studies', erected — a makeshift gimcrack structure — near the old ropeworks, then destroyed by fire in 1744 and rebuilt in a street close by the Hôtel Saint-Pierre. Even churchgoing presented a chance to show oneself and bow to demure young ladies one had already met at receptions — the seminary in the Rue des Jésuites founded in 1686 to provide naval chaplains, including one for the *gardes*, had a chapel which the young cadets were firmly encouraged to visit.

It is La Jonquière who, through his meticulous accounting of the sums entrusted to him, gives us a clear insight into Jean-François' first months as a *garde*. La Pérouse had duly handed over to him

240 *livres* out of the money his father had given him:

> On 15 December I gave him 48 *livres* to pay a month's board at the inn; on the 24th to remake his two suits and make a waistcoat and breeches 75 ℓ. 5s.5d. On 1 January to pay for power 6 ℓ. On 15 January for a month at the inn 42 ℓ. plus 9 ℓ. to pay for the second room and firewood. On 19th paid postage on two letters 1 ℓ. 8s. On the 20th to Oudart, tailor to repair two suits and make a waistcoat and breeches 7 ℓ. 4s. On 25 January paid 8 ℓ. 8s. for 6 days at the inn plus 1 ℓ. 4s. to the innkeeper, money lent for a broken glass, and 12s. for the sword, total 1 ℓ. 16s. To M. de Lapérouse for his entertainment 6 ℓ. On 16 February 16 ℓ. to the prison inn. On 15 February to repair his sword 3 ℓ. total 239 ℓ. 15s. 5d. leaving 19s. which I gave to M. de Lapérouse. Account as at 16 February 1757.[6]

From this we discover that Jean-François lived in town — and few *gardes* actually boarded at the Hotel Saint-Pierre — and spent over a fortnight in jail. The broken glass, the damaged clothing, the repairs to his sword, suggest an affray, probably more than one, possibly a duel. It is a glimpse of La Pérouse the man for which we must be grateful. All too often heroic figures are depicted in exclusively heroic stances, never telling a lie nor losing their temper, assiduous at their studies, concerned only with the career that will ensure their place in history. From La Jonquière's records emerges a more human personality, a hot-blooded young man from the region which gave birth to the dashing musketeer d'Artagnan, getting into scrapes, facing the reprimands of the stern Captain de Chézac and the short sentence which involved no dishonour but some salutary discomfort.

La Jonquière closes his accounts on 16 February, handing over the modest residue of Victor-Joseph's original allocation, possibly now supplemented by a further allowance sent from Albi. The young Jean-François no doubt left his cell to move to the Hotel Saint-Pierre. It was only for a few days. La Jonquière was readying his ship, *Le Célèbre*, and Jean-François was to sail in her. For the first time, the young man stepped on board a naval vessel, not as a visitor but as one of her complement. He took his few belongings to a corner of the main cabin — the *gardes* seldom qualified for a cabin of their own, especially in time of war — and started work, familiar-izing himself with the ship and helping to supervise the loading of the stores.

It was 22 March 1757. *Le Célèbre* was about to sail for French Canada where the final struggle for survival had begun.

Notes

1. Quoted in Le Gallo, *Histoire de Brest*, p. 140.
2. Saint-Florentin was nominally Secretary of State in charge of Protestant affairs; he was effectively a minister without portfolio.
3. Levot, *Histoire de la ville et du port de Brest*, II, p. 107.
4. Anon, *Histoire de l'Ecole navale*, p. 326.
5. Levot, *Histoire de la ville de Brest*, II, p. 113.
6. Manavit, 'Ce que La Pérouse doit à La Jonquière', *Revue de Tarn*, p. 168.

3

The First Battle

THE CONFLICT which was to become known as the Seven Years War had begun while Jean-François was still at school.

A cold war had opposed the French and the English in North America for some years. The previous war, that of the Austrian Succession, ended in 1745 with the Treaty of Aix-la-Chapelle, but it had solved nothing. In Paris, a saying had entered the language: 'As stupid as the Peace'. France received back the key fortress of Louisbourg at the entrance of the St Lawrence Gulf, in exchange for Madras, but the boundaries of New France, as French Canada was then known, remained ill-defined.

Enterprising colonists and ambitious administrators from either nation could hardly be expected to refrain from encroaching on land occupied only by hapless Indians and certainly underpopulated. The New Yorkers were edging north along the Lake Champlain route; the French were anxious to establish a solid settlement at Detroit and to regain Illinois and Ohio. Communications between French Canada and French Louisiana through a series of posts down the Mississippi and along the Illinois River and the shores of the Great Lakes, were an essential feature of France's strategic plan, but it penned in the English colonies along the Atlantic coastlands and the Alleghany chain. Between the two, a conflict was only a matter of time.

Battin de la Galissonière, Governor of New France from 1747 to 1749, was a naval officer with a broad concept of the situation. He convinced the Paris government of the need to defend the Ohio, and following the death of his successor, the Marquis de la Jonquière in Louisbourg, he was able to influence the next appointment. The post went to the Marquis Duquesne de Menneville who promptly organized an expedition to fortify north-east Ohio. It was largely successful, but it brought home the enormous logistic problems involved in defending wide tracts of unsettled land: Duquesne was shocked by 'the pitiable state' and the 'emaciated faces' of the militiamen who returned, while the French government recalled the *intendant* Bigot to France to explain why the expedition had cost close on four million *livres*.

Not surprisingly, the English reacted. London authorized the Governor of Virginia to erect forts in the Ohio valley and attack the French should they again encroach on British territory. And since the demarcation line was as unclear as ever, a clash was inevitable. It came at Fort Duquesne in 1754, near present-day Pittsburg. The leader of the British troops was, interestingly enough, a young officer named George Washington. The Sieur de Jumonville who had been sent with 30 men to report on Washington's advance and warn him off was attacked and killed with 10 of his men. There was no warning, and French survivors claimed that the attack came while Jumonville was asking for a parley or indeed in the middle of reading out the terms of his commission. The French had no doubt that Jumonville had been assassinated — there was, after all, no state of war at the time — and when retaliation followed and Washington was compelled to surrender, he was required to sign a document acknowledging his guilt. It would take the War of Independence and Washington's prominence in American affairs for the incident to be relegated to obscurity.

London had meanwhile decided to send reinforcements to the Virginian colonists. Two regiments embarked at Cork in January 1755. In June, their commander, Major-General Braddock, led a force of some 2,000 men 'over steep rocky Mountains and almost impassable Morasses' to Fort Duquesne. There he was defeated by the French; Braddock himself was killed, along with 500 of his men and officers; and into his enemies' hands fell not only all his guns and supplies, but his plans for attacks on French posts at Niagara and Fort St Frederic. It may be necessary to bear in mind that the two countries were still officially at peace.

The two next major incidents had repercussions which spread far beyond the North American continent. Both sent a wave of indignation into France and throughout her ports. The people of distant

Albi cannot have remained unaware of them. They confirmed the view that the English were perfidious and war only a matter of time.

Acadia, part of what is now known as Nova Scotia and New Brunswick, had been settled by the French in the early seventeenth century. Most of it had passed to Britain as a consequence of the 1713 Treaty of Utrecht, but the French settlers remained a source of disaffection and potential danger in time of war. Charles Lawrence, the Governor of Nova Scotia, issued instructions to deport this French-speaking population 'to distribute them amongst the several colonies on the Continent' and to 'fall upon some strategem' to hold the families, seize their boats and above all prevent them from fleeing to French Canada where they would reinforce the French colonists.

In all, between 6,000 and 7,000 men, women and children were deported in the period September to December 1755 and scattered among the various American colonies of the Atlantic seaboard, where it was hoped they would be absorbed among the English-speaking population. Deportations continued for some years until the Acadians were reduced to less than 30 percent of their original number. The tragedy was to enter literature with Longfellow's *Evangeline,* where it was still echoing in 1979 with Antonine Maillet's famous novel *Pélagie-la-Charette.* It was to spur Bougainville into establishing a French colony in the Falkland Islands to settle some of the Acadians who had succeeded in fleeing to France.

The second incident affected the French navy far more directly. While the French Ambassador, the Duc de Mirepoix, was being granted plenary powers by Paris to reach a settlement and agree to the neutralization of the Ohio and the destruction of the French forts there, Admiral Boscawen sailed for Canada with secret instruction to capture or destroy 'any French ships of war or other vessels having on board troops or warlike stores'. As it was, he only managed to capture two ships, the *Lys* and the *Alcide*. The British assured the French that the attack had been 'a misunderstanding', but their duplicity was too blatant.

Still the two powers remained at peace, and the shouted assurance of the British captain as he had borne down on the *Alcide* that the nations were not at war was grimly true, even though it was at once followed by his guns firing at the French. British naval superiority made it unwise for France to declare war, but London soon showed her that she had nothing to gain by delay: instructions were issued to all British commanders to capture merchantmen as well as ships of war. In October and November, Boscawen and Hawke seized some 300 commercial vessels in the Channel and the Atlantic. British politicians like Granville might sneer at these actions as little more than 'vexing your neighbour with a little muck', but over 6,000 French sailors were taken prisoner, some being pressed into service aboard British ships. This was the equivalent of the crews of 15 ships of the line and it placed the French Navy at a severe disadvantage when war finally broke out on 18 May 1756 and naval mobilization was announced, for although naval registers were detailed and up to date many of the men listed were already in enemy hands.

However unjustified the British actions might have been in moral terms, they reflected an understandable anxiety about French moves and the rebirth of her navy. Events in 1756 proved how well-founded this was: La Galissonnière landed in British-held Minorca and held it against Admiral Byng who was forced to return to Gibraltar. Byng was then court-martialled and shot for his pains. Had La Galissonnière not died and his successors not been so convinced of British superiority and dared to build on his achievements, France might have had more victories to her credit. As it was, in Canada, Montcalm had landed with reinforcements and in August he captured Fort Chouagen on Lake Ontario, taking 1,700 prisoners; earlier in the year Gaspard Léry had destroyed the strategic supply base of Fort Bull; and François de Nilliers had taken Fort Granville in Pennsylvania. There were to be other victories during the long war: D'Aché successfully led a squadron and 4,000 men to India, and an English attempt to effect a landing near St Malo ended in disaster; but the eyes of the French Court were firmly fixed on the European theatre of war. There the armies marched and retreated in complex and seemingly endless manoeuvres. There would be much incompetence and much bravery, until eventually war weariness supervened, fed by financial troubles and the constant drain on men and resources. The European map would not be greatly altered, but France's overseas empire would be in ruins, with Canada, India and Senegal going to England, and Louisiana to Spain.

As 1757 dawned, the port of Brest was feverishly preparing to send supplies and reinforcements to the French in Canada, who were isolated by snow and ice in what was a particularly hard winter. The Governor, Vaudreuil, modestly asked for 1,800 men, but Versailles, which knew more than he did about British plans, considered that five times that number were needed. There was no point in sending ships in winter — the St Lawrence was frozen over — but delays occurred which held the French supply ships until March, which meant they did not reach Quebec until mid-year.

The *Célèbre* was a ship of 64 guns, part of a squadron led by the Marquis de La Motte. Emmanuel-Auguste de Cadiheuc du Bois de La Motte was as famous as his name was resounding. He had sailed with the great Duguay-Trouin on the 1711 expedition which resulted in the capture and ransom of Rio de Janeiro. In 1751 he was appointed governor of the Leeward Islands. In 1755 he had taken Vaudreuil to Canada. Now in his sixties he was assembling his squadron for a last crossing of the Atlantic before retirement. It was to be a mixture of success and disaster.

The squadron sailed from Brest on 3 May 1757. There were two great vessels of 80 guns, the *Formidable* and the *Duc de Bourgogne*, four of 74, three of 64, and two frigates of 32 guns. The sight must have looked impressive indeed to the young Jean-François, sail crowding on as the sailors worked feverishly among the rigging, shouted orders from the petty officers below, the red and gold of the officers' uniforms on deck, and the ship moving under him as the arms of the bay opened out and they reached the open sea.

La Motte, however, was not out to provide a grandiose sight, but to complete the crossing as expeditiously and unobtrusively as possible. There were fast English frigates about, ready not to engage in unequal combat but to report his movements. His first aim was to elude them, to set out at dusk and preferably under the protection of the light Breton rain. Fog and wind mattered more than guns to a squadron whose purpose was to carry supplies, not win battles. As he neared the western approaches of Canada, he knew that the naval nets of Boscawen, Hawke and others were stretched out to catch him. Luck was with him: unnoticed until the last moments, the La Motte squadron put into Louisbourg on 19 June.

For young La Pérouse, the voyage was an opportunity to put into practice the naval theory he had learnt at the Brest School. There was probably little opportunity for the routine training prescribed for *gardes* on board ship, for this was wartime, there were extra lookout duties for all, and the vessel was crowded with stores and supernumaries; but Jean-François was in his naval 'godfather's' ship, and La Jonquière would have made certain that the youth was given every opportunity to learn. Jean-François was a good pupil. The sea was his vocation, his protector's eyes were on him, and France desperately needed officers for her navy.

Louisbourg, a port of great strategic importance on Ile Royale, now known as Cape Breton Island, northern Nova Scotia, was defended by a garrison of 3,500 men. Its defences had been repaired, new entrenchments built, guns positioned in expectation of a British attack. Boscawen's base port was Halifax, a mere 200 miles to the south. The British, under Vice-Admiral Holburne, could muster 15 ships-of-the-line, sundry small craft, three brigades of four battalions each and various auxiliaries. The safe arrival of the La Motte squadron saved the Ile Royale for another season.

Jean-François was well received by the commander Augustin de Drucourt, and for more than his mere presence among a naval force whose arrival was so timely: Drucourt had been in charge of the school at Brest and always extended a special welcome to any young *garde* who chanced to land in Louisbourg.

The *Célèbre* and the *Bizarre* took the troops they had brought with them on to the mainland and left for France ahead of the main squadron. It was always necessary to seize a chance to sail when fog reduced visibility or a storm scattered the blockading British ships, as one did on 24 September, sinking two of them and damaging a number of others.

La Pérouse was back in Brest by 4 November and was given brief shore leave prior to his joining the frigate *Pomone*. It was possibly fortunate for him that he did, for as the last of La Motte's squadron limped home on 9 December, typhus swept through Brest, raged on until the following April and cost an estimated 10,000 lives.

No one has disputed the claim that the La Motte squadron, its own men sick and weakened, and taking back to France many sick from the Louisbourg garrison who were only a burden on the town, was responsible for the great epidemic. An estimated 4,000 sailors and soldiers landed by La Motte's ships had to be transferred to makeshift hospitals. Barracks, churches, even the *Hôtel des Gardes*, were taken over. To prevent the epidemic from spreading, 150,000 *livres* was sent urgently from Paris to pay off all valid men, but it was too late. Boyer, the King's doctor, hastened from Versailles to take charge. He issued instructions to isolate the areas surrounding the hospitals: private individuals were required to send to them any sick they were nursing. It was all to little purpose in a period when the main remedies were purging and bleeding. The convicts on whom the town depended for many of its services fell ill as well, so that refuse was no longer being collected and disposal of the dead became a problem. The stench of death and corruption rose over the plague-stricken port and hung over it until the epidemic burnt itself out.

Jean-François spent December and January in the *Pomone*, commanded by the Chevalier de Ternay. In February he followed Ternay in the frigate *Zéphire*. Once again, he was to sail to Canada. First, the *Zéphire* went down to Rochefort and then to the nearby island of Aix where she joined a convoy under the command of Louis-Charles du Chaffault who had recently distinguished himself when captain of the *Atalante*, a vessel of 34 guns, by capturing the *Warwick* of 64.

It was Ternay, however, who was La Pérouse's commanding officer and would soon assume a considerable role in his life, far greater than that of his first mentor, La Jonquière.

Charles-Henri-Louis d'Arsac de Ternay, a bachelor, was the second son of the Marquis de Ternay. Born in 1723, he had entered the navy as a *garde* at the age of 15, sailed in the Mediterranean, been appointed ensign in 1746 and fought in Santo Domingo and Louisiana until the Peace of Aix-la-Chapelle. He had then joined the Order of Malta and spent three years in Malta as a novice, but did not take his final vows. He returned to the Navy, sailing to Canada in 1755 under La Motte. A miniature of the time shows a slightly tense man with finely drawn features, the lips a little pinched, the eyes somewhat distant and visionary under delicate eyebrows. Aged 35, he had made up his mind that his future lay with the Navy rather than with the Order. He assumed command of the *Zéphire* with the rank of *lieutenant de vaisseau*. Quiet, he was essentially a kind man who took at once to the young *garde* from Albi and fulfilled his responsibilities as a guide and teacher with his usual earnestness.

Du Chaffault sailed in the *Dragon*, the only ship of any size in the motley division. There were two frigates in addition to the *Zéphire*; four vessels sailing as storeships, which meant they carried no more than half their guns; and a privateer from St Malo, the *Prince-Edouard*, with 150 soldiers for Quebec. The division made the Atlantic crossing in good time, passing to the north of Boscawen who was as usual patrolling the western approaches. Du Chaffault landed the troops he was carrying at Port Dauphin, as Louisbourg was now effectively blockaded. It was far from easy. Ternay was given the unenviable task of landing stores and men in heavy seas along an inhospitable coast with the knowledge that 60 English vessels were converging on Louisbourg. The operation began on 3 June and was completed on the 6th, soldiers, their belongings and supplies being taken off from the various ships in small boats, rowed ashore and hastily mustered inland. They then had to struggle down to Louisbourg. They reached the French port just as 8,000 English soldiers were landing to complete the siege of the city which was being blockaded from the sea. They were still there on 27 July when Louisbourg fell.

British naval superiority not only sealed the fate of Louisbourg as it would the fate of Quebec and of the whole of New France, it forced vessels like the *Zéphire* to hug the coast, seek temporary shelter in unfamiliar bays and make wide detours. Engagements with the enemy were to be avoided at all costs. Undoubtedly, back in Albi, Marguerite Galaup was worrying about the dangers her son was running in North American waters, but in fact young La Pérouse was gaining invaluable experience in coastal navigation. The *Zéphire* was sent back to France by Du Chaffault who was going to Quebec. It was urgent to report to Versailles on the situation in Nova Scotia, and ensure that such supplies and men as the government was willing to spare be directed to the mainland. But the massive naval force brought together to blockade the fortress of Louisbourg compelled Ternay to sail north around western Newfoundland, through the Straits of Belle-Isle.

This involved a cautious navigation along an unfamiliar coast, black cliffs lapped by angry waves, swift tidal currents, sudden swirls of fog, and a lonely seascape across which only an occasional fisherman's boat appeared, to flee at once from the threatening stranger into the safety of a cove. Precision, vigilance, attention to detail, were essential to survival. Ternay helped the young *garde*, and taught him much that was to prove invaluable to La Pérouse in years to come.

The *Zéphire* sailed along northern Newfoundland, well clear of the land, and eastwards in higher latitudes to avoid the English. Not until she was approaching Ushant did young La Pérouse have his first encounter with the enemy. It was brief and inglorious: Ternay manoeuvred to avoid the blockading ships, sailed away, veered back, crowded on sail and entered the outer roadstead of Brest.

Jean-François left the *Zéphire* on 21 July. He had three weeks shore leave: time to relax, to visit friends, to write letters to Albi. He could reassure his parents who were naturally more concerned about the events in Canada than most of France — for the government was concentrating on the endless manoeuvres of the armies in Europe and most courtiers were quite prepared to share Voltaire's view of Canada as nothing more than 'a few acres of snow'. The key fortresses were falling — Fort Duquesne, Frontenac, Louisbourg and although Du Chaffault's mission enabled the defenders of Ile Royale to hold the British back for long enough to make it impossible for them to attack Quebec until the next season, the capital of New France was doomed nevertheless.

Brest was showing the effects of war. The port had barely begun to recover from the frightful epidemic; ships were being fitted out for expeditions that were cancelled at the last moment; British vessels patrolled off the coast like hungry wolves waiting to pounce. The sense of frustration was deepening. We can take it all the same that Jean-François visited the taverns with other young *gardes*, that they compared notes on their brief campaigns, boasted a little, exaggerated the dangers they had run, joked and flirted. He was, for all the maturity that wartime adds to youth, only 16.

Admittedly, his seventeenth birthday was almost on him. He celebrated it, with toasts in good southern wine, aboard the *Cerf*, a storeship of 300 tons, fresh and clean, for she was only two years old, commanded by Béreul de la Melaine. There were to be no adventures this time, not even the dangerous dash into port to escape the marauding enemy, but an opportunity to advance his studies a little further and gain experience. When he was paid off the *Cerf* on 16 November 1758, he had spent a total of 19 months on board ship — in two frigates and a storeship. He had twice sailed to the Canadian coast, seen some action, lived the life of a naval officer on active service, met army officers and watched with amusement the constant exchange of jokes and insults between the sailors and the soldiers they were transporting.

Now it was winter. La Pérouse went back to his studies — to Bouguer's ponderous mathematics manual, Romme's treatise on masts and riggings, Duhamel de Monceau's work on naval architecture. There were examinations to be passed as prerequisites to promotion. Wartime might provide more opportunities for going to sea, but one's long-term career still depended on meeting the requirements of the *Ecole des Gardes*.

In May 1759, La Pérouse was told of his posting to the *Formidable*. After inspection, he had to admit she was a fine ship, of 80 guns, with a total complement of 971 officers, men and servants, commanded by the Chevalier de Saint-André du Verger. It was no secret in Brest that it would form part of an expedition to England. It was indeed no secret even in London: 18,000 men were being gathered under the order of the Duc d'Aiguillon, Governor of Brittany, for a landing somewhere in the British Isles, and a force of that size could not easily be concealed from the eyes of English informers nor the gossip in naval officers' homes kept from their ears. What remained undiscovered was the likely date and the chosen location of the landing. It was concern enough for the English government to know of the project and be kept on tenterhooks by the presence of thousands of men near Best, linked with obvious preparations for a major naval undertaking.

Jean-François went on board officially on 1 June. Ten of his fellow *gardes* were with him, together with 17 senior officers, including the commanding officer's own brother. There were 200 fusiliers, grenadiers drawn from the Saintonge Regiment, and 146 men from the coastguard defence force, who were to carry out the landing which, it eventually transpired, would take place in Scotland with, shortly after, another at the mouth of the Thames.

Thus, for the first time, the young La Pérouse was to take part in a formal engagement – but only if the squadron could slip past Admiral Hawke and avoid Commodore Duff's fleet stationary in Quiberon Bay to the south.

It was not until 14 November that the French commander, 69-year-old Maréchal Hubert de Conflans, found the opportunity he had been waiting for. A storm had raged across the Breton coast, driving Hawke's ships out to sea. Coastal watchers saw no sign of the English vessels when the weather improved, and a convoy from Canada reaching Brest reported having seen no enemy sails. Conflans rightly concluded that Hawke had been forced to his home base for repairs – he was in fact in Torbay – and he ordered his ships to sail immediately.

It was necessary to go south to Quiberon, where the expedition's transport vessels were waiting, watched over by Duff who would therefore have to be faced and destroyed before Hawke returned. Naval engagements between opponents of equal strength seldom produced decisive victories. Maurepas, who had been Minister of Marine for so many years had put it pithily: 'Do you know what a naval battle is? I will tell you: the fleets manoeuvre, come to grips, fire a few shots, and then retreat . . . and the sea remains as salt as it was before.'[1] He might have added a comment on the role of the weather – which had allowed Conflans to leave Brest and then delayed him so that it took him six days to reach Quiberon, by which time, although he did not know it, Hawke was right behind him.[2]

Duff, anyhow, had been forewarned and was ready for the battle. Conflans, whose 21 ships were arranged in three divisions, one of them led by the *Formidable*, gave the signal to attack when at dawn on the 20th he sighted eight ships of the line and three supporting vessels ahead of him. The wind was rising and the seas were lashing the coast, but time was of the essence.

At 9.30 a.m. the French were in pursuit, with Duff's ships retreating, when a fleet appeared to the west. It was Admiral Hawke with 21 ships of the line. Conflans was now outnumbered and attacked from two sides, with his ships in some disorder since Duff had divided his small force in two groups and thus effectively split Conflans' as well.

The French had little time to regroup. The westerly wind was rising to gale force, helping Hawke, but driving Conflans towards the shore. The Marechal decided to seek the shelter of Quiberon Bay, an oblong-shaped gulf protected by islets and rocks. Keen though his officers and men might be to stand and fight, his instructions were to organize an attack on the British mainland, not to risk France's Atlantic fleet in an unequal engagement.

The weather worsened as Hawke's leading ships reached the French rearguard. The first shots were fired by the *Magnifique*, but the *Formidable* was soon engaged, struggling to come to the aid of the *Magnifique*. She faced in turn 15 British ships which poured the fire of their guns into her as they sailed past. At one time, the *Formidable* was being raked by cannon from four enemy ships. Her captain was dead, half her masting had crashed down, her rudder was torn away. She was drifting helplessly, her guns still firing, when as dusk fell the English captain of the *Resolution* sent his people to take her over. It was then that they realized the extent of the carnage.

The chief surgeon of the *Formidable* drew up his own report, estimating that 300 men had been killed and over 150 wounded; he had no means of assessing the number drowned:

The squadron leader Saint-André du Verger [had] his head smashed by a cannon ball; his elder brother, the post-captain second in command, cut in

The end of the battle, Quiberon Bay.
(National Maritime Museum, Greenwich.)

half by a ball. Lieutenant d'Arcouges a ball in the chest. Monsieur Colline, a Danish officer, completely cut in half by a cannon ball. M. de Grammont, sub-lieutenant, back broken. M. de Chaulne, *garde*, cut in two, M. d'Herneville, *garde*, head blown off. In the Saintonge Regiment, M. de la Picotière, lieutenant, riddled with bullet, a cannon ball in the stomach. M. de Montluc, a leg carried away, died of wounds. M. Durienne, assistant medical officer, leg carried away, dead. M. du Cluzel, sub-lieutenant, head blown off.[3]

Among the wounded, six *gardes* are listed, including Jean-François de La Pérouse with minor wounds to the stomach and to one arm. For him, the Battle of Quiberon was over. He was now a prisoner. During the next day, the struggle continued, but the French were primarily concerned with escaping from the pursuing British. Seven ships of the line, three frigates and a corvette found refuge in the narrow esturary of the Vilaine River; eight fled south to Rochefort. Five ships had been burnt or had sunk; one, the *Formidable,* had been captured. English losses included the *Resolution* which eventually sank with two of the unfortunate *gardes* from the *Formidable*, although one of them, Bouteville, was found two days later by a Dutch merchantman and brought back to Brest. Thus, of the 11 young *gardes* on board the *Formidable*, three lost their lives and six were wounded.

Admiral Hawke had neutralized the Atlantic fleet, just as Boscawen had all but destroyed the Mediterranean fleet at the Battle of Lagos off the Portuguese coast. Britain was safe from invasion, her mastery of the seas restated. Hawke, anxious to show how fierce the fighting had been, had the *Formidable* repaired — enough at least to sail her to Plymouth with a makeshift crew. It was to be her final voyage: further work on her was considered pointless and the Admiralty ordered her broken up in 1767.

Hawke's decision saved La Pérouse from imprisonment. The English admiral knew it would be hard enough to get the ship to an English port without cluttering her up with wounded as well. Jean-François was sent ashore as a prisoner on parole, to be exchanged against a British prisoner of equal status captured during the abortive 1758 English landing in northern Brittany.

Precise details are lacking as some of the documents relating to the prisoners are missing. La Pérouse was certainly not among those sent on board the *Resolution*, nor does his name appear in the 'List of French commissioned officers as have been taken and brought into Great Britain 1755-1762' in the Public Record Office.[4] No mention of him appears anywhere until late 1760 when he is listed as 'present at Brest'.

The Duc d'Aiguillon gave priority to the case of the *Formidable*. 'Her crew has shown such bravery and firmness that I felt it incumbent on me to see to their exchange before anything else', he wrote to the Minister,[5] adding: 'The English never cease to praise them'.

Jean-François came under Clause 4 of an agreement signed by Hawke and D'Aiguillon:

> 4. The other officers and *gardes* of the *Formidable* will be allowed to return to French soil and to remain there giving their word that they will not serve again until they have been exchanged.

We can assume that he remained hospitalized for a few weeks in the neighbouring town of Vannes. When he was fit to travel, he returned to Brest. Whether he was given leave to visit his parents in Albi remains uncertain. In view of his age, his bravery, his wounds and the fact that he had not been home for over three years, it is not unreasonable to suppose that he was, but this was wartime and such evidence as we have tends to suggest that he may not after all have made that long journey into Languedoc.

Notes

1. Quoted in Trammond, J., *Manuel d'histoire maritime de la France*, Paris, 1927, p. 459.
2. The Battle of Quiberon (or of the Cardinals, from the name of rocks at the entrance to the Bay) has been analysed in detail by Admiral de Brossard in his 1978 book on La Pérouse.
3. Archives Nationales, Marine. B4-88, fo. 162 ff., quoted in Brossard, p. 30-1.
4. P.R.O. Kew, A.D.M. 103/502.
5. Aiguillon to Berryer, Vannes, 4 December 1759, quoted in Brossard, p. 45.

4
The End of a Disastrous War

JEAN-FRANÇOIS remained nominally a prisoner of war until late 1760 when he was released from his bond in exchange for another prisoner. This did not mean he could not return to the Navy, but rather that he was not to take any part in the continuing war. He had little choice in the matter anyhow, since the French fleet, so recently battered by the English, remained blockaded in Brest.

He still had the opportunity of resuming his studies, returning to the Hôtel des Gardes and consolidating with additional theory the practical experience he had gained. There was much to be done: the science of navigation, mathematics, astronomy, naval architecture, geography. Monsieur de Chézac supervised work, firmly but with some indulgence towards the young man who had shown daring and bravery, and who had lost several of his friends in the sea fight off Quiberon.

Brest cannot have been a happy town. The feeling of frustration felt by officers in the permanent naval service was exacerbated by the disdainful indifference of those who had come to the war as to a diverting activity, suitable for gentlemen, but not to be regarded with too much seriousness.

There were dinner parties, gambling evenings, a mediocre theatre, the occasional ball; but they could not hide the fact that the port was a prison, isolated from the rest of France by bad roads and wild country, and barred from the open sea by the waiting English squadrons. Supplies of food and wine were irregular, trade was slowing down, shortages were pushing prices up. And the news was mostly bad. Quebec fell, Montreal soon followed, then Detroit and one by one the French outposts along the Mississippi.

The reaction of French intellectuals was one more blow, incomprehensible to those who had fought so hard for French Canada, and based on a dismal lack of sympathy: Voltaire, who had sneered at New France in his *Candide* of 1759 as 'a few acres of snow', not only congratulated Frederick of Prussia on his victories over French armies in Europe, but wrote to the Foreign Minister Choiseul begging him 'on his knees' to get rid of Canada. The tangled skein of the European campaigns was not easy to visualize from the port of Brest: there were victories, but they never seemed to be followed up, while personal rivalries between the commanders undid what the courage and sacrifice of their men had achieved.

Individual initiative replaced what the Navy could not attempt to do. Corsairs set off on raids from St Malo or other ports to harry English shipping, returning with a prize or rich booty. It was dangerous, but it could be rewarding. Above all, it broke the crippling monotony of life in the blockaded ports.

Freed from his parole, La Pérouse wrote to a shipowner of Bordeaux, a Monsieur Gradis, begging him, 'should the opportunity arise, to remember him and retain the assurance that no one in the world has more determination'.[1]

A better occasion was to present itself, more in keeping with the status of a young *garde de la marine*, and involving the colourful Chevalier de Ternay.

Six ships had taken refuge in the mouth of the River Vilaine during the later stage of the Battle of Quiberon, and there they remained, safe enough from the patrolling British but of no use to anyone. There were no facilities ashore, no stores, no yards, hardly even a tavern. Faced with total inaction, the senior officers were granted leave and eventually were posted to other ships. It was proposed to pay off much of the crew, but the impoverished treasury could not really afford it. Ternay who had fought on the *Inflexible* which was now declared to be too badly damaged for further repairs, found himself, as the consequence of the departure of his fellow officers, one of the senior officers on the river. He was only a lieutenant, but the Duc d'Aiguillon supported him. The minister was also behind Hector, who was sent to the Vilaine to plan the complex operation of preparing the ships without arousing English suspicions for the high-tide, dead-of-night run towards the open sea. Unfortunately, Marion du Fresne was sent out as well — and he was a merchant navy officer. 'Temporary gentlemen' with naval experience were essential in time of war, but they were deeply resented by the officers of the royal navy.

Ternay was a determined defender of the privileges of the nobility. No one could question Marion de Fresne's professional skills or his courage — he was eventually to sail to the Pacific and to die at the hands of the New Zealand Maoris. But friction could not be avoided. Two of the ships slipped out in January 1761, but Marion du Fresne returned to St Malo and the more compatible messrooms of the *Companie des Indes*.

Promoted to captain, Ternay was requested to bring out the *Robuste* and the *Eveillé*. It was scarcely a propitious time for the undertaking: the British had just captured Belle Isle, across the bay from the Vilaine. D'Aiguillon, not a little irritated by the whole situation, grumbled about the lack of determination of sailors 'who always find excuses in the winds, the tides and the moon'. The facts were that supplies were critically short and Versailles was more interested in channelling funds into the continental campaigns — it looked by 1761 as if Frederick of Prussia would finally be forced into some compromise, if not downright surrender — than into re-equipping ships which, bottled up in the Vilaine, would end up bottled up in Brest or Rochefort.

Nevertheless, Ternay was displaying great energy. Officers were sent down from Brest, including La Pérouse who joined the *Robuste* on 1 May. The ship was in a poor condition, and with no facilities for repairing her in the Vilaine she presented a serious risk. When finally, on 28 November, she struggled over the bar in company with the *Eveillé*, she was making water at the rate of three feet a day. Winds and the need to avoid enemy patrols led Ternay down to La Coruña on the northern coast of Spain. By the Family Compact signed a few months earlier, Spain had been brought more firmly into the French camp, so that the port authorities could at least help in repairing the ship.

The Spanish were twice given the opportunity to display their attachment to the French cause: on 2 December when the ships arrived, and again on the 16th when, driven back by a storm, they limped back.

The *Robuste*, with La Pérouse on board, finally reached Brest at the end of the year. He received a bonus of 300 *livres*, as did the other *gardes*, which he was able to start spending ashore when he was discharged on 12 January. Ternay received an annuity of 3,000 *livres* which made up for the personal funds he had been forced to spend to bring the operation to a successful end.

Jean-François was back aboard the *Robuste* by early May. The war was struggling towards its lamentable ending. The death of Elizabeth of Russia had brought the pro-Prussian czar Peter II to the throne, and Russian troops were beginning to withdraw; Havana was being threatened and would soon fall to British troops; Rodney had already captured the French West Indian island of Martinique. Peace talks were to proceed throughout 1762, under the direction of the Duc de Choiseul who had taken over the Foreign Affairs portfolio. French efforts were now directed towards securing the best possible terms. This meant harrying the English to increase weariness and seizing what bargaining counters might be available. Ternay was despatched to Newfoundland on such a mission.

Choiseul was a pragmatist uninterested in the anti-colonial views of the *philosophes* who were prepared to sacrifice all France's overseas outposts in exchange for a less ambitious foreign policy that would enable France to pay more attention to her internal problems. They might well be right, but he had a peace to conclude — some might add he had a career to foster — in which hard negotiations and every diplomatic asset would be required. Born Comte de Stainville in 1719, he had served in the army during the War of the Austrian Succession, had learnt the art of diplomacy as French Ambassador to Rome, then to Vienna, and had been made *duc et pair* in December 1758 when he became Secretary for Foreign Affairs.

He was a man of noted wit and charm. Scarcely handsome, he had had the good fortune to marry the daughter of the financier Gozat, who brought him an immense fortune and the advantages of youth and gentleness. Her wealth and his talents made an irresistible combination. In January 1761 he added the portfolio of War and, in October, of the Marine — which meant the Colonies as well. He had become the most powerful man in France; even when he gave the Ministry of Marine in 1766 to his cousin César-Gabriel de Choiseul, Duc de Praslin, he retained his influence since the two men substantially shared the same views. They were both to lose their power at the same time, in 1770, so that the decade 1761-1770 can justly be called the Choiseul Period.

They inspired confidence in others through the very confidence they displayed in themselves. The Minister of Marine, Berryer, for a time the protégé of Madame de Pompadour, wrote to Choiseul-Stainville on 20 August 1761:

> I am utterly in need of your assistance. Only with time and plentiful resources organized with complete orderliness and economy could one succeed in restoring this unhappy machine which it seems everything is conspiring to destroy.[2]

Berryer was not exaggerating. The Mediterranean squadron had been virtually destroyed at Lagos, the Brest squadron had fared no better at Quiberon, Canada had been lost, Lally-Tollendal was surrendering the last French possessions in India, the English were in occupation of Belle Isle in Brittany. The war to all intents and purposes was lost. What now mattered was a peace that would enable France to win the next war. Neither of the Choiseuls had any doubts that there would be another war and that the enemy would again be England. 'England is the declared enemy of your power and our state. She will always be', wrote Choiseul-Praslin to Louis XV. They were right in their views, although their belief in the inevitability and even the desirability of a confrontation with Britain would lead eventually to their dismissal. And they had the consolation of living long enough to see their policies vindicated and Britain lose her grip over her North American colonies.

When Choiseul-Stainville took over the Navy, he realized how parlous its state was:

> What little remained in the stores was being auctioned off; we had nothing

with which to repair and refit the vessels that had survived M. de Conflans' battle; since M. de la Clue's fight, the port of Toulon was no better than Brest; the ships were in a state of abandonment; the stores were empty; the navy was in debt to everyone and did not have a penny; all the officers were in a state of utter discouragement, and the Minister who was in charge of this Department was at the point of bitterness and relinquishment.[3]

His first task was to restore the Navy's finances. His personality and drive found some response among lenders, but he also discovered some funds overlooked by Berryer and in one or two cases concealed and about to be manipulated into private hands. He prevailed on the States of Languedoc to offer the King a ship of the line; other provinces were persuaded into following suit and even some cities joined the trend — Paris and Marseilles followed the example of Burgundy, Flanders, Artois and Guyenne. The clergy contributed a million *livres*. In this way, 15 ships, from 54 to 90 guns, were built, backpay claims were settled, the naval stores were restocked — and at the end of the war, in 1763, the state of the navy was better than it had been in 1761.

Thus it was possible to send Ternay to Newfoundland. Choiseul had few illusions about the final outcome of the war, but like Pitt he knew the importance of the North Atlantic fisheries. In 1761 Pitt had stated his intention of holding on to all of Canada, including the valuable fisheries which he regarded as 'a great nursery for sailors' and 'the best of schools for the French navy'. The issue of the fisheries became the most important point of difference in the continuing negotiations between France and England, with some of Pitt's colleagues arguing against his obduracy, and Choiseul remaining determined to hold on at least to the right for the French to fish in the Gulf of St Lawrence, even if France could not retain a territorial foothold.[4]

Ternay's instructions were to destroy fishing settlements along the coast of Newfoundland, clear it of English influence, and thus prepare the way for a late offensive in the Gulf. The true, diplomatic motives were not revealed to Ternay: they were no concern of his. He was given the *Robuste*, the *Eveillé*, the frigate *Licorne* and the storeship *Garonne*, together with an infantry force of 570 men and 31 officers under the orders of Colonel d'Haussonville. La Pérouse was aboard the *Robuste*.

Ternay's hopes were high and the young *garde* found his enthusiasm catching. As the division sailed from Brest on 8 May 1762, the two men and their fellow officers began to scour the horizon for two English convoys which spies had informed them were about to depart from Cork. One was bound for Canada with supplies, the other for Lisbon. Confident that the seas had been cleared of French raiders, the English authorities had provided only one warship, two at the most, to escort the convoys. Furthermore, May was the time of the year when English fishing vessels set out for the cod grounds around Newfoundland. So there were rich prizes to be had, prisoners to be taken, much-needed supplies to be re-routed to Brest.

Unhappily, the seas remained empty — no sails appeared, whether to herald the presence of a following convoy, or to spell danger. This disposed of the problem that nagged Ternay — how to take home ships he might have captured at the outset of a voyage intended to take him to Newfoundland.

La Pérouse, less experienced and more eager for a spectacular revenge on the English, was disappointed, but there were minor engagements. By the time the division reached Newfoundland, on 20 June, three small merchantmen had been captured and burnt. Closnard in the *Garonne*, however, had given chase to one ship which had finally eluded him and, no one could risk doubting it, had by now reached the British settlements and raised the alarm.

Accordingly, Ternay took his ships to an isolated cove south of Saint John's. He set the troops ashore and they marched off to cover the 25 miles to the main port. Very sensibly, the forewarned British were looking out to sea for the French ships, Their watch was justified when the *Robuste* appeared. But by that time, d'Haussonville's soldiers were attacking from inland. Caught between two fires, Saint John's surrendered.

To be fair, the port was undermanned: the French took 82 officers and men prisoners — which was the total extent of the garrison. The crew of the *Grammont*, a frigate anchored in the harbour, provided a better catch — 125 men. Some 40 fishing boats and all the port's equipment and stores were destroyed. There was no sign of the main fishing fleet, so the French had to be content with destroying fishing boats and shore facilities from Fort Trinity to Harbour Grace. But summer was passing, it was obvious the main fishing fleet would not make for the trap set for it at Saint John's, and a British attempt to recapture the town could only be a matter of time.

For someone like La Pérouse, July and August were dull months of shipboard duty and routine tasks. There was little glory to be gained from burning fishing smacks and cod drying platforms. Ternay had grander plans. His troops, now strengthened by Irish volunteers from the Newfoundland coasts, would fortify Saint John's and hold it through the winter; by springtime Choiseul would have sent him reinforcements; he could then attempt a landing on the Quebec coast or Ile Royale where the local French population would rise in support.

Cold reason soon prevailed. Supplies were scarcely adequate for the French to last out the winter, the sparse local population was pro-British, an attempt to recapture Saint John's might occur well before the real winter set in. Rumours that an expedition was being prepared against him in New England were reinforced by sightings of sails out at sea. Ternay called his officers together on 8 September. His orders had been satisfactorily carried out: he would not endanger his ships by waiting for the English to attack and destroy them bottled up in the harbour. The port could be held for the winter months by a garrison of 300 men; Ternay would sail back to France, report on the success of his mission and return as soon as he could with whatever ships Choiseul gave him. At any rate, if it were true that the English were about, he would go out and fight.

The winds on which so many plans depended in the days of sailing ships had the final word. The French started to embark d'Haussonville and the balance of his troops, whereupon the winds changed and prevented their departure. On the 12th, the British force arrived — four ships, two frigates and 1,500 men in nine transports. Generously, the wind now dropped to a light breeze, enabling the British soldiers to land without trouble. Ternay had not worked and plotted so hard to get the *Robuste* and the *Eveillé* out of the Vilaine rivermouth merely to lose them off the coast of Newfoundland. D'Haussonville and his soldiers were put back ashore to reinforce the French garrison, and at night on the 15th while the early autumn fog rose around the coast Ternay slipped away. D'Haussonville politely capitulated three days later.

Jean-François might feel that the expedition had not been markedly glorious, but Ternay, impassive on the quarter-deck, knew that it had been as successful as the Minister had dared to hope. The current war was almost over: to some extent the raid was a test of what the French navy might be able to achieve during the next one. Ternay was bringing back an English frigate, three captured vessels as prizes, and 350 Irish volunteers whom it was not wise to leave behind to await British reprisals — they would be able to join France's Irish brigades.

On 29 September 1762, the French were nearing Ushant. The English squadron was waiting for them. Ternay tried Port-Louis to the south. He sighted more enemy sails and wisely decided to sail down to La Coruña, capturing a corsair of 26 guns on the way.

Choiseul sent him a courier from Bayonne, with instructions to remain in Spain and await the signing of the peace treaty. There was no point in taking any risks. The preliminaries were signed on 3 November. A month later, the British Parliament debated them; they were approved without a division in the House of Lords, and by a majority of 319 to 65 in the Commons. In spite of Pitt's concern about the concessions made to France over the North Atlantic fisheries, and some extremists' anxiety about what they viewed as leniency in the West Indies and India, opposition to the peace terms could only be of a token nature, and the bribes which the government had, traditionally, used to sway the last waverers were unnecessary: Britain had driven France out of North America and out of India, and established for all to see British supremacy in commerce and naval matters.

Ternay did not have to await the formal signing of the Treaty of Paris on 10 February 1763. The British blockading fleet was going home; corsairs were transforming themselves into peaceful merchantmen. He sailed from La Coruña on 9 January 1763. On the 20th he was back in Brest.

Jean-François was now 21. He was still a *garde de la marine* and for the first time in his career he was serving in time of peace. What prospects could there be for promotion now? His immediate future depended on the government's policies. If Versailles decided to retrench, his career would vegetate. There was, after all, very little money left in the king's coffers. Everything depended on Choiseul.

Notes

1. Quoted in *Supplément du centenaire,* Société de Géographie, 1888.
2. Quoted in Lacour-Gayet, *Choiseul,* p. 21.
3. Op. cit.
4. The protracted negotiations are detailed in Rashed, *The Peace of Paris.* Liverpool, 1951.

5

Interludes of Peace

IN 1763, Jean-François went home to Albi. The war had not quite by-passed the city, but it had not affected it much either. There was the inevitable slow see-sawing of fortunes — a slide into decay here, a rise to wealthy status there — but, in spite of his parents' regular letters, the quiet town had moved into a remote background. It was all so very different from the cold grey mists of Brittany and the restless world of the sea. He recaptured memories of holidays at the Go; people stopped to greet him in the streets, but each meeting entailed an effort of recollection and gossip about marriages, news of births and deaths served merely to underline that he and those he had known were growing apart.

Victor-Joseph Galaup may have raised the issue of marriage, but without conviction, more to sound out his son about possible attachments in Best than with any serious project in view. Jean-François was still young, with his career ahead of him and, although he was the only son of a family of some standing, there would be time enough to plan a match. How many years would elapse and how startling and inappropriate the match would turn out to be in his eyes was something that Victor-Joseph was spared from imagining.

Soon, the young *garde* set out on the long journey back to Brest. His immediate future depended on his passing a final set of examinations. It was not enough simply to have served and to be a nobleman: to the dismay of many who considered it the prerogative of noble birth to be placed in command, Choiseul was insisting that the king's ships should be run by professionals, and if he did not go quite all the way and throw the doors open to middle-class officers, there were sufficient instances of unorthodox promotion to cause ripples of indignation among the less qualified, and to stiffen the resolve of the studious — which indeed was the wily Minister's aim.

French naval officers could console themselves with the thought that whereas Lord Grenville was reducing the Navy's budget to levels which many considered to be far below the minimum required for national security, his French counterpart was pressing forward with new works at all the major ports. The port towns were being cushioned against the usual economic rundown associated with the end of hostilities by Choiseul's programme of development. A new arsenal had already been opened at Marseilles to complement Brest, Rochefort and Toulon; in due course Lorient would be added. Artillery brigades were set up at each port from 1764, while the great *Ordonnance* of March 1765 reorganized the administrative structures and Martinique in the West Indies, and the Ile de France in the Indian Ocean.

Admittedly, the French navy had suffered heavy losses — 93 ships totalling 3,880 guns — and was therefore rebuilding from a position of weakness while Britain was cutting back from one of strength, but the First Lord of the Admiralty, Lord Egmont, could fairly complain in 1764 that 'we have not now in Great Britain (guardships included) seventeen ships of the line complete'. For once, at least on paper, France was achieving parity and Grenville's anxiety to bring the budget back to a peacetime level, however understandable in political terms, would take a major part of the blame for the failure of the British navy at the start of the American War.

The French treasury was in no better state than Britain's, but the two Choiseuls could at least make their plans without looking over their shoulder. Lord Grenville had to contend with a Parliament of noblemen and yeomen who disliked taxation and could do something to express their displeasure. The Choiseuls needed only to persuade the king and his advisers. Lord Grenville and his successors at the Treasury were plagued by the need to placate taxpayers at home, and were consequently driven to tax British colonists overseas. Thus a confrontation and a rebellion became inevitable, and the war which the Choiseuls had foreseen came about. A different political system enabled the French to ignore the pleas of their taxpayers and watch with smug satisfaction the English lose their American colonies; but the Choiseuls were walking a tightrope and when France finally reached the edge of bankruptcy the entire structure collapsed in the great Revolution of 1789.

All this lay in the future. For La Pérouse, opportunities were waiting which might not have existed for young naval officers across the Channel. On 1 October 1764 he finally passed out of the *corps de garde* and received his commission as ensign, or sub-lieutenant.

What mattered now was to gain more experience, and in as many fields as possible. He kept back a natural ambition and a certain impatience — which pierced through his correspondence in later years — and sought any appointment he could find, not omitting to call on his protector Ternay for assistance.

Already in September 1763 he had sailed in the *Six-Corps* under Chézac, the commander of the Brest *Compagnie des gardes*. The *Six-Corps* was named after the six merchant guilds of Paris which had answered Choiseul's call for contributors to the restoration of the Navy. The voyage was a short one: built and launched in Lorient, the *Six-Corps* had to be sailed to Brest. It took, all in all, four weeks. Nearly two years would elapse before La Pérouse had another chance to join a ship.

Thus, 1764 was a year of studies, of modest socializing, and of speculation about the future. The great event of the year was the death of Madame de Pompadour in April, which threatened for a while the influence of Choiseul. Without the powerful favourite, Louis XV might begin to rely more heavily on his son, the Dauphin, who was a declared enemy of Choiseul. Matters were not eased when in November, Choiseul persuaded the king to sign a decree suppressing the Jesuit Order. The Dauphin, like most of the royal family, was a firm supporter of the Jesuits.

La Pérouse shared many of the opinions of the reformist *philosophes* of his day, but he cannot have been unmoved by the outlawing of the Jesuits: like most educated young men, he had studied under them. He may not have been one of their academic stars, but he was no failure either. Now one more sentimental tie with Albi was being severed. In earlier skirmishes between the more puritan

Jansenist magistrates and the powerful Order, colleges run by the Jesuits — which meant in effect most educational institutions of standing — were ordered to be closed. Gradually their properties had been sequestrated. The final blow had now fallen. It made more enemies at Court for Choiseul, but it gained him friends in the Paris parliament.

Then the king's son fell ill with tuberculosis; his decline continued during 1765 and in December the Dauphin was dead. Choiseul, who would have been instantly dismissed had the Dauphin come to the throne, was now safe. The Dauphine remained his enemy, with a growing influence on the grieving Louis XV, but she too was soon to sicken and die.

The drawing-rooms of Brest echoed with conjectures about the future of France and intrigues at Versailles. Gossip often flourishes best when knowledge is vague and second-hand. There was little enough to do. Louis de Bougainville had succeed in organizing an expedition to the Falkland Islands to settle Acadian refugees deported from New Brunswick, but the day of the great voyages of exploration had not yet dawned. La Pérouse could only manage to sail for a few months from 20 August 1765 in the *Adour*, a storeship transporting timber.

Beggars could not be choosers. He was not the only young officer looking for a chance to sail and gain practical experience. Life ashore was dull at the best of times, and one could hardly hope to add to one's all-important *dossier personnel* — the officer's personal file — by frequenting the few salons of Brest or gambling for modest stakes in the backrooms of the better taverns. Even Ternay himself could only manage coastal work in a corvette of 80 tons.

The *Adour* was commanded by the Baron de Clugny who took her down to Bayonne, close by the Spanish frontier, to load timber from the Pyrenees for the naval yards at Rochefort and Brest. Bayonne was going through a period of prosperity, supplying not only timber, but tar, hemp, anchors and guns. Trade indeed was so profitable that the ship-chandlers and merchants of Bayonne began to fear that the king might take over the port.

Jean-François was to get another chance to sail down the Atlantic

The Duc de Choiseul
(Musée de la Marine.)

coast. This was in no small way due to Clugny's favourable report when the *Adour* completed her voyage in January 1766: 'Messrs de La Mettrie et de La Pérouse, *enseignes* ... through their vigilance and determination added to the few resources we had.'[1] This time, in May, La Pérouse sailed in the *Dorade*, commanded by Kergariou. The pay was minimal but the experience invaluable. The *Dorade* sailed down to Bayonne and back by way of Bordeaux and Roche-fort. More than sailing was involved: young Jean-François met timber merchants, sundry shipchandlers, bankers. The complex world of shore suppliers and financiers, of bills of lading and bills of exchanges, opened before him. And the day was not too distant when he would be as much at home in it as on the seas. In July, Kergariou gave up his command and another precious report found its way into La Pérouse's slim personal file: 'Messrs de Kergariou and La Pérouse, *enseignes*, behaved with all the ability their diligence has developed in them'.

The war, with all its disasters, was receding into the past. Things were improving under Choiseul's drive. The *Dorade* was back in Brest in July. Almost without a break, on 16 July, La Pérouse joined the *Gave,* with his friend La Mettrie, on their way to Bayonne for more timber; but they later had an opportunity to go further — to Toulon, which La Pérouse had never seen. Going through the Straits of Gibraltar into a new sea was another experience to add to his growing stock, but it brought him in sight of an English naval base from which the victors of the Seven Years War kept watch on passing ships — he could only feel bitterness at the thought that they knew that the *Dorade*, for all the braid and colour of her officers, was merely doing a merchantman's work.

Back in Albi his parents must once again have wondered whether his choice of career had been wise but soon he was able to send them news which made them proud of him: he had been given his first command. True, it was only the *Adour*, but it was a beginning. He took over on 10 September 1767. The storeship was slow and un-glamorous, but she was serviceable. On 14 November he transferred to the *Dorothée* which he commanded until 18 May 1768.[2] The time had come for other work. In July he saw Ternay who, following a spell of hydrographic work in the *Heureuse*, was in command of the *Turquoise*. The Queen, Marie Leszczynska, had just died, and in this official period of mourning the officers wore black stockings and a black crepe armband even in the *Turquoise* which was a small corvette commissioned for coastal survey. It was part of Choiseul's plan to make Brest impregnable by fortifying the island of Ushant and having such precise charts of the coast that French vessels could beat any blockade by sailing blind at night. It required painstaking survey work, and it was to provide one more invaluable experience for La Pérouse.

Choiseul's problem had been that Ushant was privately owned. Given by Henry IV in 1597 to the Comte de Rieux, it was still held by the family. Such private property might easily fall to English raiders. Choiseul had persuaded the count to sell it in 1764 for 30,000 *livres* down and an annuity of 3,000 *livres* extinguishable only on the death of the countess and her son. Considering that the stormracked island had produced a return on average of a mere 708 *livres* a year, the Rieux family could not resist the offer.[3] But at last Choiseul could have the island fortified and fitted into his overall defence plan.

La Pérouse sailed with Ternay from 14 July to 14 September 1768. The *Turquoise* threaded her way between the rocky islets and the shore, around the jagged granite lashed by the foam, struggling against the swiftly racing tide, cautiously watching for the sudden changes of wind channelled capriciously down the lateral valleys. It was mid-summer, but no one could be certain that a sudden storm would not sweep in from the Atlantic and blot out the dangers around them. Ternay however knew what he was doing:

> My plan is to repeat the runs I made last year and attempt to pass at night through waters I have already sailed through by day. This undertaking will be more difficult, but it can be necessary in time of war when the Iroise is occupied by superior forces.[4]

Jean-François spent the winter months ashore. There were no immediate prospects in sight for him in early 1769, and he asked for a lengthy period of home leave. This was granted without difficulty, so that he left for Albi on 1 March and did not return to Brittany until the end of September. It was the first request of this kind he had made since his arrival in Brest thirteen years earlier, and it would be many years before he would again be able to spend such a long period in his native district.

His father was turning 60; the old man's eyesight was beginning to fail, but his back was straight, his manner dignified, as befitted a leading citizen of an old provincial town. Victor-Joseph was in every respect a patriarchal figure, brooking no challenge to his authority. The matter of Jean-François' marriage must have been raised several times and the names of suitable young ladies mentioned. Apart from Jean-François, only two children had survived, both girls, so that unless he married and produced an heir the name of Galaup de La Pérouse would die out. But nothing eventuated. Jean-François was not ready to marry — at least, none of the suggested matches appealed to him. He was still only 28, having celebrated his birthday at the Go before leaving for Brest; but for his father especially, the 'only' was beginning to sound hollow.

Jean-François impressed him with his maturity, his knowledge of the world, his self-confidence. Even his tendency to put on weight, against which he struggled all his life, suggested that La Pérouse was no longer just a youth; some consideration needed to be given to the headship of the family and the unborn generations of it. Old Victor-Joseph shook his head regretfully at his son's comments about being only 28 and in no hurry to settle down.

Jean-François' thoughts lay elsewhere. Things were happening in his own world, which was not the steady peaceful semi-rural world of Albi.

In December 1766 Bougainville had sailed to the Falklands to bring down the curtain on his attempt to colonize the island, and this done 'he had gone on to the Pacific Ocean, arriving in Tahiti in April 1768, following Samuel Wallis and preceding James Cook. Not many months later, when garbled reports of Wallis' voyage reached India, the French hastily organized the Surville expedition to forestall a possible British settlement in the Pacific.

The race to the South Seas had begun and France, now well on the way to recovery after the Seven Years War, had no intention of being left out of it. Her rival, Britain, had enough troubles of her own to even out the contest. George III was beginning to show signs of mental instability, the American colonies were growing restless, the Stamp Act had to be repealed in the face of their opposition, and this was followed by growing agitation against the Mutiny Act, while in the East the issue of the renewal of the India Company's charter led to an acrimonious argument between the Crown and the City. If the French *philosophes* were submitting the French political system to pointed analyses, much the same thing was happening across the Channel: Edmund Burke's famous pamphlet of 1770 was significantly entitled *Thoughts on the Present Discontent.*

When La Pérouse returned to Brest, he was posted, after the usual winter months ashore, to the *Belle-Poule*. It was at last a warship, a frigate of 26 guns, heralding the long awaited end of coastal duties on dreary storeships. There was even a possibility of war. The arguments over the Falkland Islands had moved into a new phase. Bougainville had bowed to Spanish pressure and given up his plan of colonization, but the British had their own claims to the group and were now confronting Spain. The Choiseuls were far from averse to a conflict between these two countries, from which France, and probably the restless American colonists, might gain. As part of their manoeuvres France had signed first a treaty with Genoa in 1764, then another in 1768 which resulted in France acquiring Corsica — thereby, interestingly enough, ensuring that Napoleon Bonaparte would be born a Frenchman and become the powerful enemy of Britain which Choiseul dreamed of being. Now a struggle between Spain and England might weaken France's hereditary rival in areas where Britain would be most affected: in her overseas empire and her trade routes. Spain would be unlikely to win, but the gamble had its attractive aspects. The *Belle-Poule*, under Thomas d'Orves, was only one of the royal ships being readied for an eventual war.

French fishing boats and coastal vessels were kept close to the shores by their masters who remembered the sudden pouncing raids which had preceded the outbreak of the previous war. And indeed two English frigates were sighted off Ushant. Choiseul had had the island and the coast fortified, but there was no satisfactory signalling system between these defences and the port of Brest. La Pérouse, whose work along this coast was remembered, was sent out in October 1770 in an ammunition lighter, a *bugalet*, with seven or eight men to check on English shipping movements and set up signalling posts. The little boat was so insignificant that its name has not been recorded. He returned to the *Belle-Poule* on 30 December.

Tension was rising all along the Channel and Atlantic coasts, but neither France — nor indeed Spain — was ready for war. The emergency faded away and with it went the power of the Choiseuls.

The end of the Choiseul era had become inevitable, in large part because the Duke had underestimated the influence of the new favourite, Madame du Barry, a grievous miscalculation by one who should have remembered how much of his power he owed to her predecessor, Madame de Pompadour. It may have been too much for the Duke to accept that the illegitimate daughter of a tax collector and a former courtesan could have gained such ascendancy over the ageing king — Louis XV was 60 and Madame Du Barry was 24 — and it was rather more than he could bear to pay homage to her. But there were ambitious men, such as the Duc d'Aiguillon, behind her, and Choiseul himself did not lack enemies.

On Christmas Eve 1770, the Duc de la Vrillère handed Choiseul a letter from the king instructing him to place his resignation in the hands of the Secretary of State and retire forthwith to his country estate. Choiseul's fall had numerous repercussions, including a minor one in Brest: La Pérouse had been put forward by the local commander, Rosilis, to take command of a three-year-old corvette, the *Lunette*. The request was not actioned, and for the first time, but not the last, La Pérouse wrote a letter of complaint. He was no longer a young officer, he was a man of experience and tireless energy; the time had come for him to be heard:

> Monsieur de Rosilis requested for me from the Duc de Praslin the command of the *Lunette* so that I could complete my work on signals which M. Hector, port superintendent, decided required certain modifications. Such, my Lord, was my situation when the Duke de Praslin was

dismissed. I had been chosen by a commanding officer who is still by
your side, I had earned through my diligence the support of M. de Rosilis,
I had carried out a brief campaign without payment in spite of the meagre-
ness of my fortune: those are my qualifications, and I was so confident
that I had already purchased some supplies for my future campaign. I
had furthermore already been in command of two small vessels used for
the transport of masts, and the Duke de Praslin had had the kindness to
tell me that he would remember my zeal when the time came.

Having been in the Service for over fifteen years, I have been on twelve
campaigns, I was wounded in the most murderous battle of the last war;
in spite of that, M. de Tromelin, a port officer for the last six months,
is reaping where I have sown: he obtains the command M. de Rosilis has
sought for me.

I seek, my Lord, in my past life, the reasons that might justify so harsh
a treatment . . . . [5]

The Minister replied a fortnight later — most promptly when one
considers the slowness of mails between Brest and Versailles in
winter and the fact that Choiseul-Praslin's replacement had only
just taken over the portfolio — that Tromelin, who had been given
the command of the *Lunette*, was senior to La Pérouse and that it
was 'appropriate to take him off the frigate *Belle-Poule* which may
receive instructions to sail at any time and where M. de La Pérouse
will be of far more use'.

It was not a mere placatory gesture. The *Belle-Poule* did sail in
early May 1771 for the West Indies. She was to be away for just
under six months. With La Pérouse sailed another *enseigne*, Fleuriot
de Langle, who was to be his companion on his great voyage of
circumnavigation. The second in command was Armand-François
Cillart de Suville (or Surville) who had served with distinction in
India and been in the *Robuste* during the 1762 Newfoundland expedition. Jean-François was among friends. His work on board was
appreciated and Captain d'Orves would report on his return: 'La
Pérouse. Very well-read and knowledgeable. A young officer in
whom one places great hopes'.[6]

The French West Indies were going through a period of prosperity,
eclipsing even British and Spanish trade figures. A thousand ships
a year traded through the ports of Santo Domingo and the islands of

Guadeloupe, Martinique and St Lucia. There was a healthy export surplus — 200 millions *livres* as against 70 millions of imports in an average year — largely because more than half the total exports consisted of sugar and its by-products, such as rum which was not favoured by the wine-drinking colonists who were too few in numbers to require a significant volume of imported manufactured goods. Coffee came mainly from Martinique, indigo from Santo Domingo, sugar from everywhere. Santo Domingo, the western part of the large island of Hispaniola — today's Haiti — still had much virgin land that could be developed without fertilizers. The French had opened two free ports, Mole St Nicolas in Santo Domingo and Le Carénage in St Lucia, where foreign ships could trade with a duty rate limited to one per cent. Traders came from New England, selling grain, fish and barrels, in exchange for rum, molasses and sugar — which, being cheaper than Jamaican sugar, was frequently re-exported to Britain as English colonial sugar.

The sugar plantations depended on slavery. The British had the major share of the slave trade and supplied most of the Spanish and French colonies. Thus when the *Belle-Poule* reached Santo Domingo La Pérouse was confronted by a totally different world from that of French Canada: over eighty per cent of the population was black, most of them slaves. The proportion was much lower in Martinique and Guadeloupe; but in Santo Domingo one gained the impression of being in Africa.

The centre of administration was Port-au-Prince, but the first port of call was Cap Français on the north coast and by far the larger town, with a population of 12,000 — twice that of Port-au-Prince — including 2,500 whites. As the main port of a prosperous colony, it was not unattractive. The town had been laid out in straight lines, so that the streets intersected at right angles. Covered with sandy gravel, they were pleasant in summer and reasonably free of mud in the wet season. The Cours Villeverd, its main street, was lined with stone houses, mostly single storied, with building materials often imported from France, including tiles from Normandy and slates from Anjou. As befitted a port, Cap Français had over 20 taverns, and a hospital with 100 beds, well filled when a ship came

in with scurvy cases, or in the months of June to October when
fevers and dysentery multiplied.

When Jean-François visited Port-au-Prince, he found a smaller
town, with a higher proportion of whites, wider streets but far more
mud: it was, wrote one unimpressed visitor, 'like a Tartar camp . . .
if it rained overnight you cannot walk in the streets which are like
great muddy tracks lined with ditches where frogs are croaking'.[7]
Matters had not been made any easier by an earthquake which had
destroyed much of the town the previous June, so that the authorities
forbade all building other than in timber or timbered masonry.

Society, as was often the case in the smaller colonies, was split
horizontally between the rich planters and merchants — the 'grands
Blancs' — and the shopkeepers, artisans and clerks — the 'petits
Blancs' — but also vertically between the locally-born Creoles and
the French-born administrators who stayed only for short periods.
In spite of receptions, balls and visits to the theatre — there was
one in Cap Français and one in Port-au-Prince — the social cleavage
was all too plain to the officers of the *Belle-Poule*. The strain was
made worse by the growing controversy over slavery, an institution
viewed as essential by the local planters. The philosophical movement then gathering momentum in France challenged slavery on
ethical and economic grounds.

Montesquieu, in his *Lettres persanes* of 1721 and in his *Esprit
des lois* of 1748, had been a lone voice crying in the wilderness
when he wrote, 'Slavery is of use neither to the master nor to the
slave'[8] but by the 1760s much factual reporting was beginning to
work on French minds. Chanvalon published a *Voyage à la Martinique*
in 1763, Le Cat a *Traité de la peau humaine*, Maupertuis his *Vénus
physique* in 1765, and Demanet a *Nouvelle Histoire de l'Afrique
française* in 1767; the highly influential anti-colonialist *Histoire
philosophique et politique des établissements et du commerce des
Européens dans les deux Indes*, by the Abbé Raynal, had just been
published and would run to 30 editions in 20 years. The work of the
great *encyclopédistes*, of Diderot and Rousseau, provided a cement
which united these various views into an impressive whole. It was
furthermore the age of the Physiocrats, the economic wing of the

philosophes, who were subjecting economic forces to scrutiny. Viewed from a rational standpoint, slavery was uneconomic. Moreau de St Méry calculated that 200 slaves produced 150 tons of sugar, and that as many as half this labour force were children, old people and servants, so that true productivity was about 1.5 tons per head.[9] If one took into account the capital invested in housing and the cost of policing estates to prevent escapes and uprisings as well as raids by the bands of 'marron' slaves ensconced in the hills, the slavery system was hard to justify.

La Pérouse later found similar arguments in Mauritius. The issue was more acute in the West Indies because of the islands' involvement in the actual slave trade, but the impression he took back with him was that the ownership of labourers was motivated as much by a desire to maintain a social status as by the need for labour in underpopulated islands. His views were always dispassionate and realistic; in many respects he shared the views of the Physiocrats, but essentially he was a Galaup, the descendant of merchants and local administrators whose rise was due to objective minds and a down-to-earth approach.

The *Belle-Poule* completed her mission, keeping watch over British and Spanish naval units, protecting trade vessels and ready to intervene should France's interests be threatened. In October 1771 she was back in Brest and La Pérouse signed off on the 14th.

The winter months were not all to be spent ashore. The *Belle-Poule* was being refitted and copper-bottomed in readiness for a long voyage. The command passed from Thomas d'Orves to Jean-François' protector Ternay who had been named Governor of the Ile de France and the Ile de Bourbon, which are today Mauritius and Réunion. The days of storeships and brief coastal surveys were mercifully over. La Pérouse was to sail for the East.

Notes

1. Brossard, *Lapérouse*, p. 123.
2. Archives de la Marine, B2-C6-378.
3. Levot, *Brest*, pp 148-9.
4. Archives de la Marine, B4-112:22.

5. La Pérouse to Ternay, the new Minister of Marine, 14 Jan. 1771, in Archives Nationales, Marine, C7-165.
6. ANM B4-117:103.
7. Giroud, *La Vie quotidienne de la société créole à Saint-Domingue au 18e siècle*, p. 82.
8. Part I, xv, ch. 1.
9. His *Description de la partie française de St Domingue* was published in the U.S. in 1797. A Creole from Martinique, he had served as councillor in Santo Domingo.

6
The Ile de France

JEAN-FRANÇOIS returned to the *Belle-Poule* on 22 January 1772. Within a few days she was ready to sail from Brest, going down to Lorient for further supplies on the 25th and finally leaving the French coast three weeks later. Ternay was in command, Cillart de Surville was his second; among the other officers Kergariou-Locmaria and Grenier were to have particularly brilliant careers. All were of a rank acceptable to the royal navy, but they can only have been relieved to forsake the tensions that were daily growing in Brest. The split between the 'blues' and the 'reds' had become more marked after almost 10 years of peace: the blues seemed more than ever interlopers, in that there was no emergency to justify their role in the Navy. The port administrators, mere clerks in the eyes of many, were at loggerheads with the navy officers, and the reforms initiated by Choiseul, however overdue they might have been, merely exacerbated the irritation of those who felt the privileges conferred on them by birth were undermined by claims of a more efficient administration.

The government sought to improve matters by sending the Comte d'Estaing to Brittany with the double title of Inspector-General and Commander of the Navy: but d'Estaing had spent more years in the army than he had in the navy. He had a tendency to underrate the rights of the nobility — although no one, least of all probably himself, could imagine that a day would come when he would serve in a republican navy. Haughty of manner, he was courteous towards the blue officers and their middle-class wives, and rapidly earned the support of the people of Brest. In counterpart, he was snubbed by the red-uniformed naval officers.

La Pérouse was spared the climax of this growing enmity, which came in December, when the majority of the officers in port stayed away from the ceremony of the blessing of the colours. The rector of the seminary seized the occasion to give a homily which said very little about the navy, but praised the Count, his family, his vast knowledge and the services he had rendered France on land and on sea. The crowded congregation of shore officials and merchants was enraptured, but the ball which d'Estaing gave in the evening was boycotted — even the young *gardes de la marine* staying away until d'Estaing, angered by the teenagers' snub, sent for them to come and dance 'in the King's name'.

Jean-François was to find a different society with its own set of social prejudices in the Ile de France. The Indian Ocean was weeks, usually months away. News reached the colonists irregularly, so that France turned into a strange and remote world, lacking the realities of everyday life.

As a preliminary to passing the invisible gateway to the East, he had to undergo an initiation, the Passage of the Line, a strange and irreverent ceremonial, with echoes of ancient saturnalia and the medieval Feast of Fools. It was a ritual the sailors never failed to follow, even although few of them understood what the imaginary Line represented. If nothing more, it was a relief from the boredom of the long repetitive weeks at sea.

Initiation ceremonies, like all traditions, are not easy to rationalize for outsiders or those who are their victims. The latter become their defenders once they no longer have to submit to them: the uninvolved usually retain a sense of superior detachment. We do not know how Jean-François reacted, but an outsider from a voyage across the Pacific, Philibert Commerson, has left a precise, if disdain-laden description of one contemporary crossing of the Line:

> Here at last is the day the sailors have been waiting for so long. The day before we received the most absurd of letters addressed by Father Tropic to the ship's captain, warning him to observe the customs and traditions of the Navy and consequently not to allow the uninitiated to cross the Line without having been made worthy of it by the sacred baptism . . . etc . . . . Signed: Father Tropic, son-in-law of Father Line.
>
> As a result great preparations from early morning in the tops where all the ship's boys had climbed up with the boatswain and other confederates to prepare the masquerade. Meantime all the candidates were lined up on the quarter deck, for there were no fewer than 30 or 40, in two rows,

the officers on the starboard side, the others on the port side, all of them having both thumbs tied up with a rope which stretched from one end of the deck to the other. After making sure that no one had escaped, Father Line came down from the tops with all his acolytes. Imagine a masquerade of devils. All the ship's boys as naked as your hand but covered from head to toe with oil and lampblack or tar with feathers stuck all over their bodies. All great masqueraders covered in sheepskins, horned, armed with tails and claws, some walking on all fours, others dancing like bears, seized by convulsive movements, and all of them whinnying, growling, mewing, barking with an accompaniment of twenty ram's horns and all the galley's saucepans. After parading several times, Father Line, distinguished by his three-tiered horned tiara and an outfit that was more ridiculous than the others, went and sat on a throne they had prepared for him, and his chancellor held up a notice which everyone in turn had to go up and read, the rough purport of which was a promise that you will do unto others what is done to you, that you will never make love to the wife of an absent sailor and so on. At this point I could not help laughing at the sight of the horns on the masqueraders . . . We still had to put our offering in the basin held out by the other assistant, but we had agreed that, without forsaking the rights of *buena malo*, we would do so only after being well and duly baptised, since we had no wish to decline the *lavabo* and had prepared ourselves for it. We merely set aside the vulgar bawdiness reserved for the sailors, so that we all received a thorough wetting, firstly by the officials of this ceremony, then by ourselves, all endlessly throwing buckets of water at each other, no one being left out. As for the common martyrs, they were all made to sit over a tub filled with water, with an oar under their buttocks which was removed as soon as the formula had been sworn to, so that the candidate fell into the tub, even held down forcibly by strong pairs of arms until, under the pretext of helping him up, he was thoroughly smeared with lamp black. The scene was carried out at the foot of the longboat which had been filled up with water, from which fifteen or twenty men threw bucketfuls of water on the baptisers as well as the baptised. After this, the boys were whipped on the forecastle and all the bucket carriers ran about until bumps and bruises given and received during this pleasant exercise had wearied the actors. Finally came sundry evening rejoicings, bacchic libations in the honour of, and at the expense of the neophytes. Could one believe that such a dull ceremony has been widely adopted by every nation and that no ship has ever failed to follow it? There is more: if the ship herself has never crossed the Line, the captain has to pay for her.[1]

The *Belle-Poule* crossed the Line in May, after brief calls in the Tagus and at the island of Goree off the coast of West Africa. It was a period of dreary calms with the great grey sails hanging heavily in the still air; intolerable heat raising new stenches from below decks; the dense blue of the tropical sea; sudden strange phenomena such as fish that flitted above the water, phosphorescent waves surging eerily in the black night; St Elmo's fire dancing on the tip of the masts — so many new mysteries explained by the older sailors from their store of sea tales and superstitions to wide-eyed boys sitting in a circle on deck, long yarns in the slowness of the day, broken by an argument, a fight or the excitement of sudden danger. The voyage from Goree to False Bay, on the eastern side of the Cape of Good Hope, took over six weeks.

There was no other suitable port of call for ships bound for the Ile de France with a chance to buy fresh supplies, and to talk French with those descendants of the Huguenots who still retained something of the old tongue. Then too, there was an exchange of visits with officers of the *Nourrice* which had put in at the bay on her way home to France.

The *Belle-Poule* stayed over a month at the Cape, from 18 June to 22 July. Just under a month later, she reached Port-Louis, the capital of the Ile de France. No one could have known in advance the date of her arrival. The retiring Governor François du Dresnay Desroches was not there to meet his successor, but in the neighbouring island of Bourbon. Etiquette required Ternay, and therefore his officers, to remain on board until proper arrangements could be made for a formal reception.

The frigate dropped anchor off the Pavillons, outside the port. Jean-François could only scan with his eyeglass the small town, contained in a valley at the end of the long harbour, with steep mountains climbing up on all sides and barring the horizon in a jumble of peaks, blue haze covered at times, barren and burntlooking at others. Deforestation was beginning to make itself felt as the colonists cut trees down to create new farms. Anxious though the authorities were to retain them along the shores to hamper landings by potential enemies, they were helpless in the face of settler pressure.

The problem was made no easier by a two-headed system of government. The island group, known as the Mascareignes, had been administered by the French India Company until 1764 when following the bankruptcy of the company they reverted to the Crown. Delays in providing an alternative structure had led to an uneasy interregnum of three years, until General Dumas, as Governor, and Pierre Poivre, as Intendant, arrived in Port-Louis.

In theory, the separation of powers between the military and the civilian should have worked well, but in an island which was prized above all for its strategic value and was a natural naval base in the Indian Ocean, on the route to India and the Far East, defence considerations affected every aspect of island life. Finance was the irritant: military matters – and that included maintaining the sea links with France and the remaining French Indian settlements – cost money and were not visibly productive. Pierre Poivre had plans for the economic development of the islands; he was all vision and drive,[2] but his ideas required capital, and not all his schemes were profitable. The presence of the *Conseil supérieur*, a local council of notables, chaired by the Intendant, and given responsibilities in the administration of justice, did little to soothe relations. Dumas and Poivre had fallen out almost before they reached Port-Louis. The general was replaced by a naval captain, Desroches, in the reasonable belief that an island situated on a crucial sea route would be best governed by a man of the sea, but Desroches had also been given instructions to reduce expenditure. By the time the new Minister, Des Boynes, recalled Desroches and despatched Ternay in his stead, the Governor and the Intendant were no longer on speaking terms.

Poivre, himself was being replaced by Jacques Maillard du Mesle, *Conseiller du roi* and *Commissaire-général de la Marine*, an experienced naval administrator. Efficiency and restraint were called for; economies were insisted upon – Ternay, for instance, was to be paid 50,000 *livres* a year, or 30,000 less than his predecessor.

Politically and militarily, the island was a burden on France, but its economy had progressed under Poivre. Coffee grew well and was exported to Europe. Cotton was being successfully established. Fruit products included mangoes, guavas and pineapples. The cattle trade was growing, although bullocks still had to be brought in from neighbouring Madagascar which also supplied the islanders with rice. Cereals came from the Cape. Trade extended to India, Manilà and China, and there was of course a whole range of commercial activities associated with the arrival and departure of shipping: it is interesting to note that one of Ternay's earliest actions was to reduce the number of taverns in Port-Louis from 125 to 30, close them entirely on Sundays, and prohibit gambling.

The economy was based on slave labour. The 1776 census gives a total population of 32,739 inhabitants, including 25,154 black slaves and 6,386 whites. Most came from Mozambique and Madagascar, some from India. Escaped slaves, known as the *marrons,* roamed the interior, representing a danger to the more isolated settlement. Ternay was to make a determined effort to flush them out, struggling against the twin problems of inadequate roads and poor transport, since the island suffered from a perennial shortage of horses.

The town itself was unattractive to the eye. The first thing La Pérouse saw on arrival in the outer harbour was the wrecks of ships that had fallen victim to cyclones in the previous March and April. A drought had followed, and the *Africaine* had been sent to Madagascar to seek urgent supplies. Port-Louis cannot have appeared very impressive, if we can accept the description left by the novelist Bernardin de Saint-Pierre, author of *Voyage à l'Isle de France:*

> The Town or Camp consists of single-storied wooden houses, each one isolated and surrounded by palissades. The streets are well aligned but have no trees. Everywhere along the ground you see rocks jutting up so that you cannot take a step without risking your life.

He might have added comments on broken glass and refuse littering the streets, something which Ternay and Maillard were to try to eliminate by decree — an inexpensive if ineffectual approach to the problem.

But there were greater delights in the country and Bernardin himself was to leave in his pre-Romantic *Paul et Virginie* coloured and indeed sentimentalized descriptions of the Mascareignes. There were shady valleys, with cascades of clear water, the chattering of birds, and the intense blue of the sky so different from the Atlantic storm

Arrival of a fleet in Port-Louis, Mauritius. (Musée de la Marine.)

clouds and the silent mists of Brittany.

In one respect at least Port-Louis was not unlike Brest: local society was as divided and as petty in its rifts as in the Breton port. One of Maillard's early tasks, in association with Ternay was to reorganize the *Conseil supérieur*, to rid it of corruption and put an end to seemingly interminable wranglings. Then they set to work drawing up a set of rules to regulate precedence at church services . . .

La Pérouse's first taste of the tensions that can develop in a small isolated colony came soon enough. On the 24th Desroches was back and ready to receive the new Governor. It was with infinite relief and measured excitement that Jean-François finally stepped ashore: 48 hours is a long time to wait in the outer harbour after more than six months at sea. The pageantry made up for the dreariness of the waiting. The men of the various regiments stationed in the island stood at attention, almost two thousand of them, on the Champ de Mars, a large square near the centre of the town — admittedly stony and treeless as Bernardin has pointed out. The periphery was lined by local notables, shopkeepers and their wives, colonists who had ridden down from their holdings or been brought down in palankeens by their black bearers, sailors from the ships, slaves with special status allowed out for the day. All the shops and even the taverns had closed.

Ternay reviewed the troops in the company of the retiring Governor. Pierre Poivre followed a few steps behind with Maillard du Mesle. Poivre and Desroches had arrived separately; they neither spoke nor looked at each other during the entire ceremony, and they went their own way afterwards like the perfect strangers they had become.

The review over, everyone formed a procession to walk over to the church and later to the *Conseil supérieur* where Ternay and Maillard were to present their letters of appointment. Desroches who was still nominally Governor walked a step ahead of Ternay; Poivre, staring at nothing, kept a step ahead of Maillard; then came the members of the council, the senior officials, the officers, military, naval or merchant; the tradespeople and property owners, in a silent but determined tussle for precedence, manipulated into position by their tightlipped wives; and then the crowd of nonentities, petty

officers, artisans, sailors, urchins, and the blacks, for whom the occasion provided a break from routine, tinged with a touch of derision.

Into this the officers of the *Belle-Poule* had to find their place,
Cillart de Surville firmly to the fore, shepherding with dignity his
friends, Kergariou who was a count, as was the *enseigne* Bizien, as
he was himself, as La Pérouse would be one day. They were red
officers, defenders of the privileges of a doomed nobility, and they
kept together, forming a wedge of superiority before which the
locals parted, not merely impressed but anxious not to challenge
men who were so close to the Governor-elect and potentially powerful.

Thus Jean-François found a seat in the front part of the nave, an
area much prized on this occasion, and there, unaware of the jostling
and elbowing that went on in the back, he watched the apostolic
prefect, Fr Contenot, lead the Te Deum in thanksgiving for their
safe arrival and pray for the success of Ternay's mission. Five years
later, when he was sailing away in bitterness, Ternay may have remembered this ceremony and reflected that prayers are not always
answered.

The religious ceremonies over, the official party moved on to the
Council rooms, where Ternay and Maillart were formally installed.
The crowds thinned, off to their shops or their farms, or to the
thriving taverns. Jean-François and his fellow officers walked back to
their ship to complete their packing. Cillart de Surville was to take
over the *Sensé* and sail her back to France with Desroches; Grenier
was to command the *Belle-Poule*, and La Pérouse went to the *Africain*.
In the meantime, they took lodgings ashore, visited the town, paid
calls on residents to whom they had been given letters of intro-
duction, and attended inaugural receptions given by the new
Governor and his Intendant.

Ternay had offices in Port-Louis, but his official residence was
Le Réduit — sometimes referred to as Le Château de Réduit — five
miles out of town. Compared with most buildings in the Ile de
France, Le Réduit could be termed a castle, or at any rate a manor
house. Built in 1748 by a previous Governor, Pierre David, it stood
in a large wooded space between two tributaries of the Grande

Rivière. The site was pleasant and peaceful, suitable for garden fêtes and official dinners, and it was to remain the home of successive governors, French and English, for 200 years. Ternay, in accordance with the custom, had to buy from Desroches the furniture and paintings within as well as the cattle, poultry, farming implements and blacks without.

Maillard had his Hôtel de l'Intendance in the centre of Port-Louis, where the administrative offices were located, but he too had his country house. An imposing symbol of the estrangement between Poivre and Desroches, it stood outside Port-Louis, but on the opposite side of town to Le Réduit. Called less austerely Mon Plaisir, it had been purchased by Poivre in 1770. Some 20 years older than Le Réduit, it was a wooden house with a long verandah onto which opened the drawing room and two bedrooms. The estate comprised some 70 hectares, a small lake, a vegetable garden and a large aviary. Poivre's interest in botany and, more especially, in widening the economic base of the colony by introducing new species, was revealed in the gardens, laid out in the symmetrical French style, where grew spice plants from the Dutch East Indies, roses from China, cherry trees from Japan, mango trees, tea shrubs, coffee trees, and the famous breadfruit trees which were to be the cause almost 30 years later of the mutiny in the *Bounty*; today all this is Mauritius' botanical gardens. Mon Plaisir also owed something to the advice of the Ile de France's most celebrated botanist of the moment, Philibert Commerson.

Commerson was then 45 and in poor health. Maillard described him as a soured character and a libertine. Difficult he certainly was, but his reputation as a libertine may have been largely due to the fact that his valet, on his voyage across the Pacific with Bougainville, was a woman disguised as a man. Both had arrived with Bougainville in Port-Louis in March 1768, and both were still in the island, Commerson living some miles along the west coast in the area known as Le Flacq. Whatever his personal faults, he was an outstanding botanist, respected by Linnaeus and elected — as it transpired, just after his death — in 1773 to the Academy of Sciences. Poivre persuaded him to side with him in his disputes with the Governor and had enough skill to avoid upsetting the cantankerous scientist. A passion for botany united them, and Mon Plaisir offered a wealth of interesting material.

Island society, divided and limited though it was, included others associated with Bougainville's voyage, in addition to Commerson and his former valet, Jeanne Baré. Charles de Romainville, cartographer on board the *Etoile* had transferred to the local regiment and was highly regarded for his skill and his good nature; he was, in 1778, to be sent to the Seychelles to set up a colony. Charles Oger, a *pilote* from the *Boudeuse* was also still in Port-Louis.

La Pérouse had numerous opportunities to discuss the great voyage of exploration with them. Other, less successful voyages were the subject of ceaseless gossip: the disastrous expedition of Marion du Fresne who had sailed from Port-Louis in October 1771 with Ahutoru whom Bougainville had brought back from Tahiti but who had died of smallpox soon after setting out for this last stage of his return journey; and the hasty voyage of Kerguelen who had returned to Port-Louis from southern waters in March 1772 with reports of remarkable discoveries which had enthused Poivre and Desroches. For once, the two men had been in agreement: 'All that the eyes have been able to see,' wrote Desroches, 'seems to indicate a country that is inhabited and carefully cultivated.'[3] 'M. de Kerguelen has discovered for France, in the space of two months, a new world,' added Poivre.[4]

Kerguelen had triumphantly sailed for France shortly after, preceded by a letter to de Boynes, the Minister of Marine, claiming: 'I have had the good fortune to discover the southern continent.' But only a few days after La Pérouse arrived in the *Belle-Poule* and Ternay had officially taken up his post, Port-Louis was thrown into a state of turmoil by the appearance of the *Gros-Ventre*, Kerguelen's consort vessel.

Both ships, it turned out, had merely discovered what is now called Kerguelen Island, an uninhabited desolate spot in the southern Indian Ocean. That was the land Kerguelen had spoken of so glowingly in February 1772. The reality was quite different. The French had found it bleak, cold and foggy. The *Gros-Ventre* became separated from Kerguelen's *Fortune*. After waiting for Kerguelen to reappear and after a second attempt at landing on the rocky ice-bound island, her captain, St Allouarn, decided to make for Australia in accordance with their prearranged plans. The *Gros-Ventre* reached the Australian continent safely, sailed up the west coast, obtained supplies from the Portuguese in Timor and the Dutch in Batavia, and made her way to Port-Louis. St Allouarn, who had been in bad health for most of the voyage, died shortly after.

It thus fell to Maillard to advise Versailles that whatever Kerguelen had seen in the southern seas, it certainly was no new continent. Appending the death certificate of François de St Allouarn, aged 35, he reported:

> The King's flute, the *Gros-Ventre*, commanded by M. de St Allouarn, which had accompanied M. de Kerguelen, commanding the *Fortune,* on a voyage aimed at discovering the southern land, returned to this port on 5 September; from her disembarked Messrs de St Allouarn and Maingaud, who were very ill, and the other officers, as well as the crew, greatly wearied by this voyage. Messrs de St Allouarn and Maingaud died soon after landing, and some officers are still very ill.[5]

He added comments on other unsuccessful undertakings, including Marion du Fresne's, and concluded:

> All the expeditions, My Lord, which aimed at some kind of discovery or the transport of spices, have cost the King prodigious sums, and the colony meanwhile is short of everything, even of bread . . . I hope that those that will be despatched by us will make voyages of greater usefulness, and that, at a smaller cost, they will repay the King for the very real service they will render the colony.[6]

Maillard's report reached the Minister too late to stop Kerguelen who was already on his way to the Ile de France with a new and far more costly expedition. Port-Louis once again split on the issue, many of those who had supported Kerguelen now changing their minds while others, unwilling to admit that they had been duped, remained loyal. But Maillard and Ternay were faced with the evidence: recent expeditions had been expensive, over-ambitious and ineffective. In his report, in addition to Marion du Fresne's *Marquis de Castries* and

Mascarin which had then still not returned, Maillard mentioned the *Heure du Berger,* the *Curieuse* and the *Etoile du Matin*, all sent out by Poivre to seek the island of St John of Lisbon — which did not exist.

The new Intendant was simplifying a situation which was far more complex than he had yet had time to realize. The *Heure du Berger,* commanded by the able Lieutenant de Saint-Félix, accompanied by the *Curieuse,* commanded by Bougainville's former *pilote*, Charles Oger, had been sent primarily to take formal possession of Rodriguez Island, approximately 600 kilometres due east of the Ile de France. There had been reports of an island still further east and to the south, St John of Lisbon, and Saint-Félix was provided with a Berthoud chronometer to fix the position of the island should he find it. He did not, any more than did the *Etoile du Matin*. Similarly, Kerguelen was to be asked to seek the island of Nagtegat — the fact that he did not bother to look for it was due as much to his belief that it did not exist as to his own cavalier treatment of his instructions.

Maillard and Ternay had received orders to enforce whatever economies they could on the islands they had come out to administer, but they had only begun to appreciate the pressure of strategic imperatives which had led Poivre and Desroches to back these costly expeditions.

If St John of Lisbon really did exist — and, however deficient in precision, the reports were firmly anchored in local beliefs — then it was important that the French and not some other power should control it. The Ile de France was essential to France's economic survival in the East. With the adjacent Ile de Bourbon, it represented an important port of call on the way to and from the Indies or China, reducing or eliminating dependence on the Dutch-held Cape settlements. If French influence could extend to Rodriguez in the east, the Seychelles and the Amirantes in the north and Madagascar in the west, the security of Port-Louis would be greatly strengthened. St John of Lisbon, Kerguelen's island and, if it could be found, the coast of a fabled southern continent, would enhance it yet further: France would then hold a line of bases stretching from the coast of

Africa to the deepest south. Bougainville had bolstered Poivre's determination by telling him of his own attempt to settle French colonists in the Falkland Islands and thereby establish a key base near the Straits of Magellan. English eyes were turning towards the Pacific; the French were responding by trying to place sentries at the entrances.

The non-existence of islands could be proved only by actual exploration, just as the legendary southern continent could only fade away as a result of the voyages of a succession of explorers, each paring away a portion of the imagined land mass. Maillard cannot be blamed for interpreting a negative result as a costly failure: it is only human to prefer a tangible discovery to evidence that rumours are unfounded. He was caught furthermore by Versailles' need to reduce expenditure and by the presence at the Ministry of men far less prepared than the Choiseuls to plan things on a grandiose scale.

Yet the Court was not always unwilling to find money for undertakings it considered warranted. Kerguelen's second expedition, even now sailing towards the Ile de France, was costly indeed — two large vessels, fully laden, and a total complement of 700 men and officers. It was to be 'the finest that has ever been undertaken', as the instructions put it.

Anglo-French rivalry remained the spur. Strategic and economic considerations, ever present, were reinforced by national pride. The figure of James Cook was now dominating naval exploration. The French might call him 'the incomparable', but they still saw no reason why they should not attempt to emulate him. Bougainville had acquired a reputation of his own, but his hydrographic work lacked the painstaking professionalism of the Yorkshireman. Kerguelen at least could be called a professional. That he had fatal weaknesses of character was still at this time obscured, and the government gave him support to an extent it could ill afford. Maillard and Ternay, who knew far more about the realities of Kerguelen's first voyage, were less sympathetic.

Thus, around Jean-François, the complex pattern was beginning to form which one day would send him into the Pacific on the great voyage that would indeed rival the epic efforts of 'the incomparable Cook'.

Meantime, there were more urgent problems to be dealt with. Uppermost was the shortage of food brought about by the great cyclones of March and April, which had caused extensive damage to shipping and to plantations already badly affected by the cyclones of 1771. La Pérouse was transferred to the *Africain* (or *Africaine*) commanded by Claude-Joseph Du Chayla, with instructions to proceed to Madagascar, the Ile de France's main source of rice.

It was no easy task. The *Africain* was one of the ships driven ashore by the April cyclone, but fortunately unladen at the time, she was refloated without too much difficulty. But she was a heavy storeship of 1,000 tons, and had suffered some damage, so that it was October before she could sail from Port-Louis. The crossing to Antongil Bay on the east coast of Madagascar took a little over a week.

Before they could buy supplies, Du Chayla and his first officer had to persuade the local tribes to stop fighting. For the time being at least, a chief named Yavid had the upper hand, but a judicious mixture of diplomacy and bribery persuaded him to lay down his arms — by telling him, La Pérouse was to claim in a slightly disingenuous report, that 'Mr de Ternay desired it and ordered it'.

The *Africaine* made several expeditions to the east coast of Madagascar and to the island of Bourbon, bringing much needed supplies of rice and bullocks. Then, on 21 April 1773, La Pérouse took over command of the *Seine*, a ship of 700 tons, carrying 30 guns, with a complement of 110 officers and men. A solid vessel, launched in 1768 as a storeship, the *Seine* was still sailing 20 years later on the eve of the French Revolution.

Jean-François' orders were now to sail to India. The long dull months spent ferrying supplies from Madagascar were at an end. A new world, far more complex than the petty provincialized society of the Ile de France, was about to open to him.

Notes

1. Journal of Commerson in Taillemite, *Bougainville*, ii, pp. 422-30.
2. He was the author of *Voyages d'un philosophe*, published in 1768.
3. Letter to the Minister of Marine, 20 March 1772, B.N., N.A.F. 9438-78.
4. Letter to the Minister of Marine, 21 March 1772. B.N., N.A.F. 9439-91.
5. Letter to Minister of Marine, 8 November 1772. B.N., N.A.F. 9438-107.
6. Ibid.
7. Report of November 1776 on Madagascar, A.N. Colonies, C5-A6, No 12. We can presume a very precise implied threat behind this flat statement, in that if Yavid did not comply with Ternay's wishes the French would attack him.

7
India

TWENTY YEARS earlier, France was a power to be reckoned with in India. The great Dupleix had built on the foundations laid by earlier French representatives in India, such as Lenoir and Dumas, and capitalized on the fears of native princes anxious to find another power to hold the British in check.

In spite of the Peace of Aix-la-Chapelle which left only the towns of Pondicherry, Mahé, Chandernagore and Karikal to France, Dupleix manoeuvred, cajoled, conquered and bribed until he controlled a territory that stretched from the Narbada River in central India to the southernmost tip of the subcontinent. 'Controlled' might be regarded as too definite a term: Dupleix's empire was a house of cards, held together by the sheer force of his personality and an experience of Indian politics gained from his many years residence on the continent. It collapsed under the superior generalship of Robert Clive and the greater resources which the deeply alarmed India Company was prepared to grant him, while Dupleix was not only inadequately provided for, but recalled in disgrace by a government anxious to avoid military entanglements in the distant East and by colleagues jealous of his power and his wealth.

The outbreak of the Seven Years War put the remaining French possessions once again at the mercy of the British. Chandernagore fell in 1757, an attempt by Lally-Tollendal to take Madras in February 1759 turned into a failure; two months later the British captured Masulipatnam. Supplies from Mauritius depended on control of the sea, which France did not have. The defeat of Lally by Eyre Coote at Wandewash in 1760 and the fall of Pondicherry a year later completed the British victory. Bengal, Oudh, Behar and Orissa were all effectively under British control.

Yet, when peace came, France was not totally driven out of India as she was out of Canada. Pondicherry was returned, to become

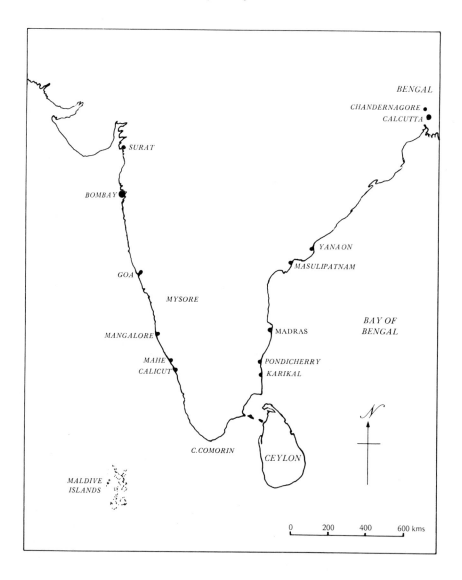

Main European settlements in India in the 1770s.

once again the centre of French administration, as were Chandernagore, Yanaon and Karikal on the east coast, and Mahé on the
west. There were other minor posts, but nowhere did French influence extend beyond the ports' environs. There were French agents
still travelling to the courts of friendly princes; men such as Law de
Lauriston, Governor of Pondicherry, still harboured hopes of neutral-
izing English influence in certain states; the British themselves
viewed French activities with unremitting suspicion. The fact remained: the Indian continent was sliding inexorably and perceptibly
into what was to become the British Empire.

Legally, however, the Indian possessions were administered not by
the British government, but by the East India Company. And like
the restless colonists of America, the Company's shareholders were
under pressure from an economy-minded government. Theoretically,
the Company traded while the local Indian rulers, under supervision,
carried out the administrative work. This dual system presupposed
that the Company's servants would not abuse their privileges and
that the Indian princes would be content with their state of reduced
independence. On this assumption the Company's shares had steadily
risen on the stock market. When news arrived in London that Haidar
Ali of Mysore was invading the Carnatic and likely to reach Madras,
prices dropped dramatically.

In 1770 and 1772 a famine devastated Bengal, causing the deaths
of an estimated one-sixth of the population. Revenue from this
province formed an important part of the East India Company's
income. The drastic fall in revenue coincided with the rise in military
costs necessitated by the threat of invasion.

There was no way by which the Company could avoid extra
military expenditure. The Haidar Ali threat was dealt with, but the
Company's gradual absorption of the Carnatic raised the fear of the
rulers of Hyderabad and Mysore. The collapse of the Mogul empire,
advantageous to the Company on the surface, brought it face to face
with the resurgent Hindu states, the warlike Mahratta confederacy
and a number of independent princes. The commercial company
might have no clear wish to turn into a military power, but it had to
be prepared to defend its gains.

By 1771 its finances were at crisis point. Bills of exchange total-ling one-and-a-half million pounds were about to fall due. The collapse of the great Scottish banker, Alexander Fordyce, in June 1772, added to the sense of economic uncertainty. It was a bad time to borrow money. The East India Company was forced to appeal for help from the government.

For the French in India there remained the hope of fishing in troubled waters, but little more. The paradox of a great Company — which in a span of 10 years had become the most powerful force in India, which ruled entire provinces and whose employees were among the wealthiest Englishmen of the day — now teetering on the brink of bankruptcy might puzzle the English Parliament and cer-tainly worry its own shareholders, but men like Law de Lauriston knew that its underlying strength would protect it. The French had little to hope for. Parliament would come to the rescue of the Com-pany, for many members were financially linked with it. What the French could angle for was better trade agreements, and a strengthen-ing of diplomatic ties with the independent princes, especially those who were still safe from the 'protected' status. This policy, modest as it was, required some exercise in flag-showing — and this in turn required resources.

The nearest French naval base was Port-Louis, the harbour of which was still littered with the wrecks of ships destroyed by the cyclones. Ternay could only promise Law to send him one ship annually, of five to six hundred tons, for a period of six months. Thus was the *Seine* despatched on 18 May 1773 under La Pérouse's command.

Coincidentally, 1773 was the year when the British government came to the conclusion that England could no longer maintain the pretence that her interest in India could, or indeed should, be con-fined solely to trade. It made a loan of just under one-and-a-half million pounds to the Company, thus ensuring its financial stability and putting an end to the hopes of those who still thought it might share the fate of the now bankrupt French *Compagnie des Indes*. But it also passed the Regulating Act which provided for a governor-general and contained the first steps towards transforming India into a British-run empire. It sounded the knell of the East India Company, but by the same token it confirmed the impotence of the French in India.

☸

Jean-François' *Journal de la flute du roi la Seine* is held in the naval archives in Paris.[1] Proudly, he headed it up with the words:

> under the command of M. de la Pérouse, *enseigne* of the Royal vessels. Sailed from the Isle de France on 18 May 1773 bound by way of Bourbon and the islands of Séchelles [sic] and Praslin for the East Indies.

Bourbon, today known as the island of Réunion, provided supplies which the Ile de France, more heavily populated and so badly affected by the cyclones, still lacked. On 24 May, La Pérouse sailed for the Seychelles, a group of scattered islands identified from old Portuguese maps by Lazare Picaud in 1742 and formally claimed by France two years later.

The islands were off the India route and spread over an area of some 150 square miles. D'Après de Mannevillette, the great hydrographer, author of the *Neptune oriental*, was still uncertain of their correct position and his only information was what could be collected from passing captains by his Port-Louis correspondent, Sirandre. But few ships passed that way — a mere eight or 10 in the previous quarter of a century.

Sailing north, La Pérouse had to compensate for westerly currents but above all for the lack of a chronometer, essential for determining a longitude with any accuracy. Like all captains of his day he made use of a wide range of indications: the presence of land birds, floating branches or fruit, the type of bottom — mud, ooze, sand, broken shells — when it was possible to use the soundline, an operation which slowed the vessel's progress.

On the 30th, the usual midday observations placed him in latitude 16°S — at least latitudes were ascertainable at that time — which is that of Sandy Island or Tromelin Island, as lonely a place as one can find, but he was not sure whether he was east or west of it. Somewhere to the north-west lay Nazareth Bank, but closer to his route waited the Agalega Island — and again he was unsure whether they were to the north-east or the north-west. The westerly currents had to be allowed for, at an estimated 24 knots a day:

> I saw at 11 this morning [2 June] a quantity of birds of all kinds which shows that I am not far from land, but the sailors I have placed permanently on the topmasts have seen nothing. Throughout the night I sounded every two hours but did not find bottom.

The next problem was Coëtivy Island, which he failed to sight. It was 5 June and he had reached the southern Seychelles. On the evening of the 6th, he sighted Frigate Island, the most easterly, bearing N by NW. His longitude was 150 miles out, which making allowance for the unreliable charts, the lack of chronometer and the general unawareness of the problem of compass deviation (which would not be solved until 1801-03 with Matthew Flinders' work) is a highly creditable result.

The islands were idyllic. The temperatures were warm, but kept moderate by the south-east monsoon. The *Seine* was there in the dry season: the blue of sky and sea contrasted with the stretches of coral sand and the heavy green of the coconut trees.

Life ashore belied the promise of nature. The first permanent settlement, on the small island of Mahé, was barely five years old and in total disarray. La Pérouse had hardly dropped anchor when a canoe came up, bearing a man called Silord who implored his protection against another named Anselme.

Anselme was the offical agent of Brayet, a resident of the Ile de France and the promoter of the Seychelles colony. Brayet had been backed by Poivre who hoped to develop plantations of spice plants on the Seychelles to compete with the Dutch East Indies. But the project was undercapitalized and ill-organized. Rats were eating up stocks of maize, a few huts sheltered the 20 or so squabbling settlers, the few acres of cleared forest were invaded by weeds. La Pérouse saw only half a dozen nutmeg trees and one clove tree. The best of them is the size of sail thread, with five or six leaves on it and is about a foot high, he reported.

Ternay had given him instructions to reorganize the settlement. Anselme, cowering in a leaky hut, had his authority restored, not as

Brayet's agent, but as Ternay's representative. A sailor who had threatened to kill Anselme was flogged in the presence of the rest, and the leading troublemakers taken away aboard the *Seine*: Silord, who was a boatswain and the leader of the opposition to Anselme, and his wife; Montagnier, a priest, together with a black woman he seemed to be living with; and half a dozen others, who seemed to be so dissatisfied with their lot that the frail community would have finally disintegrated as a result of their sense of despair.

La Pérouse sailed on 26 June. His task had not been easy either from the point of view of navigation or from that of administration, but he had acquitted himself well on both counts. It would be exaggerating to claim that after his intervention the future of the Seychelles was assured, but at least their worst days were over. Nature, always prodigal to the small island group, could now be expected to respond to the modest efforts of the remaining colonists.

The *Seine* reached Pondicherry on 21 July by way of Eight Degree Channel and Cape Comorin, and there she remained until 27 August 'waiting for the end of the sickness season in Bengal'.

Pondicherry was the main French establishment in India, the residence of Jean Law de Lauriston, the Governor since 1765. Although, as his name indicates, Law was of foreign descent – he was the nephew of the famous Scottish financier, John Law, who had introduced the idea of state banking and fiduciary banknotes to France with eventually disastrous results – he was a strong patriot. His energies were devoted, in unseverable equal parts, to countering English power and to making money.

He had found Pondicherry a mass of ruins, following its capture by Colonel Coote in 1761. By 1769 when a census was taken, the town consisted of over 3,000 dwellings, over a third of them still in ruins, with a population of close on a thousand Europeans and over twenty-six thousand Indians.[2] A French visitor in that year gave Law the credit:

> Three years and more had elapsed since the sack of Pondicherry: weeds, brambles and thorns had covered part of the ruins of the town which gave one a feeling of confusion and horror; Pondicherry, so famous and flourishing in the days of M. Dupleix, a mere twelve years ago, had become, like

Jerusalem, a haunt of snakes and vipers. But at last M. Law arrived in the name of the King . . . in a short time the streets appeared, the houses rose again, and today Pondicherry is an object of admiration for all who see it, knowing that three years earlier it had been nothing more than a heap of ashes, stones and dust. The Governor . . . brought together several thousand workers who, in a short space of time, enclosed the city within a wall, with a parapet and sixteen bastions, to protect it from a sudden attack . . . The Governor's palace . . . will be a very fine single-storeyed building, and the Governor . . . will have quarters as good as those of the Governor of Manila.[3]

Law had expended a great deal of his own money on the work of reconstruction, but by the time La Pérouse arrived the venture was paying off. He recorded the presence of three other French vessels in port, and two more appeared shortly after. Private trade and public administration were all one. With his chief associate, Jean-Baptiste Chevalier, the Governor of Chandernagore, Law had effectively replaced the old bankrupt *Compagnie des Indes*. What he did was no different from what the English India Company was doing: whenever official firmness was required to maintain control, he acted.

Thus he had despatched Surville in the *Saint Jean-Baptiste* to forestall a rumoured British settlement on a newly discovered island in the Pacific, but also to trade. Thus Trobriand was being sent in the *Etoile* to avenge the massacre of the crew of the trader *Eprouvé* in Borneo. Thus La Pérouse himself, commanding a ship of the royal navy, was to be sent to Bengal to show the flag, but also to carry supplies and goods for private traders. Versailles had no wish to complain: Law was no Dupleix – he was not building up a great empire, but he kept the French presence alive in the East and, an even greater blessing, he did so at no cost to the struggling French treasury. He was an efficient thorn in the side of the British administration, as they were to recognize, a bare five years later, when Sir Hector Munro stormed Pondicherry and, once again, its walls were razed to the ground.

The monsoon had spread over Bengal, bringing with it the fever-bearing intense humidity, and now it receded. It was safe — or at least safer — for Europeans. La Pérouse sailed north, to Balasore, near the mouth of the Hooghly, to wait for a pilot. He had to learn Eastern patience: 'at night we set up lights and fired guns'. Two days went by; then the pilot appeared and the slow advance began up-river towards the French settlement. It took nine days. Continually sounding, responding to the quiet calls of the pilot, the French manoeuvred their way through a strange world of muddy water, half drowned islands, settlements of fishermen built on land that seemed never to have been meant for human habitation, and the tragic flotsam of decaying vegetation, dead animals and occasionally men, bobbing their way down river to the bay.

Gradually, they reached the higher land, with ricefields and more prosperous villages – Raipur, Ulubaria, Nangi, and the approaches to Calcutta. French Chandernagore being upriver from Calcutta, the *Seine* had to sail past the British city, the heart of Bengal.

It was humiliatingly imposing. Rochegude, the other great sailor that Albi has given France, was in Calcutta in 1768 and estimated its population at 700,000 people, nearly all Indians; La Pérouse's estimate was a population of half a million, an impressive enough figure, equal to that of Paris. By contrast, nearby European settlements were stagnating.

The Danish post of Serampore was in ruins, the Dutch one at Chinsura held a mere 150 soldiers, the Portuguese had abandoned their trading post at Bandal. Chandernagore, thanks to Chevalier, was reviving, but constrained by the terms imposed by the British after the Seven Years War. The French had jurisdiction over an area enclosed within a periphery of 10 miles, surrounded by a ditch not more than 20 feet in width; the garrison was limited to 20 Europeans and 200 sepoys.

Chevalier had stressed the need for irrigation works so as to add some defences, but he was constantly the victim of petty and not so petty vexations from the powerful India Company. Nevertheless, with a determination equal to Law's and an even greater gift for intrigue, he maintained Chandernagore as a viable port, sending ships to the Near East and the Orient, and keeping contact with the Ile de France and Europe. A number of minor factories or trading posts were still active and dependent on Chandernagore; the most important of these was Kazimbazar, the centre of the silk trade; others were situated at Patna in Bihar province, at Dacca, at Joudhia to the east and at Balasore in the west. These small posts, usually manned by a single French agent, suffered from constant British interference and did not long survive.

In Chandernagore, La Pérouse took on supplies and more trade goods for Law: 'a cargo of comestibles to be taken to the Ile de France as freight on behalf of private traders' as Chevalier reported to the Minister.[4] He had become reconciled to the King's vessels being used for private commerce, and before long he would take part in it himself — whatever rules applied in Europe had little validity in this eastern world of intrigue and large profits.

In mid-December, the *Seine* began the slow voyage downriver to the mouth of the Hooghly, accompanied by the *Etoile* and watched suspiciously by a British guardship. Already, while the *Etoile* was loading rice and biscuit, a boat had come up to carry out a search and had only desisted when her captain, Trobriand, shouted down that the first Englishman who tried to set foot on board would be thrown into the river. There were signs of activity on board the guardship when the *Seine* approached, but together the two French vessels carried enough guns to defend what freedom of navigation there yet remained on the Hooghly.

As 1774 dawned, the *Seine* was in the Bay of Bengal, making for the small French post at Masulipatnam and, further south, Pondicherry. It was a form of coastal trade, providing valuable experience though little glory, but Law in Pondicherry expressed his gratitude — and filled the ship with more supplies and trade goods, this time for the Ile de France. Eventually their friendship would lead Law's son Jean-Guillaume into the *Astrolabe*, to join La Pérouse's expedition to the Pacific and to die in that great ocean which his father had once dreamed of as a possible source of wealth for French traders from India.

Jean-François was anxious to return to Ternay. He sailed on 3 February, making south-east and south-south-west to keep clear of Ceylon. The north-east monsoon, westerly currents, charts with too many approximations — the problem of longitude reappears. Bird-watching assumed an importance often tinged with anxiety or irritation:

> We saw several birds of the type which does not go far from land and throughout the night we could hear the cries of sea-swallows. At midday [on 10 Feb.]we were in the latitude of Gama which D'Aprés places on his chart in 72 °. Maybe it is further east. Possibly we have developed an appreciable difference in our longitude.

The Chagos Archipelago had to be avoided, tempting though it would be to use it as a check. His journal reflects the empty seas through which the *Seine* was sailing:

> Sighted many flights of birds around the ship . . . fog . . . no altitude reading . . . the lookout sees nothing . . . sounded without finding ground . . . our horizon barely extends beyond half a league.

On the 12th he reached 19°40', the latitude of Rodriguez Island and changed course to due west. 'The boat was sent ashore to collect a few turtles of which I was in dire need; all my supplies had been totally used up.'

On 24 March 1774 the *Seine* dropped anchor in Port-Louis after an absence of 10 months. La Pérouse was to be granted a respite of five months ashore before he sailed again in the *Seine* for what he hoped would be his final voyage to India before his return to France.

He was 32, an age when promotion begins to assume an importance coloured by nagging anxiety. France had been at peace for more than 10 years. Advancement could only be slow and La Pérouse was still only an *enseigne*, surrounded by others of his own age, all competing for the attention of the naval authorities. Under the Ancient Regime, birth and connections mattered greatly. La Pérouse had protectors like La Jonquière and Ternay, but others had well-placed relatives. A 'red' officer he might be, but he lacked the uncle at court, the well-connected cousin, the sister married into the old nobility which others could call upon to place a good word in the best ears at the right moment. And the Indian Ocean was so far away from that Versailles where beat France's administrative heart.

His family, in the few letters he found awaiting him in Port-Louis, did not share his growing concern. They had faith in him and they accepted that the destiny he had chosen for himself, so unusual for a Galaup, should take him far away from them for long years. His sister Jacquette sent him news of his home town and in return he wrote her an account of life in distant islands.

His father, now in his sixty-fourth year, his eyesight beginning to fail, was feeling concern about his only son's continuing celibacy. The Galaups did not marry young, but old Victor-Joseph had taken a wife by the age of 31 and had ensured within twelve months that a son would carry on the family name. Jean-François was no Don Juan: his shape was stocky, he had a tendency to increase his girth and was finally surrendering to it, although his manner was lively, his slightly southern accent attractive, the appeal of the red and gold uniform with all the mystique of the sea undeniable. But little of this mattered. Marriages were arranged by parents, not born of romance. And one could not arrange a marriage from half a world away, let alone send out a bride to a distant colony. Anything else than a suitable match in France, preferably in Albi, was wellnigh unthinkable. So when would Jean-François return?

Jean-François was in fact in the process of falling in love. With his friend, Mengaud de la Hage, he had rented a house on the hills overlooking Port-Louis, to spend in peace and quiet and some comfort the time he would still have to serve out in the Ile de France. There were some attractive homes not too far away: the Réduit where Ternay retired when life in Port-Louis became too tiresome; the house of Vicomte du Chayla who had commanded the *Africaine;* and the home of Abraham Broudou in the Plaines Wilhems, not far from the main road that led from Port-Louis to the smaller harbour of Port Bourbon in the north.

The Broudous came originally from St Quentin, in Picardy, but had moved to the prosperous port of Nantes. In 1768, Broudou had been sent to Port-Louis to manage the naval storeyards and supervise the hospital. He had two daughters, Elisabeth (or Elzire) and Louise-Eléonore, born in Nantes on 15 May 1755.

Jean-François may have met Eléonore soon after his arrival in the

Ile de France, at which time she would have been no more than 17. The Broudous, although previously in trade and now in government service, were people of some standing in island society. They were nevertheless clearly of the middle-class. La Pérouse could not have been unaware than any union between a Galaup and a Broudou must be regarded as a misalliance, but he fell in love . . . . Whether this was love at first sight as so many writers have claimed, or a gradual process, no one will ever know. It is enough to say that, within a year, La Pérouse was seriously contemplating marriage and that eventually he pushed all obstacles aside with his characteristic determination and married her.

Abraham Broudou may have harboured hopes that both his daughters might find suitors among the young naval officers in port. Mengaud de la Hage was usually invited with La Pérouse, so that the proprieties were observed, and he later joined Jean-François in the purchase of a property at Eau Coulée close to the Broudou home. Abraham Broudou could provide his daughters with a modest dowry, but not one that was appropriate for a marriage to an officer in the royal navy. Whatever secret hopes he may have cherished had to be laid to rest when it was clear that Mengaud enjoyed Elizabeth's company, but was essentially there for La Pérouse to confide in and to lean on when required.

The time came for them to sail again, Mengaud for Madagascar, and La Pérouse once more for India. It was initially another of those voyages in which private trade and public need are mixed: he went on account of M. de la Rochette, a local trader, with goods for the Malabar coast, accompanied by *Les Trois-Amis,* commanded by La Rochette himself.

In Pondicherry on 20 September 1774, he was sent by Law to Mahé by way of Cochin and Calicut. He reached Mahé on 20 November, spending a fortnight at this French fortified port, and then continued north along the Malabar coast.

He was nearing the northern edge of the area controlled by Haidar Ali, the Mysore leader who was fiercely defending his independence against the British Company and was consequently friendly towards the French. He was the effective protector of the Mahé outpost. And the *Seine* was bringing him arms supplied by Law. Not surprisingly, when La Pérouse dropped anchor at Mangalore, Haidar Ali put on the kind of display at which Indian princes excelled and which men like Dupleix had used so dazzlingly to impress the Indians in return:

> I was granted the honours accorded to an envoy extraordinary. Six thous-
> and sepoys were lined up presenting arms when I asked to set foot ashore,
> and the Governor made me the gift of a curved sword on behalf of his
> master.[5]

A pleasant stay ensued which lasted 10 days; it was then time to go on north, to Goa, where the Portuguese were far from friendly. The *Seine* to them was a trading vessel and as such was liable to a visit by customs officers; but at this point it was convenient to re-assume the role of a naval vessel. La Pérouse turned the customs men back and formally protested to the Portuguese viceroy who rejected his complaints. The *Seine* remained off Goa harbour a full week, quite literally showing the flag. Then she went on her way, still sailing north, for Surat.

Now at last La Pérouse encountered action. It was on 5 January 1755. A Mahratta fleet of three ships of 40 guns and more than 20 light vessels carrying 8 to 10 guns hove into sight. He veered towards them and after a gunfight lasting two hours they fled back to the safety of their home base. This was a more than welcome change from carrying trade goods along the coast. Jean-François may be forgiven for a report which contains a few triumphant notes:

> My men were not in the least frightened by the number of enemy ships
> we had to face and they all expressed their despair when the wind advant-
> age and their greater speed compounded to form an insurmountable ob-
> stacle to the desire I had to get within a pistol's shot of them.[6]

He spent a fortnight in Surat, sailed back to Goa with no further trouble and went on to Mahé. To his astonishment, he found the port besieged by a force of ten thousand led by the Malabar prince Cherikal. Not improbably, in view of the complex and constantly shifting political pattern of India, they included some of the sepoys who had welcomed him ashore three months earlier.

India

Cherikal was the ruler of 'Colastry' — in all probability Kolattiri, the most northerly of the Malabar kingdoms, centered on Badegara, just south of Mahé. The French were supporters of the ruler of 'Coringote', his rival, whom we can identify as the Prince of Calicut (Kozhikode).

The situation was as serious as it looked. Some pressure was no doubt being put on the besiegers from pro-French Calicut, but what saved Mahé was the arrival of La Pérouse in the *Seine*, with La Rochette's *Trois-Amis*. The town itself was highly vulnerable:

> Mahé is scarcely more fortified than the village of Charonne; a simple bamboo hedge forms the palissade while a crumbling fort and a few other small batteries represent our power on the Malabar coast. M. de Repentigny (the commander) is bedridden following a stroke which has left him half paralysed and helpless. All the inhabitants were extremely anxious: only a small river separated them from the enemy army.[7]

La Pérouse, the senior officer by virtue of the local commander's incapacity and his own standing as Law de Lauriston's agent, took over:

> I promptly fortified a small entrenchment which had been started beyond the river; in the evening I had two guns set up, and I left about 40 sailors there. The Mahé garrison consisted of 60 Europeans and 200 local soldiers — on whose behalf we were fighting this war [presumably soldiers belonging to the ruler of Calicut] ... I placed 150 of these in the fort with our sailors, putting them in charge of one of my ship's officers named Du Drésil.[8]

His caution proved advantageous, for Cherikal attacked under cover of darkness with 600 men and was repulsed by the defenders and the grapeshot from the two guns:

> I instructed M. du Drésil to strengthen the defences of his post; we placed 6 guns and 100 sailors there, 50 from the *Seine* and 50 from the *Trois-Amis*; and no sooner were we set up than, one hour before daybreak, all of Cherikal's army came up to attack us. Our grapeshot once again put them to flight. M. du Drésil allowed two-thirds of our garrison to make a sortie against the fleeing troops, a great number of whom were killed. The sailors cut off at least 100 ears and nailed them to the palissades of

the fort. I was not put out by this ferocious behaviour because the season was pressing us: from the month of May the Malabar coast becomes untenable for ships; mine moreover was leaking and in no condition to sustain a storm. We had only eight killed, including three Europeans.[9]

Cherikal retreated to a camp he set up on the shore. It was time to put an end to a threat which Mahé could not resist on its own for very long. There was a small galliot, the *Expérience,* at anchor in the port. La Pérouse transferred Closnard to her, with orders to attack the camp and above all, prevent supplies of rice reaching Cherikal. Robert de Closnard, or Clonard, was then 23. One day, he would sail with La Pérouse on his great voyage to the Pacific and perish with him. Several raids were made on Cherikal's entrenchments, during one of which Clonard was wounded in the thigh and, during another, lightly in the head.

Cherikal counterattacked on Mahé, being twice repulsed, but Haidar Ali and Law were negotiating for an end to the fighting. In April, Law sent Repentigny orders to make peace. An agreement was signed on the 25th, and three days later La Pérouse sailed for the Ile de France 'where I arrived almost sinking, with two pumps going night and day.'

Notes

1. A.N. Marine C7-165, 123-145.
2. 'Le Recensement de la population de Pondichéry en 1769'. *Revue d'histoire des colonies françaises,* 1927, No. 3, pp. 444-5.
3. Le Gentil, *Voyage dans les mers de l'Inde,* pp. 631-1.
4. Chevalier to Boynes, 6 Oct. 1773, A.N.M. C7-165.
5. Report in A.N.M. B4. 125 f.234.
6. Quoted in Brossard, *Lapérouse,* p. 261
7. From La Pérouse's report in A.N.M. B-125/234, quoted in 'La Campagne de Lapérouse dans l'Inde', (anon). *Revue de l'histoire des colonies françaises,* vol. xxxii, 1929, pp. 301-6. Charonne was a village outside Paris, now absorbed by it and part of the 20th arrondissement.
8. Ibid.
9. Ibid.

8
The Landowner

PORT—LOUIS had quietened down under Ternay. The old quarrels the islanders nurtured in their midst had settled down into new patterns, but the sun still beat down, the cane plantations prospered, trade remained profitable and, far away in the hills the escaped slaves organized themselves into squabbling, marauding gangs.

But in Europe an entire world had come to an end. Louis XV had died after a reign of almost 60 years. Frenchmen had been born, had raised families and had gone to their grave knowing no other king than him; but the unthinkable had happened and now a new king had ascended the throne. He was only 20, ill-trained — indeed, untrained — for a task that would have been daunting enough to a man of genius. And Louis XVI was no genius, merely a young man of moderate ability, married to an attractive Austrian bride wholly devoid of political sense.

He did at least have the benefit of goodwill. There is a honeymoon season for kings as there is for new governments. Louis XV had been called 'the Well-Beloved' by his subjects — at least in the early part of his reign: when he died his corpse had been driven away to the jeers of lackeys. The Ile de France decided to erect an obelisk in Port-Louis to mark the welcome beginning of a new reign. Was there not something endearing about a king who called upon a new Chief Minister to take office by writing to him: 'I am only twenty'? Compared with the imperious absolutism of his two predesessors, was such modesty not worth a monument? There would be time enough to change one's opinions, and the year 1793, when the executioner would hold up Louis XVI's severed head to a shouting multitude was still far away in the future. Ternay led a week of celebrations, once the period of official mourning for the old king was over. There were messages of loyalty to be sent to Versailles, speeches, banquets, and everyone went home well satisfied, to talk over events.

Peace seemed assured for some years at least. The new ministers were more interested in reforming the economic system than in foreign adventures: an attempt to bring Choiseul back into the government was foiled and England's old enemy went back to his country estate. Across the Channel, Lord North was being equally cautious. He had his own problems to deal with: the intricate finances of the India Company, a troublesome John Wilkes agitating for parliamentary reform, and above everything else, unruly colonists in North America. If the French government had to deal with riots over the price of flour, the English had to contend with Bostonians throwing tea into the harbour. There was worse to come. The first shots were fired at Lexington in April 1775, heralding the American War. To the colonists in Port-Louis, when they learnt of it four months later, it seemed a matter of minor importance, an embarrassment to Britain one could chuckle about over a glass of wine.

For Jean-François there was no sea voyage in view. It was a welcome relief, even though it meant office work, the checking of maps and harbour works, the issuing of permits, the quiet boredom of a small colonial town. But he had no real desire for great adventures. A post ashore meant opportunities to visit the Broudous. He had begun to nurse the thought of marriage. Was he not now 34? Too unsure of his father's reaction to tell him directly, Jean-François decided to broach the subject with his sister first, and even this approach was circuitous:

> My dear sister, in the three years I have been in India I have only received one letter from you. I have just made another cruise on the coast of Malabar. I was attacked by pirates whom I trounced, and returned safely to the Ile de France. I have managed fairly satisfactorily my little fortune and, at the present moment, I have a 90,000 *livres* share of prizes due to me. You can be assured that I have not forgotten you and that I will bring you some Indian cloth . . . I am a little in love with a young person from this island, and this could well end in a marriage, but nothing has yet been decided.[1]

Later the same month, he bought a property of some 156 *arpents* (roughly 150 acres) in the Wilhems Plains district, along the Mesnil

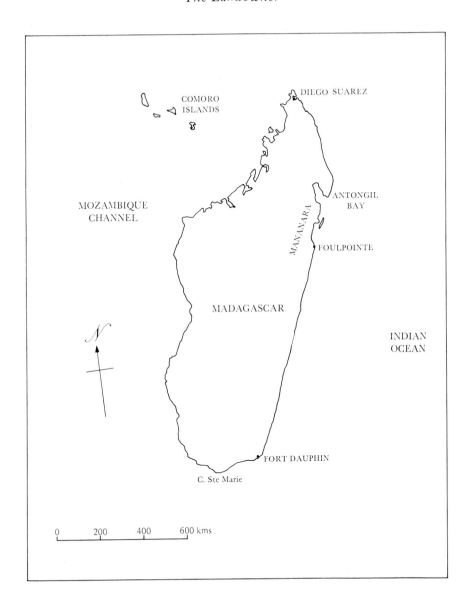

Early French links with Madagascar

river, and conveniently situated on the road that led to the Broudous' residence. The price was 6,000 *livres*, but the property was purchased jointly with his close friend Charles de Mengaud, a *lieutenant de vaisseau* from a distinguished family: Mengaud's younger brother had sailed with Kerguelen's expedition of 1772 and had gone on to Western Australia and Timor with St Allouarn. Kerguelen had come back to the Ile de France in 1773 to face the coolest of receptions from Maillard Dumesle and Ternay. As we have seen, they had little reason to be enthusiastic Kerguelen had told the French government that what he had discovered was nothing short of the fabled southern continent, as a result of which a costly second expedition had been authorized, but in the meantime St Allouarn's *Gros-Ventre* had limped into Port-Louis, her crew sick and weary, to set the record straight: Kerguelen Land was a bare-looking, storm-lashed and snow-covered place, probably an unpopulated island of modest size and to all appearances quite uninhabitable.

Kerguelen still hoped for help from the Ile de France, in particular with supply ships. Originally it had been decided to give him Mengaud in the cutter *Sauterelle*, but the orders had already been countermanded from Paris, and Mengaud went instead to Madagascar.

Living in Wilhems Plains enabled both men to keep as much as they could away from the arguments and factions which divided island society and eventually drove Ternay to beg to be relieved from this governorship. There was not only Kerguelen, whom many viewed with disfavour, but a prolongued argument between Maillard and Grenier. The latter was a well-known naval officer who had carried out valuable hydrographic work in the Indian Ocean. The problem was that trade and naval operations were constantly interwoven, as La Pérouse had discovered to his surprise but also to his advantage. There was rarely a clear dividing line between the king's service and assistance to local traders, or indeed trade on one's own account. At least in Eastern waters such activities were not considered demeaning for naval officers, and for the hard-pressed administrators of the isolated colonies they were essential to economic survival.

Grenier had gone to Madagascar in *La Belle-Poule* to rescue the men of the *Fortune* which had run ashore. Maillard provided Grenier with muskets to barter for food supplies, but none of the French traders were interested in the guns — they required piastres or bills of exchange which Grenier could not supply. The officers, Grenier included, bought the muskets and trade goods themselves and paid for the food out of their own pockets. Maillard claimed that if a profit had been made — and few could doubt it — then this belonged to the Ile de France treasury. Grenier made counterclaims, Ternay was asked to adjudicate, the Minister of Marine back in Versailles was notified, and the salons of Port-Louis gleefully divided into a pro-Maillard and a pro-Grenier faction. Grenier finally sailed for France at the end of December in the midst of yet another dispute, this time over a load of ebony wood he was taking to Europe.

Madagascar had begun to loom large in the preoccupations of the islanders. One of the world's largest islands — only Greenland, New Guinea and Borneo are bigger — it provided food for the Ile de France, mostly in the form of cattle, and a small but regular supply of slaves. It was rent by almost constant warfare between its various tribes, so that it seemed ripe for colonization. The Portuguese, the Dutch and the English had each in their way attempted to establish settlements, but they had all failed. People like Maillard with instructions to reduce expenditure saw little profit in doing anything more than trade with the Malagasy of the coastlands: the only alternative, as he knew full well, was a war of conquest which Versailles could not afford.

Versailles, however, was not averse to adventure on a moderate scale. What if France's perennial rivals, the English, did establish a base on the island, thereby threatening not just the Ile de France and the other Mascareignes islands, but the very route to the Indian Ocean and the East? The fact that the only English attempt at a settlement dated back to Charles I was no argument. Versailles took a middle stance between inaction and colonization: it sent a free entreprise adventurer to Madagascar and let Ternay and Maillard do the best they could for him. Maillard was a sound administrator, but Benyowski was a charmer — and when had Versailles ever resisted charm?

There are certain men upon whom Fate showers gifts and flaws of character in almost equal measure, so that success always teeters on the edge of disaster. Maurice-Auguste-Aladar, Baron Benyowski, was born in Hungary, the son of a general in the Austrian army. He was just in time to get embroiled in the Seven Years War. At the age of 14 he fought at Lowositz under Field-Marshal Maximilian Browne — as fascinating a character as Benyowski, since he was a Swiss-born Irishman serving in the Austrian army. He fought at Prague and at Domstadt, whereupon an uncle invited him to Poland and adopted him. His father having died, Benyowski returned to claim his inheritance, found the family castle in possession of his brother-in-law, tried to capture it by force, was repelled and exiled as a troublemaker. He was barely 21.

Back in Poland, Benyowki joined the cavalry, studied in Danzig, then, the war being over, he travelled to France, Germany, the Low Countries and England. In 1768, when the Poles were struggling to resist Russian encroachments on their remaining lands, he went to Warsaw, where he married, and was appointed a colonel in Czarneski's forces. His troops captured the fortress of Landscrow, but he was wounded and captured at Kamenetz, near Cracow, in May 1769. Imprisoned in Kazan, he plotted with other prisoners to break out with the aid of disaffected Tartars, was discovered, fled to Moscow, was recaptured and this time sent to Siberia.

It would take more than a Siberian prison to hold him. He charmed the Governor of Bolskeretsk-Ostrog, as he charmed everyone else, gaining as a bonus the affections of his daughter, Aphanasia — or so, at least, he claimed. He had studied geography and navigation in Danzig, so the Governor invited him to help with the drawing of charts, which gave him a good knowledge of the Kuriles and the Aleutians. At the same time he was plotting to seize a ship and escape. Aphanasia apparently decided to come with him — it is not clear whether he had told her he had a wife in Poland — and she warned him when, inevitably, the plot was uncovered. This time Benyowski struck first. The prisoners captured the fort, killing Aphanasia's father in the process, seized the ship and sailed away with 97 men and nine women. It was May 1771.

What itinerary they followed is arguable. They claimed to have followed a circuitous route to avoid pursuit, from Kamchatka across the Bering Sea to Alaska, then back to Japan and south to Formosa. At the end of July the fugitives stopped for supplies at the small Japanese island of Miyake Shima. They possibly sailed close to Shikoku and Kyushu, but whether they risked a landing on the forbidden coast can be doubted — it would have been foolhardy by any standards, even Benyowski's. They reached Formosa in late August, where they had to fight off the locals, crossed to China proper — probably Swatow, then Macao. Sickness and exhaustion had taken their toll, and Aphanasia, as romantic a heroine as the sentimental novels of the time could have wished for, was among the 20 or so who died in China. Her death saved Benyowski the embarrassment of explaining her existence to his wife, the Baroness.

He sold the furs they had bought on the North-West coast, sold the ship as well, and sailed for France. He was now 31, battle-scarred and irresistible. He offered to found a French colony on Formosa; it was a little too preposterous for the Minister of Marine who suggested a French settlement on Madagascar instead. Benyowski, knowing even less about the place than he knew of Formosa, promptly accepted.

He was, wrote Des Roches:

> covered with the scars of old wounds, some of which disfigure him or cause him to limp. Nevertheless he has retained a powerful appearance of health and vigour; his features are pleasing and his wit sparkles . . . he has some knowledge of every science. Bellecombe credited him with 'a strength of temperament and a character quite out of the ordinary'. His portrait shows him in a rather pensive mood, with a longish nose and a full mouth.

Benyowski sailed from Lorient in March 1773. With him went his long-suffering wife, his sister-in-law, a maid, four servants and 237 volunteers. Six months later, he was still in the Ile de France arguing with Ternay, who was distinctly cool towards the entreprise, and Maillard, who was even cooler. None of the would-be colonists knew much about conditions in Madagascar. Port-Louis was full of traders and naval men who could tell them about the island, giving a favourable or an unfavourable view, depending on their own interests.

Ternay provided Benyowski with the small corvette *Postillon* so that his party could find out about 'the customs and the military resources of Madagascar'. At the end of 1773 further volunteers arrived from France aboard the *Laverdy*. Ternay could resist no longer: the charm and persistence of the adventurer was wearing him down and, anyhow, what else could be done with the volunteers, now exceeding 300? He provided Benyowski with the *Desforges*; the settlers left in February 1774.

The choice of Antongil Bay has been criticized. It was certainly an unhealthy place, but then much of the coastal area was humid and marshy and the bay at least is deep and sheltered. Benyowski set to with his usual energy. Forts were built, stores, roads, the outline of a town. But supplies were short, ill-health struck down labourers and soldiers, money ran out, the nearby tribes organized raids to drive the interlopers away.

Kerguelen came to his help in the early stages. With the *Rolland* and the *Oiseau* Kerguelen was just back from the costly expedition to the land he had discovered two years earlier. Forced to admit that it was neither the fabled continent nor a place where France could establish a colony, and being unwilling to face his critics in the Ile de France – and Ternay in particular – he had made for Madagascar to refit and to prepare for the homeward journey.

Antongil Bay was no place to refresh a crew: 14 of Kerguelen's men died of fever. Nor did he have a high opinion of Benyowski and his ramshackle settlement, but neither of the two men was on good terms with Ternay – which forged a bond of sorts between them. Kerguelen felt it politic to support a French establishment which had the blessing of the Minister of Marine, to whom he would soon have to account for his failure.

Accordingly, Kerguelen sent his men to fight by the side of Benyowski's volunteers. The very presence of Kerguelen's ships helped to impress the Malagasy, for the *Rolland* was a new ship of the line, an impressive vessel of 64 guns, and the *Oiseau* was a solid frigate of 32, backed for several weeks by the corvette *Dauphine* which Ternay, with considerable reluctance, had lent Kerguelen. Fighting continued for some time after the ships' departure, but gradually Benyowski established control over most of northern Madagascar.

Money and men were essential if this fragile hold was to be consolidated. Banking on Kerguelen giving a favourable report on his arrival in France, Benyowski sent an appeal direct to Versailles for one million *livres* and 600 more colonists. The government reacted with considerable caution. Turgot, the chief minister, believed in reform and freer enterprise, but above all he aimed at cutting France's chronic budget deficit. Bellecombe, who had been Governor of Bourbon, and was about to replace Law de Lauriston in Pondicherry, and Chevreau, a *Commissaire-général de la Marine*, who had been nominated to a post in Pondicherry, were asked to go to Madagascar on their way to India, and report back.

They arrived in Port-Louis in August 1776. Bellecombe asked for an escort to Madagascar, and Ternay requested La Pérouse to accompany him in the *Iphigénie*. It was no imposing ship of the line, but an ageing *palle* or *paille*, a small trading vessel locally built which, like so many others, served the king when the need arose, and was used for trade for the rest of the time. It was a command of a sort — and La Pérouse was not sorry to go to sea once more. Bellecombe and Chevreau were in the *Consolante*, a frigate which had brought them from France and was to take them on to Pondicherry. La Pérouse, who had sailed to Madagascar earlier, led them to Foulpointe where Benyowski had an outpost. It was in a parlous state:

> The population of this village is down by a half. The wars and the discouragement into which the Blacks have fallen as a result of the cessation of trade have destroyed agriculture . . . . Three years ago I saw ten vessels laden with rice in Foulpointe roadstead after the cyclones which had devastated the Ile de France.[2]

Bellecombe arranged a ceremony to cement peace between warring groups, some of whom were friendly, some less so, towards Benyowski. The oath of reconciliation was accompanied by drinking a potion made up of 'brandy to which gunpowder has been added, with seawater, a piastre and the tip of a lance'. The ships then went on to Antongil, where Benyowki had his headquarters. It was called

Louisbourg. Nothing could be less impressive. Wooden palissades rotting in the sand, shacks serving as homes and stores, streets that were no more than overgrown paths, rats and damp destroying everything. Benyowski's house was a single-storied wood and straw building, 60 feet by 22, divided into three rooms — living quarters, sleeping quarters, and an office.

This dismal picture suggests incompetence and wild optimism, but only in retrospect. Benyowski's undertaking would fail and he himself would be killed in 1786 in an affray with troops sent from Port-Louis. But his pioneer settlements were no more primitive than early colonists' homes in Australia, New Zealand or parts of Africa. La Pérouse spoke at length with Benyowski and wrote down comments which represent a realistic appraisal of the situation — if one bears in mind that, in the nineteenth century, when the French government decided to turn Madagascar firstly into a protectorate, then into a colony, it took them nearly ten years of military campaigns to achieve their aim:

> When I talked to M. de Benyowski about the few advantages France would obtain from his stay here, he replied that a lesson costing two million *livres* was not dear to teach the Ministry that nothing could be done on a small scale in Madagascar, but if one could establish a small navy here from private funds, give it an additional two million a year, and maintain an establishment of 600 men (which assumes a recruiting rate of 4 to 500 men a year), he believed that his colony would have made great advances in twenty years' time. I told him that 4000 leagues away from the metropolis, one should not choose for a settlement a country where five men out of six die within two years, and the remainder are weak, convalescent and unfit for military or agricultural work . . . . I asked him what his aims had been when he arrived in Madagascar. He replied that he'd wanted to bend the people to do what the King ordered, and that he had never really known what the government's intentions had been, and that in addition he knew it was easier to conquer a colony from enemies than to create a new one. I agreed with this truth which is even less challengeable if one uses Antongil Bay as an example.[3]

Bellecombe and Chevreau let Benyowski understand that their recommendation would be unfavourable. France would not — indeed, could not — support an expensive and hazardous colonization; and La Pérouse, who had been asked by several Port-Louis traders to obtain a settlement of their claims against Benyowski, could provide comfort for neither side. He told the businessmen:

> I might as well go to New Zealand to claim Marion [du Fresne's] inheritance. I remained persuaded that the 40 millions and 12000 men we would send him over twenty years, if his plan were adopted, would be added to the losses France has already sustained and that France would not by then have even 300 colonists in Madagascar or buildings and fortifications worth more than a million.

But Benyowski's personality remained impressive in spite of everything. Bellecombe, recalling the Baron's adventure-filled life, commented:

> It is hard to find a more extraordinary man . . . let people recall the very remarkable manner in which he fled from his [Siberian] exile, the good fortune he had had in standing up to this climate, and you will realise that this 37-year-old Hungarian colonel is made for great adventures.

In fact Benyowski had lost faith in France. An old Malagasy woman had recently proclaimed him to be directly descended from Ramini, a king of Mananara province, of whom it had been predicted that a descendant would one day appear to rule over his people. In September, Benyowski accepted the mantle of Ramini and the Mananara chiefs paid allegiance to him. On 28 September, he resigned from the French service and proclaimed the independence of northern Madagascar. He had little to lose. In December 1776, he sailed for France to sign a treaty of association between the country which had adopted him and the great island which he now claimed to rule over. His reception at Versailles was, once again, most gratifying. Sartines, the Minister of Marine, spoke to him at length; he received the Cross of St Louis; he was promoted to the rank of Brigadier; the empress Maria Theresa sent him a full pardon from Vienna, so that he was able to travel to Poland, and he finally was given back his family castle. But there was no income to go with it, and the French were not willing either to recognize his Malagasy title or to provide any more funds towards his colonization project.

The years went by, the Mananara people forgot their strange ruler, and it was only in 1785 that Benyowski, backed by merchants from Baltimore, of all places, could once again set foot on Madagascar, to meet total disaster and death.

The *Consolante* and the *Iphigénie* had sailed from Antongil on 5 October. Bellecombe planned to call at various islands and then make straight for India, sending the *Iphigénie* back to the Ile de France with mail for Ternay and for France. But the two ships became separated at night. Bellecombe went on to Bourbon, the second rendezvous. The days passed with no sign of the *Iphigénie*. Bellecombe asked the *Belle-Artur* which was about to sail down the Malagasy coast to keep the lookout alert for signs of the *Iphigénie*, and he penned a note for La Pérouse:

> We could not emphasize too much the concern that your absence is causing us, and we hope indeed that it will have no serious consequence.

To Ternay, he wrote that the condition of the *Iphigénie* had worried him: 'his old ship had not been careened for five years and was leaking'.

November came and almost went. On the 22nd, Maillard Dumesle completed a report for the Minister and added:

> We fear, from what the *Consolante* tells us that the King's paille, the *Iphigénie* . . . may have perished; we reckon that this may have happened because of her lateness and because of debris of a wreck sighted on the coast of Madagascar.

He was able to add a happier postscript before sealing the letter — 'The palle *Iphigénie* has just been sighted'. La Pérouse had taken 48 days to complete the crossing from Antongil to Port-Louis, much of the time being spent in pumping out and patching his creaky and waterlogged vessel.

Quite apart from the anxiety he had begun to feel for the safety of his protégé, Ternay was waiting to leave. Tired of the petty squabbles of Port-Louis, feeling increasingly powerless and ignored

in his faraway island, he had asked to be relieved of his governorship. A year had gone by. Now, his replacement, Brillane, had
arrived in July after an unexpectedly speedy voyage from France. La
Pérouse was also due to return to France and had already sold the
property he had bought with Mengaud, making a profit on the transaction of 1400 *livres*. Ternay had despatched La Pérouse to Madagascar on what he expected to be a brief mission while he finalized
matters with Brillane and organized the formal handing over. Within
a week of his arrival, La Pérouse moved his belongings on board
the *Belle-Poule* which was to take them back to France, Mengaud
included, under the command of Cillart de Surville.

Two days later, on 2 December 1776, the transfer of power
was carried out – the same set of ceremonies, now in reverse,
which had greeted them four years earlier: the reviewing of the
troops, the *Te Deum*, the speeches in the Council Chamber, the
crowds lining the streets, down from their plantations or their country
residence. Yet another fortnight went by before the *Belle-Poule*
actually sailed, by way of Bourbon and the Cape.

La Pérouse would never return to the Ile de France. From the
point of view of his career, he had little to regret. He had commanded his own ships, but not glorious vessels; the commercial
aspects of some of the voyages spoilt a little the sense of satisfaction
he could feel. Yet, in eastern waters, the duality was perfectly
normal; and in France there was no need to tell anyone of the trading element. And obviously, his four years had been financially
rewarding, as recorded in a letter to his sister: clearing pirates from
the shipping lanes of India resulted in modest but acceptable prize
money.

He could not regret leaving the Ile de France, because opportunities
for advancement only really existed in Europe. The world – at least
the world which mattered most to him: western Europe and now the
eastern seaboard of America – was in ferment. Although the news
had not yet reached Port-Louis, on 4 July, a group of American
colonists – John Adams, Benjamin Franklin, Thomas Jefferson and
others – had drawn up a declaration which would be known to
history as the American Declaration of Independence, shake the

thrones of England and eventually of France, and lead to a renewal of hostilities between the two great European powers. It was to give Jean-François the opportunity of proving to those who really mattered the strength of his character and the extent of his special skills as a sailor.

He would nevertheless have regretted his departure from the Ile de France had Eléonore herself not been on the point of sailing for France.

In his letter to his sister, Jean-François had hinted at a growing attachment. He had in fact fallen totally in love with Eléonore Broudou, had asked for her hand in marriage and been accepted. According to local gossip, Eléonore had at first rejected him and, when pressed, had told him that her elder sister Elizabeth was in love with him. 'I cannot hurt her by taking from her the man she loves most in the world.' With all the directness of a man of the sea, Jean-François called on Elizabeth:

> [who] realising how great was the love [her sister] had inspired in him, decided to withdraw. She went to stay with friends to hide her sorrow and wrote to her sister to tell her she had been mistaken over her feelings and that what she had taken to be love was a mere feeling of friendship.[4]

At this point, Jean-François spoke to Abraham Broudou, who could have no objection to such an advantageous match, and an engagement was agreed upon. But there remained the far greater obstacle of the older Galaup. Jacquette Galaup, as no doubt her brother had intended her to, had dropped hints to her mother and then to her father. Galaup's reaction was prompt: he sent a message to Ternay, formally appointing him his son's guardian and stating his objection to any marriage which could be regarded as a misalliance or in any way unsuitable for a naval officer. Jean-François was in his mid-thirties, but his plans were blocked from two directions — a parental objection coupled with an officer's obligation to marry only with the approval of his superiors. And for good measure, there was the strong bond of mutual respect and friendship between Ternay and himself.

All that could be done was for Jean-François to plead with his father, to use Eléonore's youth and gentle charm to overcome the old man's objections, and to gain his family's consent to a union which, romantic though it might be, would bring neither an adequate dowry nor connections useful to his career.

Eléonore's mother now lived in Nantes. The girl said farewell to her father and sister, and a fortnight after the *Belle-Poule* had sailed for France she followed in a merchant ship.

Notes

1. Reprinted in the 1888 *Bulletin de la société de géographie*, pp. 159-60.
2. Reports from La Pérouse to Ternay, November 1776, in AN Colonies C5-A6,, No. 13. Item No. 12 is a separate report on Benyowski's settlements.
3. La Pérouse's Report, *loc. cit.*
4. Ducray's account in his *Histoire de la ville de Curepipe* is based on little more than tradition, but the story is pleasantly romantic.

9

The American War

TERNAY and La Pérouse landed in France on 7 May and speedily made their way to Paris and Versailles.

As far as one can ascertain, this was Jean-François' first visit to the capital. There was much to be seen, calls to be made, letters to be delivered, officials to be visited. He was promoted to lieutenant, backdated to 4 April. On May 24th, he was made a knight of the Order of St Louis, the distinguished order founded by Louis XIV in 1693 but later abolished by Napoleon I who replaced it with the Legion of Honour. It was a tangible mark of appreciation, less easy to earn in years of peace than in wartime — and indeed in La Pérouse's view easier to obtain by officers who stayed in France under the eyes of the ministry instead of sailing off into distant seas.

He was not slow in pointing this out. It was a feature of his character that he never hesitated to speak his mind and lay his complaints in writing. On 5 July, from Versailles, he expressed his forthright views to the Minister:

My Lord,
Following my campaign on the Malabar coast of which I had the honour of sending you an account, you were kind enough to advise me that my lieutenant's warrant would be sent to me any day; fifteen months later it was included in a promotion list of one hundred lieutenants on which I was number forty. The flattering manner in which you granted me the Cross of Saint-Louis was of inestimable value to me, but had I remained in Europe I would have had claims for it three years earlier.

Three officers from my ship, who had distinguished themselves, have obtained the King's favours; must the captain be excluded? Finally, I have been almost these two months in Paris and I have made every effort to do what you expected of me. I have the honour to be, my Lord, with the deepest respect, your very humble and very obedient servant.

Lapérouse.[1]

He was not told to be patient or to stay in line. Ternay was there to advise him and in his own case had earlier had a disagreement over delayed promotion. Three weeks after penning his letter of complaint, La Pérouse received a grant of 300 *livres* a year 'in appreciation of services rendered in Indian waters'. It would be difficult to overlook the link between the letter and the announcement of the pension, but face was saved all round and niceties were preserved by the timing: La Pérouse's friend Clonard was offered the option of a pension or the Cross of St Louis; since he did not have the latter as yet, he did not hesitate. He chose the medal, and the money was then offered to La Pérouse.

Money and honours were items his family in their landlocked province could understand, but profits from naval prizes in distant seas and in time of peace smacked of privateering. What would the neighbours say? It was better not to explain things in too great detail to the burghers of Albi. Jean-François was eager to go south, to see his mother and his sister; less keen, however, to face his father who had thundered at him from afar when the question of marriage to Eléonore was mooted.

Meantime, there was Versailles. It was a world so different from any La Pérouse had known that he could not help but feel overawed. He was no smooth courtier, but a man of the sea, more than a little overweight, practical and down to earth, with traces left of his local accent.

But Ternay was quite at ease; he took Jean-François with him to Court, piloted him skilfully through the gilt and mirrors of the great salons, introduced him to useful acquantainces, and together they picked up the latest gossip.

War with England had not yet broken out, but relations were strained. No one could avoid gloating over the problems George III was having with his American colonists, even though the latter's republican and egalitarian opinions were scarcely palatable. But Benjamin Franklin, as their unofficial ambassador, was welcome in the drawing-rooms of the best society — this was the age of the *philosophes*, and Franklin fitted in with the middle-class, mildly scientific world of men like Voltaire, Rousseau and Diderot. Behind the scenes, Beaumarchais manoeuvred and bought supplies for the insurgent colonists, displaying all the talent for intrigue he gave to the characters of his plays, *The Barber of Seville* and *The Marriage of Figaro*. And now a young nobleman, the Marquis de La Fayette, had sailed for America with a few friends, with the entire Court's blessing and the government's sham disapproval. It was the start of an adventure that would become history.

On a lighter note, there were whispers about the visit of Joseph II of Austria, the Queen's brother. It was no state visit, but a traditional grand tour which included factories, ports and even prisons — Joseph was a serious young man. He hoped to reconcile Louis XVI and Marie-Antoinette long enough for the Queen to provide France with an heir. And indeed, a year later, Marie-Thérèse was born — she would be the only member of Louis XVI's family to survive the Revolution.

August came, the heavy month of summer when activity languishes in the heat. Ternay let Jean-François go down to Albi. They would meet later in Brest. La Pérouse had not seen his family for over five years. There were presents to give, souvenirs from the distant East, cloth from India, carved boxes, curios. But there were strains and tensions as well. His father was now blind, sensing the approach of death, and thinking of what the future could hold for his family. One of Jean-François' sisters had married and was living away from Albi. The other would also no doubt soon marry. If Jean-François did not find a wife and settle down, would there be no Galaups left in Albi? Parents had a responsibility to ensure their children married suitably; the fact that Jean-François was 36 did not lessen Victor-Joseph's patriarchal role. Names of suitable young ladies were suggested. None appealed. Eléonore was now with her mother in Nantes and had been for a while in poor health. Jean-François had no feelings to spare for another.

His father could not deny that he was at last making a successful career. Decoration and pension proved this beyond argument, but could the properties, the farm, the vineyard, the big house at the Go where Jean-François was born, be left with nothing more than an absentee landlord, a bachelor, sailing in faraway oceans?

There was strain, without doubt, and Jean-François left with a sense of relief and liberation, not unmixed with sadness. And as for Eléonore, old Galaup had expressed his feelings in a style that left his son no room for manoeuvre:

> You make me tremble, my son! You are cold-bloodedly contemplating the consequences of a marriage that would disgrace you in the eyes of the Minister and cause you to lose the protection of powerful friends! You display contempt for the opinions of your friends; you are going to lose, together with the rewards of twenty years of work, the esteem you have acquired and which you seem to have deserved by the elevation of your sentiments. We had felt flattered by it, but by lowering yourself, you would bring humiliation on all your family and your relations. You are preparing nothing but regrets for us; you are sacrificing your fortune and the respectability of your condition to a frivolous beauty and to so-called attractions which maybe exist only in your imagination.

In practical vein, he outlined problems Jean-François would encounter — In which home could she live? What coach could she have? — and rebutted his contention that a union with Eléonore would be acceptable because other officers had married girls from the colonies. The Broudous could not provide a large dowry:

> M. de la Jonquière and many others have married creoles; but what these might have lacked in respect of their birth was compensated by their fortune. Without this balancing out, they would not have demeaned themselves by marrying them.

Jean-François buried himself in work. He went back to Paris where Ternay was living. War with England had become inevitable; it had already begun in effect, in spite of all the diplomatic niceties that covered the growing active French support for the American colonists. The surrender of Burgoyne at Saratoga on 17 October showed that the insurgents were formidable opponents of Britain, even though Howe's entry into Philadelphia cheered loyalist hearts. At Court, the news that La Fayette had been wounded at Brandywine caused excited gossip. Under the care of a Mrs Beckel, whose young daughter made a charming nurse, La Fayette wrote letters to all his friends urging support for the American cause, even to Maurepas, to whom he suggested an attack by the French 'flying the American flag'.

Claret de Fleurieu.
(Private Collection)

The elderly Minister of State found the suggestion outrageous — even though Maurepas had a soft spot for energetic youths as he himself had taken over the administration of the Navy at the age of 24; but it reflected what was in everyone's mind.

Ternay and La Pérouse themselves were working on a plan to attack the British in the Indian Ocean. Claret de Fleurieu, the Director of Ports and Arsenals, gave them every support, although he was convinced, rightly, that the real blows would need to be struck much closer to home.

It was at this time that the paths of La Pérouse and Fleurieu first crossed. They would remain firm friends and associates. Charles Pierre d'Eveux Claret de Fleurieu was then just under 40, the son of a Lyons magistrate who had joined the *gardes de la Marine* at Toulon the year before La Pérouse joined the corps at Brest. Their backgrounds were similar, but Fleurieu had advanced more quickly, thanks to his interest in chronometers and the problem of time-keeping at sea. Choiseul, following his policy of improving technical knowledge in the navy, had allowed him to study under Ferdinand Berthoud, the Swiss-born watchmaker whose marine chronometer had aroused a great deal of enthusiasm. Fleurieu, together with the astronomer Pingré, had tested it for him on a voyage that took him to Cadiz, Tenerife, the coast of Africa, the West Indies, Newfoundland and the Azores. A lieutenant by 1773, Fleurieu had been raised to the rank of post-captain in 1776. His task was now to organize logistic support for the French navy when war was declared. One day he would be, however briefly, Minister of Marine.

La Pérouse outlined his ideas on India in a Memoir now kept in the Naval Archives,[2] in which he drew on his experience, but without adding anything which could be considered as particularly original. One could hardly expect anything more, so well known was the situation. Pondicherry would have to be fortified into an impregnable continental base; the Ile de France would need strengthening as the pivot of the Indian Ocean, so that the French squadrons could sail thence for India 'as fresh as they are when they leave French ports'; the Malabar coast could provide shelter and supplies, especially rice. Fleurieu thanked La Pérouse and filed his proposal among all the others that were being sent to him. They still lie there today with Fleurieu's annotations and comments.

The proposal that was finally sent to Louis XVI for his approval was drawn up by the Comte de Broglie. Not unexpectedly, the emphasis was on the Channel and Atlantic seaways. La Pérouse, with other officers, returned to Brest to prepare for its implementation.

As subsequently amended, the plan had three main sections: aid to the Americans, help to Spain in accordance with the 'Family Pact' between the two Bourbon powers, and protection of the northern French coast against possible British raids. In essence, it was a defensive programme, which Fleurieu and the bulk of the naval officers disliked. The result was a combination of isolated actions, major in themselves but ill-related to any overall objective. However, strategic plans never operate in isolation: the enemy has plans of his own and he is seldom obliging enough to dovetail them with yours. Even before the actual declaration of war, the British had decided on a new course in America, which capitalized on their mastery of the seas:

> This was to use troops only to keep footholds on the American coast and to revert to the idea of a naval war. The advent of France into hostilities confirmed them in this intention. As the defeat of France had to be the major objective, the less effort diverted to America the better.[3]

The year 1778 opened with the standard British raid on French shipping. As many as 155 merchant ships, large and small, were seized in British ports or on their way home. On 6 February, Versailles signed a secret treaty of friendship with Franklin as representative of the Thirteen Colonies. Franklin himself was received at Court of 20 March, a ceremony which implied recognition of the rebel government: the next morning, the British Ambassador, Lord Stormont, left for London. The war aims as everyone saw them were the end of British control over the colonists and the shoring up of a new country which would be an enemy of Britain and a friend to France for many years to come. The French Court had agreed to make no claims to any territory currently held by the British on the American continent; compensation could be found in the West

Indies. By this clause, France effectively abandoned the French Canadians — not that anyone in Versailles realized this, except the wily Franklin.

La Pérouse took over command of the *Serin*, a corvette of 14 guns, on 24 February. It was a mediocre vessel, with an ill-trained crew. Not one of his sailors had handled a gun before, he reported. It was the worst ship in the three ports, he went on:

> I cannot sight an English frigate from my topmasts without feeling sure that I shall be taken unless I am within a very short distance of a port.[4]

His complaints were not unjustified: he took 15 days to sail from Bordeaux to Brest, as part of a convoy which had to leave him behind because of the slowness of the *Serin*. Coastguard duties were unglamorous, albeit necessary. Twenty-one days spent tacking between Ushant and Falmouth Bay, much the same length of time spent along the Atlantic coast, all the while avoiding the enemy, was hardly the road to glory and promotion. Even so, La Pérouse showed his flair for planning. He suggested the stationing of a chain of 12 frigates and 12 luggers in the Bay of Biscay to protect the sea link between France and her Spanish ally, as preferable to the escorting of individual convoys.

He left the *Serin* on 15 May and had a month ashore — time to go down to Nantes to see Eléonore and time to discuss the course of the war with Ternay. Officially, it had still not begun. The spark that set alight the powder keg was a battle between HMS *Arethusa* and the *Belle-Poule*, in which 58 French officers and men were killed. The previous period of undeclared hostilities, which a later generation would have called a phoney war, had given time to Fleurieu to equip his ships and call up sailors. La Pérouse was sent to St Malo, where he took over command of the *Amazone*, a brand new frigate. He could no longer complain.

The *Amazone* was not ready for the first major engagement of the sea war, the inconclusive Battle of Ushant of 27 July 1778. Admiral Keppel's fleet suffered the highest casualties — 1,196 dead and wounded against 680 among the French — so the latter could claim a victory of sorts. The French Navy was entitled to feel more confident at this stage than the English which was stretched to the limit, having to keep ships continually at sea so as to maintain supply lines to the troops in America, fight the French who were threatening the West Indies, supply Gibraltar which was besieged by Spain, and guard the Channel and the Irish Sea approaches against a persistently rumoured French landing. By August, when the *Amazone* was ready, she was able to cruise, in company with Mengaud de la Hage's *Gentille* and the cutter *Guèpe*, in the North Sea and around the British Isles and capture 12 prizes without loss. The French could hardly believe their good fortune:

> The British flag was no longer seen on these seas where, a few months earlier, it had flown as a master or an aggressor.[5]

It would not last, because Britain was rapidly equipping new ships, but also because the French were still too overawed by the reputed superiority of the British navy and failed to pursue their advantage.

La Pérouse was marking time. The proposal he had made with Ternay to strengthen the Indian outposts had only been accepted as part of a broader strategy, which meant that preparations could only progress slowly, in step with other plans. For one thing, ships intended for a long campaign in Eastern waters needed to be copper-sheathed to protect them from the destructive shipworms, the *teredo navalis*. Two of the ships selected for the Indies expedition, the 74-gun *Orient* and the 64-gun *Artésien*, required this treatment. The squadron could leave earlier if the work could be carried out at the Ile de France, but no one could guarantee this. The resources of Brest were certainly strained to the limit, but Port-Louis was so far away that no one knew for certain what the situation was.

While the arguments continued, new problems arose. Although Ternay was going, he would not be in charge. The Comte d'Orves was given overall command and, by way of consolation, Ternay was supplied with a brand-new ship of the line, the *Annibal*, and raised to the rank of lieutenant-general. This promotion came to him in a letter from the king dated 7 December 1778. A week earlier, d'Orves had sailed with the *Orient* and *Artésien*.

At the end of 1778, viewed from Versailles, the strategic situation looked rather like a chessboard in the early stages of a major game. A few pawns had moved, surprisingly favourably for the French, but everywhere pieces were at a standstill. Then suddenly moves began to appear on every side.

In the West Indies, the Comte d'Estaing was poised near Martinique; in the American colonies, the British were sending out peace feelers to their rebellious colonists; in the East, the British under Hector Munro were threatening Pondicherry; in the French ports, ships were being fitted out for several different expeditions, including the one to the Indian Ocean.

Indeed, had d'Orves not been attacked by two English privateers within a week of his departure, he might have sailed on to Port-Louis, and La Pérouse might have followed him soon after with the bulk of the squadron; but the English corsairs sighting the *Orient* and *Artésien* off Cape Ortegal, northern Portugal, foolishly came within range. One was sunk and the other beaten off without much difficulty. However, a rash attack can inflict greater damage than a cautious engagement, and the *Artésien* was forced to turn back to Brest for repairs. D'Orves had no option but to go with her. For the French this was indeed a Pyrrhic victory.

News of the first move on the world chessboard followed almost at once. On 9 January Choiseul learnt that Pondicherry had fallen to the British. A month later, La Fayette arrived in Brest from Boston, seeking naval reinforcement — unofficially still, since his association with the American colonists had not been approved by the Court, but his popularity and influence were too considerable to be overlooked. Next, news came that the Duc de Lauzun had captured Saint-Louis in Senegal. And then the French learned that their West Indian island of St Lucia had fallen. Everything was beginning to point to the theatre of war being the Atlantic. The East could only be a costly sideshow.

Government policies do not change direction with the speed of a frigate. Ternay and La Pérouse had already sailed out of Brest into the roadstead. A total of six ships were in position, loading the last of the supplies, completing their preparations for the first stage of the voyage, which was the crossing to Rio de la Plata. Three other ships were to sail from Lorient. La Pérouse in the *Amazone* and Mengaud in the *Gentille* would then lead the others, since they had the greater knowledge of eastern waters. It was 25 February 1779.

Ternay, in charge from the moment d'Orves had gone ahead in the *Orient*, received instructions to sail — but to the Caribbean . . . . The Indian plan was shelved, at least until October. In fact, Jean-François would never return to the Indian Ocean.

The change of plans meant more delays. An entire convoy was to be organized to assist the Comte d'Estaing in the West Indies which the English were now threatening. More than St Lucia was in danger, for the British commander, Byron, was at last receiving reinforcements and his ships now outnumbered the French. The Brest and Lorient fleets were unable to sail until 1 May 1779, and when they did Ternay who had suffered a bad fall and Mengaud whose *Gentille* was reassigned to new duties stayed behind. Jean-François' new commander was Toussaint-Guillaume de La Motte-Picquet, a tough, experienced sailor in his late fifties who had 22 campaigns to his credit, the latest one being that of Ushant in July, where his *Saint-Esprit* had shown what could be done once the French shrugged off their sense of inferiority vis-à-vis the British Navy.

La Pérouse's journal of his months in the *Amazone* is relatively short, but it gives us his viewpoint of the struggle in the West Indies. For him, it marked the beginning of a series of successes that would lead to rapid promotion and to his appointment as commander of the great voyage of exploration.

La Motte-Picquet dropped anchor in Fort-Royal, Martinique, on 27 June. If one includes the merchant ships he was escorting, the convoy amounted to some 60 vessels. D'Estaing was overjoyed. Although he had received reinforcements earlier, the island was feeling the strain of feeding his men. The supplies brought in by La Motte-Picquet were urgently needed. But more than that, d'Estaing could now envisage an attack on the British West Indies, to make up for the loss of St Lucia and loosen the blockade on the American colonists.

The sealed instructions La Motte-Picquet brought him from Versailles were far from helpful. He was told to return to France with a convoy of merchantmen, and to leave the Comte de Grasse in charge of the Windward Islands and La Motte-Picquet in charge of Santo Domingo. History has given prominence to the Nelson touch, but the English do not have the monopoly of it: d'Estaing simply put the letters in his pocket and proceeded with his own plans. He would return to Brest when it suited him.

Almost at once, La Pérouse was back at sea under d'Estaing. The island of Martinique forms part of the lesser Antilles, in the southern part of the chain. Byron and the British were somewhere to the north; would Barbados, standing rather like a sentry to the south-east, be easy to capture before the British could react? The winds decided otherwise: during the night of 1st July the French reached Grenada. D'Estaing decided that this British possession would be as good as any to compensate for the loss of St Lucia. There were 25 French ships plus the frigates, making up an imposing force some 26000 men strong.

La Pérouse landed his troops with no opposition. There were at most 700 redcoats defending Fort St George; d'Estaing landed 2000 French marines. The ships exchanged fire with the batteries of St George, but one set of targets was fixed, while the other could manoeuvre with relative ease. By the morning of the 3rd, Grenada was ready to surrender:

> At last the dawn I was waiting for with such impatience broke, and I saw the white flag flying over the batteries and the fort. We shouted God Save the King for a quarter of an hour.[6]

The capture was followed by mopping-up operations and some celebrations. But they were short-lived. Lord Byron's fleet was coming to the rescue:

> At dawn [on 6 July] we sighted Admiral Byron coming full sail towards us, close to the land. Our frigates had sounded the alarm before daybreak, so that the General had taken advantage of night signals to order us to weigh anchor. But several ships still had a number of their boats and longboats ashore, so that at dawn only five or six ships were under sail.

> The approach of Byron had decided the General to order cables to be cut, which was done by the ships that had not raised anchor.[7]

D'Estaing was more noted for his dash — the old *furia francese* so dear to the nobility since the days of Francis I — than for his organizational skills. Chaos reigned ashore and disorder at sea. But daring and fury made up for it. D'Estaing had a fight on his hands, a real one, after the relatively easy capture of Grenada; he was not supposed to be there at all, risking France's ships, but to be preparing for his return home — he had nothing to lose and everything to gain:

> Our General sailed towards the enemy and we were so near them that it was impossible, as we sped towards them, to arrange ourselves in any regular order of battle. But the daring nature of our manoeuvre increased the confidence of our crew and reduced, no doubt, that of the enemy.[8]

Possibly, Byron was unaware that the French had captured Fort St George and he planned to manoeuvre d'Estaing into a position where both the shore batteries and his own ships could fire on the French. Whatever his plans might have been, the rapid approach of 15 ships under d'Estaing upset them and an unexpected salvo from the fort forced the English fleet to change direction urgently, veering across the advancing sails. The battle lasted most of the morning and part of the afternoon, costing several hundred lives and a thousand wounded, among them La Motte-Picquet whose thigh was crushed by a canon ball but who continued to direct operations lying on a mattress on the deck of the *Annibal*. By mid-afternoon, Byron's only concern was to extricate his ships, save what he could, and sail north to lick his wounds. Grenada was to remain French, at least for the time being.

La Pérouse's role during the battle had been to ensure that d'Estaing's signals were seen and understood. The *Amazone* spent the day sailing between the ships of the French fleet, but taking no direct part in the various engagements. It enabled him to be an observer and a far from neutral one, for while he admired d'Estaing's dash and daring, he could not fail to criticize the lack of planning and the failure to take advantage of Byron's temporary disarray.

But d'Estaing's concern was to hold Grenada. This much he had achieved. The rest could follow. A week later, the French sailed back to Martinique, leaving a garrison on Grenada. D'Estaing then went on to French Guadeloupe, where he obtained reinforcements to make up for the men he had lost, and continued on to Antigua, close to where Byron was refitting.

It was summertime, with hot days of blue skies merging with a bluer sea. None could avoid enjoying what seemed like lazy days, and the stirring sight of the 24 great ships under sail manoeuvring at their leisure past the peaceful green islands. D'Estaing has been criticized for failing to seek out Byron, but the English were at St Christopher, inside a group of English-held islands, and how difficult it would have been for the French to destroy Byron's ships must remain a matter of conjecture. D'Estaing preferred to sail on to Santo Domingo where he received a tumultuous welcome and learnt that Spain had entered the war on France's side.

This latter event did not do a great deal to swing the fortunes of war, since the Spanish Court was to display considerable inertia, but on the map at least it further endangered Britain's hold on the West Indies. Spain held Puerto Rico, Cuba and the Florida ports. D'Estaing could be justified in thinking that the American War would now be decided wholly on the American continent and that naval assistance to the rebels would finally turn the tide. But, while talk of peace at almost any price was becoming common in London, the West Indies were very much in George III's mind when he urged his ministers to carry on the fight at all costs. If the American colonists were to get their independence, then the West Indies would follow them, tied as they were to the American market. After the West Indies might come Ireland, and the final result would be the economic ruin of Great Britain. George III begged his ministers to continue the struggle in the knowledge that it was a fight for survival.[9]

D'Estaing, not surprisingly, saw things differently. And many of his officers, whatever misgivings they might have had about the wisdom of his strategic interpretations, could not avoid being stirred by the romantic elements of the American Revolution, to which La Fayette and so many courtiers and philosophers in France had already succumbed. They, of course, did not know that d'Estaing's

instructions were simply to return to France. On 16 August, responding to a series of pleas from representatives of the American
rebels and their French sympathizers, d'Estaing ordered his fleet to
sail for South Carolina with 22 battle ships, nine frigates, two cor-
vettes and two storeships, plus 15 merchantmen. Jean-François was
once again to witness a naval engagement.

On 1 September 1779 the fleet was 40 miles out at sea from
British-held Savannah, preparing its landing. The merchantmen
continued to Charleston, so that whatever element of surprise there
could be in d'Estaing's operation was soon lost. A four-day storm
did not help matters. The plan was to land the troops 12 miles
south of Savannah — but this involved marching through a network
of marshes and muddy creeks, bringing up guns and equipment
within range of the British defences. While these painstaking operations were taking place, La Pérouse, on his way to Charleston, was
presented with an opportunity for a solo engagement:

> [At dawn on the ninth] I had sight of a vessel at such a distance from me
> that I could not estimate its strength; but seeing the vessels I was con-
> voying had no more risks to run before entering Charleston, I gave chase to
> the vessel I could see, which for her part was making towards me, so that
> I was soon convinced it was a frigate . . . At eight o'clock, we were only a
> half-league away. Then she raised the English flag and fired a shot by way
> of confirmation. I too raised the English flag without confirming it, and
> the frigate at once veered off, wind astern with all sails out. I followed
> course, similarly letting out all my sails . . . At ten o'clock I was within
> pistol shot; I hoisted the French flag and fired a gun. The vessel, which had
> only twenty-nine pounders and six four-pounders, fought with a bravery
> that cannot be overpraised.[10]

The battle lasted a little over an hour. The English frigate, named
the *Ariel*, and commanded by 'Thomas Makonsay' had every one of
its masts brought down before she finally surrendered.[11] La Pérouse
lost 12 men killed, with another 13 seriously wounded. His own
mainmast had been pierced right through by a cannonball, and
threatened to break at any moment, his sails were in shreds and his
shrouds cut through. He limped into Charleston on the 11th, towing
the *Ariel*, to the cheers of his friends and of the hard-pressed
Americans.

The land operations were progressing slowly, while a succession of storms struck the French ships. D'Estaing and the American general Benjamin Lincoln were reluctantly settling down to a siege both hoped would not be prolonged, for Byron's squadron might appear at any moment. Time was not on the attackers' side. A naval bombardment in early October did little damage to the British who were dug in among sandhills. It was time for another dose of *furia francese*. On 9 October the combined French and American forces launched a full assault.

The well-entrenched British shot the attacking columns to tatters. The French lost 150 killed and 370 wounded: among these d'Estaing himself. It was time to bring out his instructions from his pocket and start thinking of returning to France. The siege was lifted on 20 October, in time to meet yet another storm which scattered the fleet, some ships making for Martinique, others for the Chesapeake, and d'Estaing for Brest.

Jean-François took his *Amazone* to Cadiz, accompanying the *Sagittaire* which had early captured the *Experiment*, a ship of 50 guns and too good a prize to be left behind, since aboard this vessel had been found General Garth and £650,000 in silver, as well as quantities of food and clothing — a number of the *Amazone*'s sailors were now wearing a strange motley of English uniforms. The *Ariel* had been abandoned, but La Pérouse evened things out by the capture of the privateer *Tiger*.

On 15 December, the four ships reached Cadiz. There was time to rest and to catch up on the latest news from Europe before each went on his way: the *Sagittaire* to Toulon, Jean-François to Lorient. It was 28 February 1780. Ternay was waiting for him, impatient to set out on a fresh campaign.

Notes

1.   *Bulletin du centenaire*, p. 255.
2.   Reference C7-165: 11-12, and 84-n150: 73-5.
3.   Watson, *The Reign of George III*, p. 210.
4.   Lacour-Gayet, *La Marine militaire de la France*, pp. 107-9.
5.   Ibid., p. 137.

6. 'Extrait du Journal de Lapérouse commandant la frégate l'*Amazone, Société de géographie, Bulletin du centenaire*, p. 238.

7. Ibid., p. 239.

8. Ibid., p. 240.

9. As evidenced by the king's correspondence. See on this Watson, *The Reign of George III*, p. 214.

10. Ibid., p. 243-4.

11. Thomas Mackenzie who had been sent out in the sloop *Hunter* to join Admiral Graves' fleet in 1775. The *Ariel*, of 20 guns, had had four killed and 20 wounded.

10
Triumphs & Defeats

CHARLES-HENRI, Comte d'Estaing was to spend the rest of the war in relative disgrace. For one thing, he was more of an army man than a sailor, which meant his fellow officers of the royal navy considered him an interloper whose relative lack of experience had resulted in a series of missed opportunities just when France seemed to hold the upper hand. Above all, he had taken a gamble and he had lost. He sat out the rest of the war like an unwanted guest. There would still be time for daring and a moment of glory when the outbreak of the French Revolution propelled him to the rank of vice-admiral with the task of reorganizing the sorely-tried French navy. And then the Terror sent him to the guillotine, aged 65, where, like so many others, he threw down a final proud challenge: 'When my head has fallen, take it to the English. They'll give you a good price for it'.

While d'Estaing's star was setting, Ternay's was continuing to rise. His task was to escort a French army to America, led by Jean-Baptiste, Comte de Rochambeau, 55, a scarred veteran of numerous campaigns. There were to be 5,000 soldiers, plus their officers and artillery support. Gone were the exciting but somewhat amateurish days of young La Fayette and his friends. Rochambeau had argued for 12 battalions, which meant 6,000 men. His request was granted. And cavalry? He could have it. What he eventually did get was less than the sum total of the promises, but that was nothing unusual and Rochambeau knew it. What he could take with him depended on the transport provided — the battlefields were 3,000 miles away.

Ternay sent La Pérouse to Versailles to discuss the massive logistic problems with Fleurieu. The naval stores had been drained by previous campaigns, the merchant vessels needed to carry munitions and supplies were dispersed in a scattering of ports; there was the usual shortage of men; there was not even enough copper to sheathe

the eight or ten warships required to protect the convoy. It was easy enough for the Minister to agree to Rochambeau's requests, which were far from unreasonable, but how much did these landlubbers know about the navy's difficulties?

Jean-François provided the first-hand knowledge so many lacked. Ternay asked him to go to Nantes, then back to Lorient and on to Brest, where the Comte d'Hector, director of the arsenals and shore installations, was struggling in a tidal wave of orders and counter-orders.

For La Pérouse, there came a dark cloud across this period of intense activity. His friend Mengaud, who had shared his years in the Ile de France, one of his most intimate friends, was drowned with 200 others when, bringing in his ship, the *Charmante*, from Lorient to Brest, he struck a rock near the Ile de Sein. Mengaud was one of the few who knew of his continuing attachment to Eléonore Broudou, still patiently waiting in Nantes where Jean-François was able to spend a few moments with her and share a few tears before returning to Brest.

By mid-April, the Ternay squadron was almost ready to sail. It was to escort 28 transport ships; Ternay would command the *Duc-de-Bourgogne*, 80 guns, and there would be 12 other naval vessels, including La Pérouse's *Amazone*. Slowly the ships made their way into the roadsteads. Thirty-two transports with a total capacity of 12,800 tons, bringing what Rochambeau called the immense paraphernalia of war, were towed out. Two ran afoul of each other and one of them was forced back for repairs. The delay did not matter too much, as the winds were unfavourable. Finally, at 5 a.m. on 2 May 1780, the convoy weighed anchor.

The crossing took two months. It could hardly be otherwise with the slow clumsy merchantmen. The speed of a convoy is ever that of the slowest ship. La Pérouse and the other frigate captain, Cillard de Villeneuve, manoeuvred around the fleet like a couple of hardworking sheepdogs. Scurvy made its appearance in the overcrowded ships, while boredom among the troops gave rise to problems of discipline. The Duc de Lauzun, back from his raid on Senegal and ready for new adventures, thought not merely of the naval officers — 'a

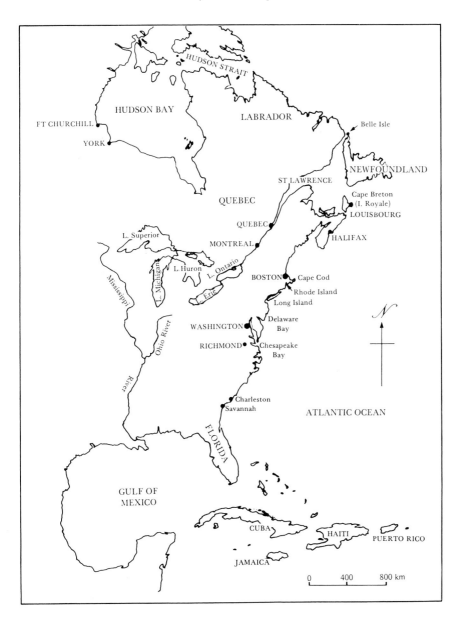

British North America in the 1780s.

corps where one breathes nothing but jealousy and insubordination'
– but also of his own men 'crammed six or seven hundred of them
per ship, unable to move, drinking water so old it has taken on a
reddish colour, eaten by lice, bugs and fleas'. He had brought his
musicians with him – fifes, trumpets, drums – and he thought-
fully helped to alleviate tedium with concerts.

On 10 June, boredom vanished. The *Amazone* gave chase to an
unlucky cutter on her way from Halifax to the West Indies with
a cargo of cod and oil. The crew were taken prisoner, the cod shared
out, and the boat sunk.

A week later, nearing the Bermudas, a sail hove into sight. It was
an English corvette his time, of 12 guns, from Charleston and similarly
bound for the West Indies. Cillart in the *Surveillante* captured her,
and thus the French discovered that Charleston had fallen to the
British who now held the entire coastline of Georgia and South
Carolina. Ternay learned also that the departure of his fleet was
widely known. It induced some caution in him when, on 20 June,
some hundred miles south-west of Bermuda, six ships were sighted.
His officers were eager to fight. The English vessels were outnumbered and could be cut off, but Ternay agreed at most to an
exchange of shots that caused minor casualties to both sides; there
was to be no pursuit. Rochambeau praised Ternay who had been
man enough 'to prefer the preservation of the convoy to the personal
glory of capturing an enemy ship', but the price he had to pay was
an orchestration of criticism among the younger officers. He displayed similar caution a few days later when two English frigates,
mistaking by night the convoy for one of theirs, tagged on behind.
Discovering their error, they fired a few shots as they veered back,
throwing overboard their spare masts and guns to lighten themselves.
The *Amazone* and the *Surveillante* gave chase, but Ternay signalled
them back: the French were too near the end of their mission to
waste time on unnecessary captures.

On 9 July 1780, La Pérouse was in sight of Land's End, in Rhode
Island. The French had arrived. Rochambeau's army would be landed
at Newport. The welcome at first was far from ecstatic. Newport
was a small, cold town, a community split by the civil war as France

would be split herself ten years later by the Revolution, and the inhabitants were no more enthusiastic about the materialization in their midst of eager French soldiers than they were about the thousand scurvy cases who had to be accommodated in makeshift hospitals. But gradually, the stiff New Englanders relaxed. By the 20th, men and stores were ashore. It was literally not a day too soon, for on the 21st the fleet of Admiral Graves, sent out from Portsmouth to track Ternay down, appeared off Rhode Island.

The French position looked perilous. Rochambeau could not start off towards New York to assist Washington without weakening Rhode Island and placing Ternay's ships in jeopardy. Washington was hardly anxious to change his own plans in order to come to the aid of this French allies. Fortunately, the British had no precise information about the size of Rochambeau's forces. They did know from their spies how much Rochambeau had asked for, but they could not be certain that he had not been granted his requests, nor did they suspect that a quarter of his men were too ill to fight. The British general Henry Clinton opted for the defence of New York. Newport could wait.

Days went by, giving the French a chance to organize themselves and regain their health. Graves did not attack. Plans were made and unmade on both sides. Rochambeau and Ternay met Washington at Hartford in September. The main outcome was that France should send more men, so that when the anti-British offensive started, it would be the beginning of the end of a war that had already dragged on for too long. La Pérouse was to be sent to Versailles with the request for reinforcements.

The *Amazone* sailed on 28 October, having aboard Rochambeau's son, a colonel in his father's expeditionary corps. It was a grey stormy day which brought down from the north the first warnings of a harsh winter. But the gale was welcome because it scattered Admiral Rodney's blockading force and gave La Pérouse a chance to avoid pursuit at the cost of few broken spars and torn sails. The crossing was almost direct, uneventful and speedy, and the frigate reached Brest in 39 days.

Rochambeau and La Pérouse left at once for Versailles. A government reshuffle had occurred in their absence. The new Minister of Marine was now the Marquis de Castries, a man with regional links with the Galaup family since he had been brought up in Albi by his uncle, the Archbishop of Castries whose see was the great glowing cathedral of Albi. In addition, Castries' son, the Comte de Charlus, was serving in America under Rochambeau and was a friend of La Fayette (he would one day become the first duc de Castries). La Pérouse's spirits were raised by these changes. Friends in positions of power at court make all the difference.

He was not disappointed. Castries could not meet all the demands, but he could go far enough to end the stalemate which was demoralizing the expeditionary force. Within a fortnight, La Pérouse was back in Brest with orders to sail at once, taking with him the assurance that reinforcements and supplies would be sent out without delay. As a tangible form of encouragement, he was entrusted with one and a half million *livres* that would put an end to the constant financial haggling the French had to resort to on the American continent to obtain necessities. Young Rochambeau remained in Versailles to continue pressing for more men — his father's army had tended to be overlooked at home and some form of ambassador at Court was necessary.

The *Amazone*, after her two wearying campaigns, needed a refit, so Jean-François was given the *Astrée*, a frigate of 32 guns, only a few months old and already copper-sheathed. But her first crossing was full of hardships. Sailing from Brest on Christmas Day, she did not reach Boston until 27 February. There, La Pérouse learned of Ternay's death. 'The worst of misfortunes was awaiting me here', he wrote. 'The Chevalier de Ternay was the best friend I had in the world; he was like my father'. And indeed, Jean-François had always felt closer to the aristocratic naval officer than he had ever been towards the stern patriarch of Albi who still harboured a grudge against the sea that had kept his heir away from him.

Ternay had died on 15 December, not so much from despair at his enforced inaction and the petty squabbles of Newport, as some have romantically suggested, as from the typhoid that had begun its ravages in the town. His health had been indifferent for some time and he had little patience with the complex manoeuvrings circumstances forced on Washington. Not all the colonists by far were supporters of the Revolution. This was obvious even in Newport. D'Estaing had discovered it to his cost in Georgia. And now Benedict Arnold, the commander of West Point, had passed over to the British side, thus becoming the United States' most famous traitor. He was, unfortunately, a skilled general with a detailed knowledge of the terrain and of the insurgents' tactics. He now became the scourge of his former friends.

The Chevalier Destouches, who had taken over Ternay's duties, had seen his men through the harsh winter months and was now about to mount a raid up Chesapeake Bay as part of a campaign to drive back Benedict Arnold's redcoats. La Pérouse was to remain off Boston, cruising in Massachussets Bay. It was routine work, policing waters where few English ships were about. Destouches, for his part, was able to engage the enemy on 16 March and give notice that the French policy of wait-and-see was coming to an end. The arrival in April of 19 transports with supplies from the West Indies further raised French morale. Destouches was disposed to raid Penobscot Bay, north of Boston, where the British had a well-defended fort. This was Massachussets country, where La Pérouse had been on patrol. There was every reason for him to expect that the *Astrée* would play an important part in the operation. Rochambeau provided 820 men. Preparations went ahead speedily, but Washington was not willing to endorse an expedition of this size for a purpose that did not fit in with the broader strategy. General Cornwallis was marching into Virginia, raiding at will and destroying a sorely battered colony. La Fayette set off to do what he could to assist. This was no time to weaken the French base by organizing an attack in the north while the south was in danger — and the reinforcements promised by Castries had still not arrived.

La Pérouse had a secret reason for feeling impatient with these hesitations and uncertaintites. Spring had finally arrived with all the enthusiatic promises of a warm summer, but the weeks were passing, and he was forced to delay preparations for a campaign he had been promised in Hudson Bay, in the isolated Canadian north. If he could preserve the element of surprise, he would destroy the forts that protected English Canada's back door.[1] But it was a door that lay open only in June and July. Once August approached the cool winds would begin to blow and within a matter of weeks ice would start blocking the narrow entrance.

On 6 May, young Rochambeau reached Boston in a fast frigate ahead of the French reinforcements. A fleet had sailed from Brest on 22 March: it was a massive convoy, but bound firstly for the West Indies which France had no intention of giving up. Hopes were raised that Washington and Rochambeau could begin their offensive once the fleet's commander, the Comte de Grasse, had refreshed his forces and sailed north from the Caribbean. But nothing is ever quite so straightforward. No one can depend on the weather.

La Pérouse had been promised the *Sagittaire* for his Hudson Bay operation — alas, the *Sagittaire* limped into Salem on 4 June, after a storm-filled 75-day crossing, with 150 sick on board. It would take a month to get her ready for a new expedition and a fresh crew would be needed. There was no hope now of reaching Hudson Bay before the first ice made its appearance, let alone of getting out again.

Jean-François remained aboard the *Astrée*. She was certainly in a better condition than the *Sagittaire* and newer as well. Admiral de Barras who had arrived from France to take over Ternay's command sent him to patrol the mouth of the St Lawrence. First of all, he escorted a convoy of six transports from Boston to Martha's Vineyard, then he made for Newfoundland with the *Hermione*. It was 1 July 1781. The war was swinging wildly from one side to another. Cornwallis was still threatening Virginia, Charlottesville had fallen briefly and toppled Thomas Jefferson in the process; but the loyalist forces defending New York under General Clinton had been weakened to bolster up Cornwallis' army, and La Fayette had rallied support for Washington who now saw his opportunity to strike at New York. Moreover, Rochambeau's men were on the move; Barras was sending urgent pleas to de Grasse to bring up the French fleet from Santo Domingo. Cornwallis, slow and deliberate, manoeuvring with difficulty and uncertainty in a country where his lines of communication were constantly threatened, moved back.

On 21 June he evacuated Richmond — 'a devastated town', wrote La Fayette who rode through it the next day. British forces began to concentrate around Yorktown near the mouth of Chesapeake Bay. From there Cornwallis planned to keep in contact with Clinton's forces in New York, but with de Grasse now on his way the balance of naval power was shifting and the British were entering a trap which the French would slam shut.

Meanwhile, the *Astrée* and the *Hermione* were cruising far to the north. On 21 July 1781, off Aspy Bay in the northernmost part of Cape Breton Island, Nova Scotia, they sighted a convoy of 20 sail escorted by several warships. Two English frigates and a corvette veered towards the French to give the transport ships a chance to seek the shelter of the bay. A series of manoeuvres saved the convoy. It was late afternoon and nightfall would enable most of the enemy vessels to escape:

> In despair at seeing everything escaping from me, I altered course towards the six warships that were the only ones still in the offing. Five hove to and formed a line of sorts to wait for me. The sixth seemed reluctant to do her duty and remained out of range. I had been far too anxious during the day to engage the enemy to be put upon by this attitude, however determined it might seem. I made for them all sails out; I did not have a moment to lose; it was 7 p.m. before we fired the first shot.
>
> The *Hermione* was still within hailing distance. I instructed M. de la Touche to sail in close order astern, as we were going to attack the enemy; he was as keen as I was; our men and our officers were moved by the same sentiments. Our sole, our unique regrets were that we could not prolong the daylight and had to fear a very dark night. The *Astrée* and the *Hermione* sailed to windward of the enemy so as to destroy any hope they might have of fleeing wind astern. They included the *Ligence*, [the *Allegiance*] of 24 guns, the *Vernon* of 24, the *Charleston* of 28, the *Jack* of 14 and the *Vautour* of 20.[2]

Naval engagements consisted in the main of sailing past the enemy, raking him with gunfire, and reforming for a second attack, by which time damage done to both sides and the manoeuvrings of the captains often resulted in a confused scrummage. The *Vulture* sailed out of line, the *Jack* hauled down her colours, the *Charleston*'s

Battle of Louisbourg, Cape Breton, 21 July 1781, by Captain Rossel.
(Musée de la Marine.)

topmast crashed down. The *Allegiance* and the *Vernon* began to sail away from the battle and eventually took advantage of the poor light to rejoin the main fleet. In all, the battle had lasted little more than an hour:

> I was unrigged to a considerable extent and I was afraid that soon, in spite of my night glass, I would be unable to see the runaways. I decided to alter course to take at least the *Jack* and the *Charleston* which remained at the rear and were the only certain fruits of my victory which the enemy might possibly have contested, attributing to their manoeuvres and their valour a salvation which they owed only to the darkness.

The *Charleston,* however, only pretended to have struck her colours; she hauled up her mizzen, and began to sail away while the French were securing the *Jack.* It was, in La Pérouse's view, a breach of the law of the sea, since he had held his fire once the *Charleston's* colours were struck. Night was falling rapidly now, and the English frigate vanished. In the morning nothing was in sight, and to make matters worse, a thick fog rolled in. La Pérouse was left to count the cost. He had suffered 15 casualties, his masts and rigging were damaged, and the *Hermione* had fared no better. It was time to return to Boston for repairs.

He had no reason to feel dissatisfied, in spite of the loss of the *Charleston.* He had been at sea for 56 days during which, in addition to the *Jack,* he had captured the *Thorn,* a corvette of 20 guns, and three merchant ships. Back in port on 17 August, he learned that the British had sent out three warships to hunt him down, and also that Captain Evans of the *Charleston* had died of his wounds.

La Pérouse was destined to miss the Chesapeake campaign that ended in Cornwallis' surrender at Yorktown. His ship needed refitting, and Barras needed someone to leave in charge of Boston while the French fleet sailed to join with de Grasse off the coast of Virginia. Thus the *Astrée* was left behind with the *Hermione* and the *Sagittaire,* and a recent arrival, the *Magicienne.*

Barras sailed from Newport on 25 August, and an unaccustomed quiet replaced the activity the New England coast had witnessed in the previous weeks. The English were concentrating their attention on the coast south of New York and on their St Lawrence lifeline. But the quiet was misleading. On the 27th the *Magicienne*, escorting a transport from Portsmouth to Boston, was attacked by the *Chatham*, a ship of 62 guns, and in spite of La Pérouse's hasty attempt at rescue, fell to the English vessel.

A report, however, went to Paris. Castries wrote back a letter of commendation to Jean-François, now promoted to post-captain:

> I read with pleasure the detail of your manoeuvres in Boston Bay on 31 August and 1 September. I note that you were prevented from coming to the aid of the frigate *Magicienne* when she was forced to surrender to the ship *Chatham*; it is unfortunate that the wind was against you, I cannot praise too much the ardour you displayed in trying to reach the enemy . . . I have drawn to the King's attention your fight against six English frigates on the 22 July. His Majesty was perfectly satisfied with your behaviour and that of M. de La Touche who assisted you.[3]

But for the next few months, there was little opportunity for further actions. La Pérouse's function was to secure an important but essentially quiet sector, receiving news from New York and the Chesapeake, and sending reports on to Paris. Admiral Hood had arrived first at the Chesapeake, and when he saw no sign of de Grasse's fleet, and thinking the French were about to attack New York, he hastened north to help Graves. Just then de Grasse reached the Chesapeake, bottling up Cornwallis' army. Hood and Graves hurried down from New York, but de Grasse beat them off. Clinton in New York organized an expedition to relieve Cornwallis, but this took time. When the British fleet sailed for Yorktown on 24 October 1781, it was already too late — Cornwallis had surrendered on the 19th.

For the next eight months the French held the mastery of the sea. The loss of Yorktown — above all, the loss of the 7,000-strong British army, which could only be made up by reinforcements sent across the Atlantic from Britain — was the beginning of the end. The peace party was gaining ground in London. In the House of Commons, Sir James Lowther moved that no more forces be sent to America: he lost by a mere 42 votes. Lord North's majority fell to a single vote in early 1782 on a motion favouring a withdrawal from the war. It was clear that the various factions were now simply

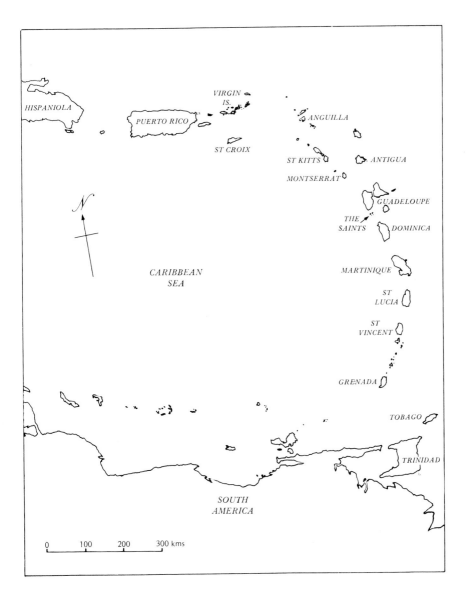

The Lesser Antilles (West Indies)

manoeuvring to gain or save whatever they could from the forth-coming peace negotiations.

For de Grasse, this meant securing France's position in the key West Indies. In November he returned to Martinique, instructing La Pérouse to escort a convoy of transport ships down from Boston. The *Résolue*, a frigate commanded by his friend Fleuriot de Langle, had recently arrived from France, bringing a sum of over four million *livres* as a subsidy for the depleted American treasury. La Pérouse decided to take the *Résolue* with him to Martinique. He was ready to leave by late November but, held up by storms lashing the coast, he did not sail from Boston until 7 December. With him went not only de Langle, but the *Sagittaire* and the cutter *Espion*. The convoy consisted of 10 French transports.

La Pérouse reached the island of Martinique without incident to find de Grasse hunting the seas to strike at Hood before the British could re-establish their naval superiority. Bad weather pre-vented the French reaching Barbados where Hood's ships were re-fitting. As a consolation, the Marquis de Bouillé was able to capture the small island of St Eustatius which he handed over to his Dutch allies. In early January, de Grasse and Bouillé set off to capture near-by St Christopher. On the 13th La Pérouse joined him.

St Christopher – or St Kitts – was a fairly representative pawn in the endless struggle between the great powers in this part of the world. Discovered by Columbus, it was first settled by the English who lost it to the French in 1666 and again in 1689. Its capital bore a French name, Basseterre – although, to make matters a little more complex for the outsider, the second largest town in French Guade-loupe, less than 100 miles to the south, was also called Basse-terre. The attitude of the residents reflected the island's chequered history: they made no effort to oppose the French landing, while the loyalist troops barricaded themselves in the redoubt.

De Grasse and Bouillé landed 6,000 men and settled in for a quiet siege – for, although La Pérouse wrote that the garrison was being 'vigorously attacked' by Bouillé's men, the redcoats held out for a month. Once again, there was little chance of glory for La Pérouse, as de Grasse sent him to convoy a merchantman carrying sugar and coffee just before Admiral Hood appeared with a fleet of 22 ships.

De Grasse had the superiority of numbers, but Hood's copper-sheathed ships were speedier. The two fleets manoeuvred around each other without coming to grips. Hood left, having failed in his bid to ease the pressure on St Kitts. De Grasse returned to Martinique at the end of February, La Pérouse with him. On the way they took the island of Montserrat. It had been discovered by the Spanish, settled by the British, captured by the French in 1668, restored to England, and now had once again changed hands. If anything, it illustrated how essential it was for France to strike a more significant blow against the British. Small islands could change hands, but major bases remained. Versailles had long realized this, and sent de Grasse instructions for an attack on Jamaica. Since Spain was now an ally of France in the war against England, Admiral Sorano's fleet, based on Santo Domingo, would join him and help to maintain French superiority, at least on paper, making up for the ships of Admiral Rodney, which had now come down to link up with Hood's.

La Pérouse still had his secret orders for Hudson Bay. It was too early to leave, as the pack ice in the far north does not begin to break up before May; but there was growing talk of peace. In London, Lord North's government had fallen and with him the Earl of Sandwich, First Lord of the Admiralty. They were succeeded by the Marquis of Rockingham and Admiral Keppel respectively. Rockingham was replaced by the Earl of Shelburne within a matter of months, although Keppel held on to the Admiralty. Britain was gearing herself up for peace as well as internal reforms, but Jean-François could expect that the war would last through the summer, and only when winter approached, with all the costly stalemate this involved, would a ceasefire be signed. He still had time to plan for the Hudson Bay expedition.

Meanwhile, the Jamaica campaign got under way. De Grasse's plan was sensible enough: it was to send the transport vessels out by night while the fleet drew away Rodney's vessels. On 6 April 1782, La Pérouse sailed south from Fort-of-France Bay. His task was to distract the attention of Rodney's watching ships and lead them towards St Lucia Channel while the transports — a total of over 100 ships — sailed north in the late afternoon. But uncertainty about the English dispositions forced de Grasse to postpone his departure and La Pérouse was driven back towards Fort Royal by two frigates and two ships of the line. The British came in close enough to see the transports waiting in the bay. Certain now that a report would go to Rodney, de Grasse decided to sail: the transports would go north and north-west at once, while part of the naval units cruised in the rear to protect them should the English appear.

Rodney effectively made his appearance, but the winds dropped. Light breezes blew up at times, adding to the confusion. On the 9th the convoy sought refuge in Basse-terre, Guadeloupe, while de Grasse manoeuvred off the islands of the Saintes between Guadeloupe and Dominica. Enough wind had now risen to enable the two fleets to face each other. There was an inconclusive engagement lasting an hour and a half. The 10th was spent reforming and manoeuvring to get away from the area, which was far from suitable for a naval engagement. On the 11th the French had made more headway than the British, but the *Zélé* and the *Jason* collided; the damage sustained slowed them down, so that they were now in danger of capture by the advancing British. At this point, de Grasse decided to veer back. 'They were only half a league from seven or eight enemy ships', wrote La Pérouse. A major confrontation was now inevitable; it was to become known as 'The Battle of the Saints'. It would end the French naval threat to the West Indies and win back control of the Atlantic for England.

As de Grasse turned back, the English reduced sail. Night fell, but preparations for the battle went on throughout the night in all the ships. At 4 a.m. on the 12th, La Pérouse was ordered to go to the aid of a vessel in distress:

> I sailed towards her, reaching her less than half an hour before daybreak. It was the *Zélé* which, in running foul of the *Ville-de-Paris*, had lost her bowsprit and her foremast. I hove to within pistol range of that vessel and sent a boat to her to set up the tow, but as my frigate was still making headway, I moved away from the *Zélé* during this operation and was forced to tack back a little to come near her again. I hove once more by her and hailed for my boat to be sent back; but the confusion of the night and of such a terrible event had slowed down the loading of the

towing ropes, and since my boat was not ready to return to me I passed her once more; I finally came back a third time; it was now becoming light. We saw ourselves surrounded by the enemy, with the French forces three leagues to windward of us and the English extremely close. There was even a frigate within range of firing her guns at us and troubling us while I was engaged in taking on the ropes which I passed through one of the windows of the [aft] council room and wrapped around the mainmast. I let out canvas at once and sailed with my tow for Basse-terre of Guadeloupe some five or six leagues distant. I was being energetically pursued by several enemy vessels and the Comte de Grasse came up with his forces to cover me. The enemy broke off its pursuit to form in battle line.[4]

Thus La Pérouse was the occasion for the battle itself which started shortly after. De Grasse could not allow the enemy to capture not only the *Zélé* this time, but La Pérouse's *Astrée* as well. He had no option but to stand and fight anyhow. The first shots were exchanged at 8 a.m. with the two fleets evenly matched. It was the wind, by changing four points to the south, which gave Rodney his chance. Gaps appeared in the French line, which the English could now sail through.

Rodney took his flagship, HMS *Formidable*, through a break near the French centre. Five ships followed him, raking de Grasse's vessels with gunfire as they sped past. A similar movement occurred in the rear, so that the French were now split into three bodies, de Grasse in his *Ville-de-Paris* with his supporting ships of the centre being isloated from the rest of the fleet. The English veered back, concentrating on the flagship. The *Ville-de-Paris*, having suffered enormous losses, was compelled to surrender; four other ships of the line were also captured — the *César, Hector, Ardent* and the *Glorieux*. And the French fleet had lost its admiral.

La Pérouse could only piece together the events of the day from disparate items of information that came to him. As soon as the *Zélé* was safely in Basse-terre, he had cut his tow ropes and sailed back to the battle:

The French squadron was still fighting courageously, and the smoke and distance prevented me from seeing which side had the advantage. Nevertheless, I had the greatest hope of victory as I could see fifteen or sixteen enemy ships disabled and no longer fighting, but shortly after, I sighted

Battle of the Saints. HMS Formidable *breaks through the French line.*
(National Maritime Museum, Greenwich.)

three frigates and a cutter hugging the winds and tacking along the Saintes, passing a league and a half to windward of me. I soon recognised from our numbered signals the *Galathée*, the *Amazone* and the *Cérès*. The latter signalled that the enemy had the superiority of numbers. I then realised that M. le Comte de Grasse's forces were in a serious predicament since the frigates had presumably been forced to abandon him. I signalled to the cutter *Clairvoyant* to come up within hailing distance, and to the three frigates to join me. They came up a little but always kept to half a league to windward. The cutter passed astern, we both hove to and her commander, M. d'Aché, came aboard. He told me the *Glorieux* had been dismasted and had remained in the hands of the enemy, although he believed they had not secured her and still seemed to be to windward of the other ships. I firstly conceived the plan of going to the rescue of this vessel if the enemy did not present an obstacle. Active gunfire was still coming from both fleets . . . Having come closer, I saw that the *Glorieux* was totally dismasted, that they were close to her and in the process of securing their prize. As night was about to fall, I sailed on the starboard tack, intending to join all the ships as well as the *Caton* and *Jason* which had sailed from Basse-terre, hoping that we might the following day recapture the *Glorieux* had it been left in charge of a weak escort . . . We all tacked about in the Saintes channel during the night. At eight p.m. I saw a great fire on the water bearing south by south-west. I had no doubt that that enemy had set fire to our ship, all the more so when at a quarter past nine we saw the explosion and the vessel blowing up. I then lost all hope of doing anything useful during the day and decided to suggest to M. de Framont, commanding the *Caton*, to return to Guadeloupe to discuss with M. de Bouillé and M. d'Arbaud what was the best thing to do in our situation.[5]

When the 13th dawned, La Pérouse surveyed the pitiful aftermath of the battle. Ships manoeuvred painfully, their masts down, their sails torn, while others endeavoured to assist them, and Rodney's fleet was struggling to keep together in spite of little more than a slight breeze. 'As we were on the field of battle we saw the sea covered with floating debris of masts and spars'. Late in the afternoon the breeze rose enough for the French to make for Guadeloupe.

The next day, from their anchorage in Basse-terre the French saw Rodney's squadron on its way north, presumably bound for Antigua. Rodney was to be criticized for not pursuing the defeated French more energetically, but he too had suffered heavy damage, and his critics overlooked the uncertain winds and frequent calms

— a warship becalmed is a helpless giant.

La Pérouse, accompanied by the cutter *Clairvoyant*, whose commander was energetic and skilful, was sent to keep watch on the English fleet. If its destination was indeed Antigua, the rest of the French ships in Basse-terre could make for Santo Domingo. This plan was carried out, but the calms held up everyone, Rodney included. By the 18th, however, the French were in sight of Puerto Rico. Two days later, still painfully struggling along with weak breezes, they had almost reached the Canal de la Mona, between Puerto Rico and Santo Domingo, when they discovered a fleet of 12 enemy ships coming up behind them.

Framont, in the *Caton*, calculated that if he could sail north through the channel, he could seek refuge in the Puerto Rican port of Aguadilla, where the shore guns of their Spanish allies would hold the English at bay. However, he gave instructions to La Pérouse to proceed direct to Santo Domingo where the French still believed de Grasse had gone and where the main Spanish fleet was waiting for the planned attack on Jamaica. Once again, La Pérouse was to be sent away before a major and disastrous engagement.

Framont was undone by the relative slowness of his ship and the capricious breezes. Once he entered the channel, having rounded Cape Rojo, the southwesternmost tip of Puerto Rico, the wind failed altogether. The *Astrée*, farther from land on her way to Santo Domingo, was not becalmed, although her speed was sorely reduced. The *Caton* was the first to fire at the advancing British who, farther south and away from the shore, still had enough wind to work with. La Pérouse's *Astrée* was only relatively better off than the *Caton* and the three other French vessels:

> I was at the time two leagues west of [the approaching vessels]. I was sailing away under full canvas with the cape to the north-east. I was being energetically pursued by a large warship driven by a strong breeze, whereas I was only making two knots. She came up to within long range. There was no doubt that I was about to be reached. Fortunately at about 5 o'clock a storm appeared in the north-east. Afraid that I was going to be reached, being at the time wholly becalmed, I lowered my larboard studding sails and set my sails to receive the wind that would come from the north-east. It fortunately started to blow at half past five; I did not have a

moment to lose as that vessel was rapidly gaining on me. The squall enabled me to make seven and a half knots in a quarter of an hour and I gained almost a league. Three ships had joined the hunter. I had four vessels giving me chase, the other eight having remained to deal with *Caton, Jason, Aimable* and *Cérès*. One of the four had given up at five and turned back to the others; another followed him at six, but the first pursuer and one other continued the chase, and at nightfall they were in my wake, one to larboard and one to starboard. The wind freshened from the north-east and gradually veered east.[6]

Night saved him. By morning he was well into the strait and quite alone. His route now took him along the north coast of Santo Domingo, not without difficulty as he found an unhelpful westerly breeze, but finally on the 23rd, he met a French squadron commanded by Vaudreuil. It was later joined by another four French ships of the Spanish fleet.

And this was when La Pérouse realized that the Comte de Grasse was a prisoner. It had fallen to Vaudreuil as the next most senior officer to gather the scattered French fleet, reorganize it, and make a decision on the Jamaica campaign. Although the Spanish fleet made up for the losses in ships the French had sustained, there was a great deal of damage to repair, and some of the ships were too slow and too old. Vaudreuil had no hesitation in postponing the Jamaican venture until fresh supplies arrived — and the plans of the English were known.

The postponement and the reorganization of the fleet enabled him to release La Pérouse. On 19 May 1782, Vaudreuil concluded a long report to Castries with the following:

[The *Sceptre*] will leave in a few days for the mission you had entrusted a year ago to M. de La Pérouse and which can be undertaken this year. I shall also give him one or two or three frigates.

The Hudson Bay campaign Jean-François had been hoping for was now on. And for it, he was being given the *Sceptre*, a solid new warship of 74 guns — one of the famous *vaisseaux de 74*.

Notes

1. The plan was elaborated between La Pérouse and the Comte de Fleurieu. Many years later, the navigator Yves de Kerguelen was to claim the ideas as his own (Kerguelen à ses concitoyens, Bib. Nat. N.A.F. 9438-179) but Kerguelen was far from reliable.
2. Report in A.N.M., B4-191: 270-1.
3. A.N.M. B4-191: 281, dated 27 November 1781.
4. A.N.M. B4. 235.
5. Ibid.
6. Ibid.

11
The Hudson Bay Raid

HENRY HUDSON was one of the seventeenth century's great navigators. He made four attempts to discover a northern passage from the Atlantic to the Pacific, the equivalent of Magellan's Strait in the far south. He lost his life in the process, but he is remembered by the Hudson River of New York and by the enormous inland sea we know as Hudson Bay.

The commercial exploitation of his discovery was handed over to private entreprise when Charles II granted a charter to 'The Governor and Company of Adventurers of England trading into Hudson's Bay'. Although protection had to be given at times to the traders and trappers, especially during the Seven Years War when British outposts were threatened by the French, the Company did not formally surrender its right to govern the territory until 1869. It was therefore in part against a trading company that La Pérouse had planned his raid. His experiences in the East had taught him how much the British depended on their chartered companies for their colonizing ventures, and how destabilizing an attack against their commercial outposts could be. He was not mistaken in the repercussions his raid would have in London — the Hudson's Bay Company had to forego paying a dividend until 1786 — even though it had little effect on the subsequent peace negotiations.

The bay is a bleak, inhospitable place, a great expanse of freezing water, relatively shallow, swept by wild northern winds that cause the temperature to drop sharply in a matter of hours, at other times invaded by cold silent banks of fog. The shore is mostly low, save in the east, but not always the bare, isolated world one might expect it to be. Spruce, poplar and balsam grow along the southern shores, and the short summer weeks glory in a sudden profusion of wildflowers, mosses and coloured lichen. There are caribou and musk ox, a multitude of ducks and loons, and overhead the soulful honking of

Canada geese; the waters still teem with fish — cod, salmon, porpoise, and the scarcer whales.

But it was a closed world, little known even to the British and far less to the French from whom the few charts the Company possessed had been withheld: 'One can truly say', wrote La Jaille of the *Engageante*, 'that for all purposes we were going to explore a country of which the only thing we knew was the name'.[1] And La Pérouse later said the same thing in a letter to his mother:

> I must tell you that I had neither a chart nor a pilot. There isn't a French-man who, in the last hundred years, has come within three hundred leagues of this bay. The English, who considered the difficulties of such a navig-ation as the best defences of their settlement, prevented the publication of the charts; and today that I am almost back from there I can swear that they were justified in thinking no one would come to look for them so far away.[2]

To reach the Company's forts, La Pérouse had to travel north through the western Atlantic, avoid British patrols, sail round New-foundland into the Labrador Sea and due west into Hudson Strait, entering it between Button Island and Resolution Island, a gap of less than 60 miles through which the tides race madly — so wildly in fact that the Strait never quite freezes over. Once inside, he had to sail for another 450 miles before reaching the island-strewn passages that lead into Hudson Bay itself, an expanse three times the size of the Black Sea, with a multitude of rivermouths and islands, and the floating remnants of the last winter ice or the first warnings of the next one.

La Pérouse was fortunate in the ships allocated to him for this expedition. The *Sceptre* had been launched only two years earlier, and was copper-sheathed. The *Astrée* went to Fleuriot de Langle who was to become his close companion and to sail with him on his great voyage of exploration. With Langle went Pierre de La Mon-neraye, who was to leave a valuable account of the expedition.[3] The third vessel, the frigate *Engageante*, 32 guns, was older but serviceable — it was to remain on active service for 20 years, until 1794; her commander was the young Marquis de La Jaille, and with him went Du Tremblier who also kept a diary.[4] La Pérouse's own second-in-command was the Baron de Paroy who had commanded the ill-fated *Cérès*.

Preparations were spread over a fortnight. They included taking on board detachments of soldiers, approximately 300 men, mostly from the Auxerrois regiment, and a number of mortars and light guns for landside attacks on the forts. But the need for complete secrecy — since it would be all too easy for spies to slip across to one of the British-held Caribbean islands — prevented La Pérouse from taking any winter clothing. Even Langle and La Jaille were forbidden to open their instructions until they had reached 45° North — the latitude of Nova Scotia.

Thus, wrote La Monneraye, having left Santo Domingo on 31 May 1782 and sailed rapidly north, they found 'the nights increasingly cold'. There was more to come:

> Our route taking us further north [off the coast of Labrador, by 3 July], we encountered the heaviest of fogs, keeping the *Sceptre* in sight as best we could, and when we lost ourselves in the fog she would sound her bell, beat the drums and fire her guns. It was then that our navigation became dangerous: the thick fog greatly limited the range of our horizon; we ran the risk of dashing ourselves against mountains of ice of a prodigious height, floating on the sea in every direction as the winds or the currents took them; they often have reef-like outcrops on which one can be broken up as on rocks.

For many of the French these icebergs were both strange and terrifying. La Monneraye waxed lyrical in his descriptions:

> We were hauling along mountains of ice of an incredible size; if the sun shone down into their crevasses, great reservoirs of thawed ice collected, which then poured out into the sea in cascades and sheets of water with a mighty roar; the sun striking its rays onto these voluminous waterfalls varied infinitely their colours and completed the picture. At times these ice mountains closed off, at a distance, our horizon; their different heights, their quite differing shapes seemed to present the appearance of a fortified city with its towers, its belfreys, its palaces of rock crystal. At other times it was a great army of three-decked ships, laid out in battle formation, that seemed to appear before us. In this field of illusions there was an infinite set of varying spectacles.

On 18 July the fog lifted, revealing the entrance to Hudson Strait;

but the great icebergs still dominated the scene. They parted briefly to tempt the French into the strait, then closed around them. The icepack tightened, and a freezing wind added to their discomfort:

> We climbed down onto these uneven ice surfaces and could thus communicate with our comrades from the *Sceptre* and the *Engageante* without the need for boats; to warm ourselves up we made snowballs, as children do, and fought battles.

After three days the icepack disintegrated and began to float away, and for the first time they saw 'Eskimos' coming towards them. At last the freezing sailors could buy warm clothes, mostly furs and sealskins. 'It was a highly comical spectacle to see our men, thus clothed, climbing the rigging and the yards, looking like bears or seals'. A few days later, La Monneraye was able to land and visit a small settlement. Was this Natural Man, the Good Savage who was so much a subject of debate in corrupt and over-civilized Europe? Whatever the merits of the arguments put forward by the French *philosophes* who sought a natural basis for a better society, encounters with primitive men and women would quickly dispel their illusions:

> Let Rousseau, the man of paradoxes, praise all he likes the freedom and independence of savage man, for my part I much prefer the loss of a part of this freedom, which civilised societies ask of us to ensure the happiness of each one and the safety of everyone. Our philosophers, of such renown, have obtained their principles and their systems merely from their imagination, and if I had been in the presence of [Voltaire] or [Rousseau], I could easily have argued with them and shown the contradictions within their ideas.

A few years later, in the Pacific, La Pérouse would echo La Monneraye's words.

It was a desolate land — Baffin Island, which forms the northern limit of Hudson Strait, a stony arid shore barren of trees, with only occasional patches of green huddling within the shelter of grey rocks. The French were glad to leave it, free now from the hardships of working the ships among the ice while clad only in summer clothing. There was more ice ahead, on 1 August, when they reached the end of the strait and started to veer south into Hudson Bay. But at least they were going south, towards relatively warmer latitudes, and the bitter north wind began to drop. The main British settlement was across the bay, to the south-west, on the Churchill River; Prince of Wales Fort defended by stone walls 18 feet high and 42 guns. From the sea it looked formidable enough as La Pérouse surveyed it on the afternoon of 8 August.

What the French did not realize until they landed on the 9th was how ill-defended the fort really was. There were fewer men available than there were guns, and those who could be mustered were traders and clerks. The real defences were isolation and the pack ice. Once these had been breached, the fort could only surrender. There was no need to fire a shot. The British commander was Samuel Hearne, then aged 37, a man notable for his exploration in the Bay and his discovery of the course of the Coppermine River in the far north; he had been at Fort Prince of Wales since 1775. After the surrender terms were agreed upon, the French dined with him, 'a handsome man, well educated and with a wide knowledge'. La Pérouse was to allow him to sail back to England in a small vessel, the *Severn*. 'When we later returned to France', wrote La Monneraye, 'we learnt with pleasure that he had safely reached England'. Later again, he would return briefly to the Churchill River, to rebuild the trading post, living through a winter so harsh that:

> All my wines froze and split the bottles and casks that contained it. Our salted provisions froze so solid that we could not separate it any more than the hardest ice.[5]

The French had come to destroy, not conquer, and accordingly once the traders and employees were taken on board with their personal belongings and the stocks of furs were safely stowed, the guns were spiked and the fort was blown up. 'Many of our people felt the ship shake under them with the explosion'. The furs carried away, ranging from beaver skins to blue foxes, to which were added over 17,000 goose quills and 300 lbs of goose feathers, were worth, by the Company's reckoning, more than £14,000. It was all over in a couple of days, the remainder of the fort being blown up on the morning of the 11th, the squadron then sailing away south to the other Company post.

This was Fort York, situated on the Hayes River, 150 miles further south. The weather was stormy, the sea shallow and rock-strewn: the French were suffering from the lack of suitable charts and, as La Pérouse reports, the prisoners quite properly refused to give them any information. A vessel was sighted: it was the Company supply ship, *Prince Rupert*, to which La Jaille gave chase, unsuccessfully, more to prevent her warning the garrison than as a prize, for she would have proved too much trouble to bring out through Hudson Strait. La Pérouse need not have worried. The southern outpost would surrender as easily as Fort York, but its less accessible situation was to exact a heavy price. The French manoeuvred in high winds around the shoals and rocks of the Hayes and Nelson rivers before landing troops along the Nelson River shore. There was no chance of a surprise landing: it took three days in perilous seas, the *Sceptre* was forced to anchor five leagues out, and at least one sloop capsized, with heavy loss of life. Swampy ground prevented any artillery from being brought up, but there were soldiers enough to overwhelm the defenders if they chose to fight. Wisely, they did not. Fort York surrendered on the 22nd. It was set on fire, the chief factor and his men being taken on board the French vessels. But on this occasion, the English had got most of their stocks away and there was little booty to carry away.

Not all the fort's traders were made prisoner. Some had time to flee inland; others were away hunting. Realising that they might starve when they returned to the ruined fort, La Pérouse left food and ammunition for them. 'If the King were here', he wrote, 'he would approve of my conduct'. More than the king of France was to appreciate his chivalry: the British remembered this action later, as they did his treatment of Samuel Hearne and his men.

The weather was wretched enough even at the peak of the summer season. The French had no difficulty in imagining what the winter would be like. In the storms, 'bears, apparently borne out to sea by the violent rush of the river currents, when they tried to cross them, came into view around our ships; often exhausted by having to swim

so far, they climbed on our cables to rest'. So reported La Monneraye, while Du Tremblier set down 25 August as 'a very unhappy
day: two of our cables broken, two of our anchors lost, our tiller
bar broken'. Sickness was affecting the crews, as the English noted:
'Many people on aboard this ship are eaten up with the scurvy and
otherwise unhealthy, which makes it look dismal to a stranger'.
On 30 August, there was 'thunder, lightning and rain. Several geese
were like to have alighted on this ship, and very often small birds
did alight'. On Saturday 31 August, 'a strong gale with clear weather.
In the afternoon many flights of wild snow geese of different species,
flying in amazing numbers, prepared to leave this coast.'

It was time to follow their example. Fortunately, an English
pilot had agreed to lead the ships out of the bay, and the *Severn*'s
men were as anxious as the French to avoid getting caught in this
bleak world by the closing icepack. On the Monday, they left with a
good WNW breeze. Four days later Hudson Strait was in sight. On
the 10th Hearne and 32 others took their leave from the French off
Resolution Island and began their journey to Stromness in the
Orkney Islands. De Langle took the *Astrée* to Brest; La Pérouse,
after some hesitation, decided to make for Cadiz, which he could
reach speedily and where a milder climate would enable his men to
recover. It was a wise choice, for he completed the crossing from
Resolution Island to Spain in 33 days.

It was, as he wrote to his mother, 'the hardest campaign ever
undertaken. Now that I know that country, I shall never return to
it'. The price paid for the Hudson Bay raid was out of proportion to
any gains. These could only be psychological in the dying stages of
a long war. But the experience he had gained in coping with little
known waters, in bitter cold and without charts, would be invaluable to him — and the French government could not fail to be impressed by the daring of the undertaking and the skills he had displayed. And as in all entreprises of this nature, there had been an
element of luck, not the least the absence of enemy ships. He wrote
to the Minister:

> I was, although I did not know it only a few leagues behind the English
> fleet. I did not have enough men left to crowd on canvas and flee if

they had chased me. Seventy men died of scurvy during the crossing and I landed about 400 sick in Cadiz. If I had remained at sea a few days more, it is likely that I would have been unable to reach any port. As I understand it, the *Astrée* is now in France; you will have been told, my Lord, the details of our campaign which would have been a happy one had it not been for the frightful sickness that came after it.

The *Sceptre* had a complement of 355. She had on board an additional 181 soldiers. Out of these 536 men, 70 had died and 400 were sick, leaving a mere 60 or so to work a ship of 74 guns. The *Engageante* had sailed with 311 men. Some had been drowned in York River, others had died of scurvy. La Jaille had a hundred men too sick to work, and of the remainder there was not a single one unaffected by illness.

While La Jaille's frigate had suffered a great deal and, a much older ship than the *Sceptre*, required extensive repairs, La Pérouse still hoped to recruit men for a new expedition — the assault on Gibraltar which had been besieged since 1779. Gibraltar had been useful in drawing British naval units away from the Atlantic, thus relieving the pressure on Brest, but an attack in September had failed, and Guichen's forces, which La Pérouse hoped to join, had not shaken Admiral Howe. The war, anyhow, was ending. The Gibraltar plan was abandoned.

The American colonists had been only too happy to negotiate terms with the Shelburne ministry. The Treaty of Alliance by which France had bound herself to assist the Insurgents required the latter not to sign a separate peace, but the war-weary colonists, their meagre treasury depleted, took little notice of such diplomatic niceties. They suspected that had England succeeded in inflicting heavy losses on the French in Europe, Versailles might have similarly sent out separate peace feelers.

Shelburne was quite happy to give away the Old North West — the area between the St Lawrence and the Ohio, the lands south of the Great Lakes — even though Canada had an excellent claim to it. In exchange the Americans recognized British rights to Canada, Newfoundland and Nova Scotia. Franklin, Jay and Adams, the American negotiators in Paris, thus signed away without a second thought any hopes the Canadian French still harboured about a land that had been theirs a mere 20 years earlier. The British loyalists who were forced to leave the new United States later settled in Canada, thus strengthening Britain's hold on the territory. France gained from the war Tobago and St Lucia, fishing rights off Newfoundland secured by the small island bases of St Pierre and Miquelon, Senegal in Africa, and the return of her old trading posts in India. Less tangible but more important was the creation of an independent country on the American continent, that would stand as a challenger to the power of Britain and remain for generations in France's debt.

Notes

1. A.N.M., 3JJ, 68, 23-3.
2. Reprinted in Fleuriot de Langle, *La Tragique expédition*, pp. 56-57.
3. Reprinted in 1888 in the Société de géographie's *Bulletin du centenaire*, pp. 268-283.
4. Reprinted in an English translation in *The Beaver*, a Hudson Bay Company's publication, in March 1951, pp. 42-46.
5. Letter of 4 September 1784 quoted in Williams, 'Remarks on the French raids on Churchill and York 1782', in *Hudson's Bay Miscellany 1670-1870*, Winnipeg, 1975, p. 94.

12
Marriage at Last

IT IS DIFFICULT in this day of televised and filmed love affairs to realize the hold a father once had on his children's future. For centuries parents had decided whom their son or daughter would marry. There had been rebellious elopements, circumventions, but these were talked about for the very reason that they were unusual. When in 1777, La Pérouse had fallen in love with Eléonore Broudou, his father had angrily rejected the idea of such a match. Jean-François was then aged thirty-six. He had submitted. 'I have a deep sorrow', he had told his sister, but that was all.

Once Eléonore arrived in France, they had been able to meet. She lived in Nantes, then in Brest, with her mother or with an aunt. Jean-François still hoped old Galaup would relent, but he had never gone so far as to bring Eléonore down to Albi to meet his parents.

Now he was a senior serving officer, a post-captain, a Knight of the Order of Saint-Louis, highly regarded by the King who granted him a pension of 800 *livres* a year as a reward for his Hudson Bay raid, a friend of the Comte de Fleurieu, whose influence in naval matters was very considerable, and almost a protégé of the Navy Minister, Castries, with whom he shared a Languedocian background. In addition the newly independent United States was about to appoint him a member of the Society of the Cincinnati, founded by officers of the American Revolutionary Army in May 1783 to commemorate the hardships and the triumphs of the War of Independence, an exclusive order of which George Washington was the President; its badge was an eagle suspended by a blue and white ribbon 'emblematic of the union of America and France.'

Jean-François was now forty-two and still had not defied his father's wishes by marrying the girl he loved. More than that, the dutiful son was contemplating marrying a girl his parents had chosen for him and whom he had scarcely seen. Thus old Galaup could die in peace, satisfied that there had been no misalliance and that heirs from a suitable blood would eventually carry on the now admired name of Galaup de La Pérouse.

Depending on our point of view in this matter, we have the vacillations and resignation of a thwarted lover, or we have the diplomatic subtleties of a determined tactician in the moves Jean-François made in 1783. Perhaps the truth contains aspects of both.

From Cadiz, while his ship was being refitted, he wrote to the parents of the girl his father planned for him to marry. They were the Vésians, of Albi, an aristocratic family, well-to-do and highly regarded. In his letters, he tactfully agreed to marry their daughter on condition that she herself was in favour of the match. And he frankly pointed out that he had loved another and had hoped to marry her. As for Mademoiselle de Vésian, he reminded her mother, with all the circumlocutions the formal style of the period allowed, that he hardly knew her daughter, and conveyed this by flattery:

> Your daughter, brought up by you and educated under your care, must be like you; I know her only through having seen her when she was still a child, and I can swear to you that if I were the most perfect man in the world, with every other possible advantage, I would prefer her to all other women . . . Born with a highly sensitive nature, I should be the most unhappy of men if I was not loved by my wife, if I did not have her deepest trust as due to her best friend, if living within my family and hers too, in the midst of her children (if we have any) did not make her utterly happy . . . I hope one day to consider you as my mother, and wish from this very day to regard you as my best friend; I open my heart to you: consult your daughter; it is up to you to see if we suit each other. Love us both sufficiently to say *No* if such is your opinion . . . I owe you my closest confidence, and so I authorise my mother to tell you the story of my former loves. I was only thirty; my heart has always been a novel . . . I hope that I shall soon be free, if then I have your reply and better still your assurance that I can make your daughter happy and that my character suits her, I shall fly to Albi.[1]

One can find double meanings in most of these lines, and it is hard to believe that he did not hope to sow doubts in the mind of Madame de Vésian. His letter to Monsieur de Vésian was shorter, but made the same point with relatively more bluntness, as if he felt that the father needed to be told more directly:

> I assure you that my feelings would suffer if I owed your daughter's hand to nothing more than that you had chosen me and that she was obeying her parents. I do beg of you therefore to place no obstacle in the way of Mademoiselle de Vésian's affections, and to think that for both of us to be happy there must have been no reluctance to overcome. I must inform you, Sir, that while my eagerness has not allowed me to delay any longer in writing to you, I have nevertheless a matter to settle which does not yet allow me to dispose entirely of myself. My mother will give you the details. I hope to be free in six weeks or two months.

The message was plain enough. He did not know Mademoiselle de Vésian; he had no wish to marry her if she showed any aversion towards a man who was almost 25 years her senior and had spent most of his time at sea; and there was someone else in the background.

The Vésians may not have been overjoyed by this reply. Here indeed was a reluctant suitor, gambling on their daughter loving someone else or not being enchanted by the prospects of a marriage to an older man. But it was not a time when the wishes of the children — particularly of daughters — were taken into account. And Mademoiselle de Vésian was of marriageable age. Her parents replied to Jean-François in sympathetic terms, without committing themselves to an assurance that their daughter was attracted to him. How could she be, when she hardly remembered him? But they did look forward to his visiting them all in Albi, where everything could be arranged . . .

The reply did not get to La Pérouse until he had reached Paris. His letters had been written on 10 February, aboard the *Sceptre*. By the time they had been delivered in Albi and family discussions between the Vésians and the Galaups had resumed in an atmosphere of slight perplexity on one side and mild anxiety on the other, the French ships were preparing to sail from Cadiz. The Spanish were keen to see them go. They had just completed an intricate set of peace negotiations, refusing Shelburne's suggestion that they regain Gibraltar in exchange for their American possessions. Shelburne had used the French to bring their Spanish allies to the bargaining table, thus effectively driving a wedge between them. Britain agreed

Eléonore Broudou, wife of La Pérouse.

to give up Florida and Minorca, but kept Gibraltar and the Bahamas. And then Lord Shelburne was overthrown. The irritated Spanish wondered whether all the peace talks would have to begin anew, with France siding with Britain. Fortunately, Shelburne's successors ratified the treaties – they had little option – just as La Pérouse sailed.

At the beginning of April 1783, he was in Brest, seeing to the laying up of the *Sceptre* which he left finally on the 16th. Soon after, he travelled to Paris where he met Fleurieu. Officially, he was on leave for three months, 'for personal business'.

The trouble was that Eléonore and her mother were also in Paris. Eléonore was staying at the Convent Saint-Antoine, not as a novice, but as a boarder. Back in Albi, where she supervised matters on behalf of her now blind and invalid husband, Madame Galaup fretted and urged her son not to call on Eléonore. He agreed, at least for the time being.

Replying to the Vésians, Jean-François stressed again the importance of feelings in a marriage relationship and added the hint that their daughter should feel happy within his own family since she would have to spend much of her time at the Galaups. There was a further touch to his letter to Madame de Vésian, so plain and down to earth that it cannot have failed to arouse some further disquiet. Was she marrying her daughter too far below her own class? The truth was that Jean-François was a plain man, honest and blunt, with no trace of snobbery. But had he underlined his plainness deliberately? . . .

> You are too good a mother to force [your daughter's] inclinations, and I have too much delicacy to try to marry a young person against her wishes; for my part, everything I remember of Mademoiselle de Vésian pleases me greatly . . . I must have a wife who can love my mother and my sisters . . *I want to love my wife as a peasant does*, have in her so much confidence that she can be entrusted, together with my mother and yourself, with all my business.[2]

Nevertheless, negotiations proceeded. But the outcome really depended on Eléonore. Faithful to his promise Jean-François did not call on her. Instead, he sent a message through a friend, asking to be freed from his promise to marry her and offering 20,000 *livres*, 'an enormous sum relative to my fortune,' as he later wrote to Castries, so that she would have an adequate dowry to make a satisfactory marriage.

Eléonore replied that she wanted no money from him, and that if he no longer wished to marry her she would free him from his word, but she would then enter a convent and withdraw from the world. There could be no other man in her life.

Jean-François rushed to see her. She had triumphantly passed the test. They fell into each other's arms. The next day he wrote to his mother.

> I had spent twenty days in Paris, and faithful to the promise I had made you I had not been to see her . . . I received a letter stained with tears, [it contained] not a single reproach, but a deep sense of pain pervaded it . . . The veil tore away at once . . . my situation filled me with horror. I saw all my crimes; I was nothing but a perjurer, unworthy of Mademoiselle de Vésian, to whom I was bringing a heart eaten up with remorse and worn by a passion nothing could extinguish; unworthy of Mademoiselle Broudou, whom I was weak enough to wish to forsake. My excuse, dear Mother, is the deep wish I have always had to please you: it was for you alone, and for my father, that I wanted to marry [Mademoiselle de Vésian].

The hesitation which Madame de Vésian had allowed to pierce through her manner were used as a further justification: 'Madame de Vésian had foreseen it, dear Mother: she knew my heart better than I did myself' — almost adding that she had understood him better than his own mother — but then Madame Galaup had been acting under pressure from her husband.

His struggle, he reminded his parents, had been between obedience to them and his word to Eléonore; there were two innocent victims — Mademoiselle de Vésian and Eléonore:

> I was stifling my remorse. I thought I was sure of myself; but I was breaking the laws of God and of man. Virtue, innocence, gentleness were being sacrificed to the framework of devotion I had built up to meet your wishes; but, my dear Mother, this motive however commendable, would be but weakness if I continued. I was imprudent in contracting this engagement without your consent; I would be a monster if I broke my word and carried to Mademoiselle de Vésian a heart that was withered and a con-

science that was torn with remorse . . . I can only belong to Eléonore. I hope you will give your consent.

As he expected, whatever explosions of anger there might have been in the Galaup household, the Vésians took it calmly. They had other suitors in mind for their daughter. Two months after Jean-François' letter reached Albi, Mademoiselle de Vésian married the Marquis de Sénégas. There was no estrangement with the Galaup family. Setbacks of this nature were by no means uncommon in the days of arranged marriages, and Jean-François had mended fences with a courteous note to her father:

> Not having had the honour of seeing her, my feelings were driven by the great wish I had to become related to you and to Madame de Vésian.

On 8 July 1783, Jean-François Galaup de La Pérouse was married to Louise-Eléonore Broudou in the Church of Sainte-Marguerite, in Paris, after signing the customary marriage contract before Monsieur Piquais, a Paris notary. Only the witnesses required by law were present at either ceremony. He was 42, she was 28. They would stay together for just two years.

He had promised not to go down to Albi until after the Vésian wedding, so in early August he took Eléonore to meet her new in-laws. The Galaups put on a show worthy of a leading local family. They intended to silence the wagging tongues gossiping about the fiasco of the Vésian match. No one would be able to claim that the victor of Hudson Bay had crept shamefacedly back to his home town. There was a great nuptial mass in the Cathedral where all those who wished to attend were made welcome. It was high summer, a time for light dresses, for gossip in the shade of the narrow streets, and for a relaxing time at Le Go. Eléonore was modest, gentle, charming. The fact that the Galaups were determined to assert before the townfolk that she was a welcome and suitable daughter-in-law must have eased her entry into the family circle where for so long she had been talked about as an adventuress.

Jean-François still had to settle his position vis-à-vis the Navy. Marriage by an officer of his rank required ministerial permission, and he had not sought it. From Le Go, he wrote to Castries:

> The great kindness you have shown towards me requires me to make a
> confession which I address, not to the King's minister, but to the Marshal
> de Castries: I am married and have taken my wife from Paris to Languedoc.
> My story is a novel which I implore you to be good enough to read. The
> Princess de Bouillon had been told and may already have spoken to you.
> Eight years ago in the Ile de France I fell madly in love with a very beauti-
> ful and charming girl. I wanted to marry her. She had no money. The
> Chevalier de Ternay objected . . .

The long letter spoke of his obeying his father's wishes, of love
cooling, of the alternative union planned by his parents, of his
attempts to break with Eléonore, of honour redeemed and love
triumphant, and it ended with an offer which we cannot fail to see
as a reflection of his recent talks with Fleurieu:

> I have brought my wife to my elderly mother . . . but I have agreed with
> her to seek to make amends in the Service, and I am ready, My Lord, to
> go round the world for six years if you order it.[3]

And Castries replied on 25 August:

> I will always feel more favorable towards this kind of union than to one
> which our customs allow to be dictated by self-interest. Enjoy the hap-
> piness of making someone happy, and the tokens of honour and distinction
> you have received from your fellow citizens. You have deserved them and,
> as a former resident of Albi, I join in them with all my heart[4]

It had, suddenly, all come right. So much so that one may wonder
whether a charade had been enacted to satisfy old Galaup. The
mention of the Princesse de Bouillon, emerging from obscurity at
this point – for La Pérouse was no Versailles courtier – suggests
some complicity in high circles. Fleurieu must have known, since he
was in almost daily contact with La Pérouse during those strain-
filled weeks of May and June. And if Fleurieu knew, was Castries
wholly unaware? Had he known, or guessed, then the letter Jean-
François sent him was merely intended for the records – for the
dossier personnel where it still lies today – and the Minister's reply
was similarly a necessary formality. The marriage between Mademoiselle de Vésian and the Marquis de Sénégas falls easily into the
same pattern; it was promptly arranged and conveniently held

Engraving of La Pérouse from an Italian edition of the Voyages.
(Rex Nan Kivell Collection, National Library of Australia.)

without anyone's feelings being injured. As Jean-François had written to his mother, Madame de Vésian had guessed the truth some time ago.

It had taken three months to get old blind Galaup to accept what his son had long since decided. If one goes back to the days of the Ile de France, it had taken over six years to wear down his resistance. In those days of dominating patriarchs, it was about par for the course. But the world was changing. Sentimental drama was replacing the harsh old classical tragedies on the Paris stage, and the first notes of the great Romantic movement had already been sounded. They had taken just a little longer to be heard in distant Albi than in the salons of Versailles.

Notes

1. This correspondence is reprinted in Barthés de Lapérouse, *La Vie privée de Lapérouse,* 1888.
2. Italics not in the original.
3. Archives Nationales, Marine, C7-197.
4. Ibid.

13
Plans and Preparations

IN LATE OCTOBER 1783, Jean-François arrived in Lorient from Albi. He had no inkling of the mind-numbing months which lay in store for him. The Battle of the Saintes in April 1782, when Rodney and Hood had defeated de Grasse, was now the subject of an official enquiry.

De Grasse, freed by the peace from his status of prisoner of war, had returned to France and laid accusations of incompetence against a number of his officers, including Louis-Antoine de Bougainville, famous as the Frenchman who had sailed around the world and brought a Tahitian native to Versailles.

François-Joseph-Paul, Comte de Grasse du Bar, was a southerner, hard and hot-blooded. He was a colossus of a man, well over six foot in height and built in proportion. He was now over 60. He had spent over 45 years at sea, fighting the English, Turkish pirates, Algerian raiders, anyone and anywhere. He had defeated Hood off Tobago in 1781, he had sailed to the Chesapeake to enforce French naval supremacy, he had played a vital part in the capture of York-town, he had taken the island of St Kitts in 1782. He was a professional sailor, a nobleman who had no time for the niceties of the Court; he was ill-tempered and impatient. He had won battles through ignoring the orders of his over-cautious superiors, and had trodden on a great many toes, including Bougainville's who loathed him. But he had lost his last battle.

He did not take criticism kindly. On his side he had Castries, the Minister of Marine, and Vergennes, the Chief Minister, but he made himself so obnoxious that Castries told him to keep away from the Court. However, he was too great a man to be court-martialled. Instead the battle itself was to be reconstructed by the Court of inquiry and the behaviour of his captains examined. His own would thus be appraised indirectly, through his log books. He was advised not to come to Lorient, but to remain at Vannes, to the south. But by December, de Grasse had stumped into Lorient and was roaring his way through the offices of the Navy.

La Pérouse found himself with nothing to do but listen to his fellow officers' complaints and to the gossiping that filled the town. Poring through journals to piece together the manoeuvres of an entire fleet is very slow and time-consuming work. While the officials struggled on, like a fleet becalmed, La Pérouse was granted permission to go to Paris for the month of December, but he was required to be back in Lorient early in the New Year. He saw Fleurieu and together they talked of the future. It is more than probable that they discussed projects for various expeditions, but it was too early for anything to develop. The war had strained France's finances to the edge of bankruptcy; the cost of Versailles and of Marie-Antoinette's extravagances threatened to drive them over the brink. France needed time to recover. There would be a command of some kind for La Pérouse, but later. He returned to Lorient.

Weeks went by. He learned that de Grasse had included him in his criticisms. At once, he dashed off a letter of protest to the officer presiding over the court-martial, insisting he be heard in his own defence. Alas, it was mere gossip; the *Président,* the Comte de Breugnon, as irritated about the dragging proceedings as anyone, turned down his request, and sought confirmation of this action from the Minister. Castries did not defend his protégé, but endorsed Breugnon's refusal with a note:

> Approved, if he is not involved, that his note be rejected.

Jean-François, feeling himself a victim of the atmosphere of Lorient, so filled with spite and rancour, and of his own impulsiveness, unburdened himself in a letter to a cousin in Albi:

> I hope that this unending business in Lorient will soon allow me to see again that region, that family, those parents I love so much and where it is my greatest wish to spend the rest of my life. I no longer know what Fate has in store for me, because having been a little heated in defending myself against M. de Grasse for whom there is now a wide feeling of contempt, it is possible that M. de Castries may have borne me some ill-

will, since that commander had been chosen by him. It is only a mere suspicion . . .[1]

Between January and May 1784, he was nevertheless able to make quick trips to Paris and indeed to Albi. Appointment to the Society of the Cincinnati was also a consolation. But time hung heavily. It was probably at this time that he wrote down his thoughts on the reorganization of the Navy.[2] This document contains two interesting references to officers achieving senior rank by a promotion taking place at about the age of 45 (he was then 43). It is in fact a sensible report, showing La Pérouse holding a middle position – possibly slightly right of centre – in the continuing argument between the 'reds' and the 'blues'.

During each period of war, the Navy was forced to call on the services of officers from the merchant navy, and after each war they were returned to the merchant service because officer rank was the prerogative of the nobility. The months that followed the end of the American War of Independence were no different in this respect. La Pérouse, like so many others, felt this situation could only work to the detriment of the naval service as a whole: 'The cause of our past misfortunes remains. They have their roots in the present structure of the Navy', he wrote. For one thing, a navy where birth rather than skills ensures advancement cannot be efficiently managed. In a ship:

> every officer, from a captain down to the most recent lieutenant, belongs to the same class. The first and second officers have often been *gardes de la marine* together with the man in command and have established that familiarity which comes from age and equality of birth, and which an ephemeral appointment to command a ship cannot eliminate.

His solution was a two-tier system, with the captain and his first officer coming from the aristocracy, and other officers from the merchant service – men 'for whom the command of a fireship and the Cross of Saint Louis after twenty-five years of service would represent a very great reward'.

The investigations dragged to an end. De Grasse was exonerated. Few cared beyond those closely involved. From June 1784, La

Pérouse spent most of his time in Paris, working with Claret de Fleurieu. What he was doing remains obscure, which suggests that it was not significant enough to be recorded. He was merely Fleurieu's assistant, anxious not to be too far from the centre of power so that, if some appointment came up, he would not be overlooked. He was torn between a desire to spend the summer months in Albi with his wife and the need to remain visible in Paris and Versailles — there were too many other officers freed from their command by the end of the war who were now competing for what little the Navy had to offer.

If only he could have had Eléonore at his side! Paris could offer some attractions, such as the strange hot-air balloons everyone was talking about since the Montgolfier brothers had sent one into the sky in June 1783, and even more so since late that same year Pilâtre de Rozier and the Marquis d'Arlandes had actually sailed in one over Paris; and now François Blanchard was crossing the Channel in one from Calais to Dover! There were plays and concerts: the music of a new composer named Mozart, and the public performance, after a six-year ban, of Beaumarchais' comedy *Le Mariage de Figaro*. There was the careless gossip of the courtiers about the indiscretions of others, not least Queen Marie-Antoinette who was just then becoming embroiled in the Diamond Necklace affair that was to erupt into a public scandal in 1785. Voltaire and Rousseau had died, but the *philosophes* still held sway in the salons of Paris and beyond. In England, the elections had just overthrown the Fox-North coalition after less than a year in office, and William Pitt was negotiating with his colleagues, mostly from the House of Lords, to put together an administration that would last and begin a much-needed period of reconstruction. In charge of the Admiralty, he placed Lord Howe. France could be said to be riding the crest of a wave, in spite of constant financial troubles. Certainly, she felt confident after the successful war:

'France had an intimate sense of her strength and her wealth', wrote Madame de Campan, the companion of Marie Antoinette, in her *Mémoires*. But it is doubtful that Eléonore would have enjoyed much of all this. She missed her husband, but she was a gentle, retiring woman, who does not seem to have found it too difficult to settle in Albi. Jean-François snatched a couple of brief stays in Languedoc, but no more. The stakes he was playing for in Paris were too high for him to risk being away for a lengthy period.

The plan that was slowly taking shape through the autumn and winter of 1784 was in keeping with France's mood of self-pride and confidence, her intimate sense of strength and wealth. James Cook had made England's reputation in the field of hydrography and exploration, but James Cook had been killed five years earlier. The temptation to emulate the achievements of the man they called 'the incomparable Cook' had tempted a previous government into backing the costly and abortive Kerguelen expedition. Sent to sail across the Pacific from west to east, from the Ile de France into the southern ocean, to New Zealand and on to Valparaiso, on:

> the finest voyage that has ever been undertaken, one that can bring the most honour to M. de Boynes [the then Minister of Marine], bring fame to the nation, enrich geography, and bring about the most benefits,

Kerguelen had sailed south to the desolate island that now bears his name and turned back home after little more than three months. Fleurieu and Castries were secretly drawn by the same desire to bring fame to France and to themselves by promoting an expedition that could stand comparison with James Cook's. They had time on their side, whereas de Boynes had been pressured by circumstances into acting too hastily. They had the Kerguelen expedition as an example of what to avoid. The result, for La Pérouse, was a period of painful uncertainty about his own future.

That something important was in the wind is evidenced by a letter a friend sent him from Lorient in response to one in which La Pérouse complained about his inability to spend any length of time at Albi. 'It is not natural that a married man should leave his own country for five or six years without having a few months to put his own affairs in order'.[3]

It seems probable that Fleurieu and La Pérouse's attention was directed towards the northern Pacific which Cook had explored just before his death. The north-west coast of America, in particular,

The Maréchal de Castries
(Musée de la Marine.)

held rich promises. It was to some extent a no man's land, where the Spanish had only a tenuous claim and where the Russians were setting up trading posts. There were great possibilities for the fur trade. There was also the nagging problem of a North-West Passage from the Atlantic to the Pacific, corresponding to the Straits of Magellan far to the south. La Pérouse's experience in Hudson Bay was invaluable. He had sailed with great skill in the narrow straits and the ice-strewn inland sea; he had traded with Indians along the coast. His knowledge could be drawn upon and his discretion ensured by the simple method of telling him very little.

It is probable that Castries approached Louis XVI at a fairly early stage, in all likelihood in the autumn of 1784. The king's interest in geography was very real. His tutor had been the elderly Philippe Buache, who was appointed the first Hydrographer in 1730. In 1756 he had composed his *Instruction historique* for the heir apparent, the Duc de Bourgogne; when his pupil died in 1760 the teacher and the text moved on to the next heir apparent, the Duc de Berry, who was to become Louis XVI. To this was added Guillaume Le Blond's *Arithmétique et géométrie de l'officier* which, in the preface in the 1767 edition, proudly claimed that all the exercises in it had been successfully completed by the Duc de Berry and his brother.

By 1769, at the age of 15, the Duc de Berry had progressed sufficiently to draw a map, in colour, of the environs of Versailles, which is still extant in the 'Cartes et Plans' section of the Bibliothèque Nationale, Paris, under the reference number C.4349. It includes blanks such as one finds on explorers' charts, labelled 'Places which have not been surveyed'. The quality of this map makes it clear that it was not the future king's first attempt.

> The Dauphin exceeded Buache's expectations. A passion was aroused in him for hydrography, the navy and the geography of discoveries, which never left him. He could understand the great geographical problems of his day and discuss them intelligently.[4]

Louis XVI would in due course play his part in drawing up the instructions given to La Pérouse for the voyage, and indeed in selecting him to command it. In the meantime, Castries was encouraged to proceed with discretion. Fleurieu was now in touch with Wilhelm or William Boldt, a native of Holland who had worked in England and in Calcutta for the East India Company. In June 1780 he was in the Ile de France, where he established contact with the French authorities; later he returned to England and eventually made his way to France where he met Fleurieu and discussed with him the prospects of a fur trade based on the North-West Coast with its primary market in China. Discretion implied secrecy, and the inevitable result is the obscurity which surrounds Boldt's activities during the winter of 1784-5. He seems to have invited an English naval officer to join him and provide the technical information which he could not supply. A remuneration of 1,200 *livres* seems to have covered the work of this informant.

La Pérouse remained in the dark. 'I am still in the same state of uncertainty', he wrote to his wife on 5 February 1785. 'Nothing is decided. M. de Castries showers me with kindness and favours, but he does not finalise anything, and I am wasting time and money far from what I love.' He did not have to wait too long. The very next day Fleurieu told him the Minister was recommending him to command a major expedition.

The plans were growing even as they were formulated. The fur trade between the North-West Coast and Asia brought in the issue of the seas around Japan about which little was known. This apparently was a suggestion made by the king.[5] Thus the expedition would travel to the north-eastern and north-western coasts of the Pacific. Requiring reports on political developments, commercial possibilities, and matters of hydrography and geography both there and on the way seemed logical. Geographical issues raised the problem of the Solomon Islands. Political matters brought in the question of a possible settlement in New Zealand. Both these island groups were added, and only much later, when an urgent report was needed on British activity in Australia, was New Zealand deleted. But by now the programme had grown to include the exploration of the south as well as the north Pacific. The shadow of James Cook still loomed large. An expedition large enough to parallel his own achievements was in preparation.

As the itinerary crystallized, the king made suggestions, amendments, recommendations. A call at Easter Island was added; Hawaii, where Cook had been killed, was more reluctantly included. The time needed for all the work to be done was calculated. It would take three years, Fleurieu informed La Pérouse. It was out of the question now to envisage an expedition centred around the future of the fur trade. As the king's interest grew and the plans unfolded, the commercial aspects receded. It would be inappropriate for the king or his ships to be associated with trade. This was France, not England. Political and commercial considerations never disappeared, but day by day they lost prominence. What mattered was exploration and scientific research — and though trade remained important, it lay concealed in secret or verbal instructions.[6]

This was after all a scientific age and the influence of the scientific societies was considerable. There were more than 20 universities in France, but they were hidebound defenders of tradition, seldom making any appreciable contribution to knowledge. Much the same can be said of universities elsewhere in Europe, with a few exceptions. such as Leyden, Göttingen and Edinburgh. The drive came from individuals and their patrons. There was a great deal of interest in the sciences, much of it admittedly superficial, but it had given rise to a number of societies or 'académies' where men of wealth and some learning gathered to promote knowledge.

The very name of the Royal Society — which played a key role in promoting Cook's voyages — was evidence of this: it had been founded in 1660 as 'The Royal Society of London for Improving Natural Knowledge'. Six years later, the French *Académie des sciences* held its inaugural meeting. Academies followed in Sweden (1710), Russia (1725), Denmark (1742) and indeed in most European cities of any size. The French *philosophes*, thanks to their elegant literary style, spread new ideas and encouraged scepticism and curiosity about the physical world, including the inhabitants and products of the furthest regions of the globe.

Collections of plants, shells, geological specimens and animals were increasing in popularity. The Paris *Jardin des plantes* or *Jardin du Roi* had been founded in 1633 by Cardinal Richelieu; the *Jardin des plantes* of Montpellier was even older, having been set up in 1593. However, systematic searches for new specimens did not develop until the mid-eighteenth century. Adanson was sent by the *Compagnie des Indes* to Senegal in 1749. Linnaeus sent Tarnstrom to South Africa, Java and China, Osbeck to Canton, Kaln to North America and Thurnberg to South Africa. Philibert Commerson went with Bougainville across the Pacific in 1767-8. Joseph Banks not only sailed around the world with Cook, but urged many others to seek rare specimens – men such as Vancouver, Ledyard, Bass and Flinders.

Administrators in the French colonies, particularly the West Indies, were required to send items to the *Muséum d'histoire naturelle,* set up in the *Jardin des plantes*, whose curator was Georges Buffon, the author of the massive *Histoire naturelle*. Even a small territory like Guiana gave rise to a surprising amount of systematic work, such as Fusée-Aublet's *Histoire des plantes de la Guyane française* of 1775, and Jean-Baptiste Leblond's epic voyage from Cayenne to the Orinoco and across the Cordillera to Ecuador.

The immense success of the *Encyclopédie* can be explained by its detailed articles and hundreds of illustrations on sciences and technology, which led Louis XVI to overlook its radical comments on society and politics. Voltaire, d'Alembert, Monge, Lalande, all wrote scientific works in the 1740-70 period: Lavoisier's first epoch-making papers on chemistry had appeared in the *Journal de physique* in 1773-4, while the *Journal économique* provided news of scientific and technological developments to bridge the gap between the pure and the applied sciences. France being an agricultural country, the scientific spirit reached into that area too. The *Société d'agriculture* of Paris, which was in the process of changing its name to *Société nationale d'agriculture,* encouraged botanists to travel through Europe to research new methods and to the tropics to seek new species. Over 1,200 French works on agronomy were published in the eighteenth century, one of the most noteworthy for its methodical approach being Duhamel de Monceau's *Elements d'agriculture* of 1760.

Many of these savants, directly or indirectly, were consulted about the La Pérouse expedition. Castries wrote to the *Académie des sciences* and to the *Société de médecine*; La Pérouse approached Buffon, then in his seventy-ninth year; Lavoisier organized his colleagues into committee; the abbé Tessier, Regent of the Paris Faculty of Medicine, started work on a programme to study the corruption of water on board ship, putting forward the suggestion that its putrefaction might be caused by the eggs of insects — a daring advance to the brink of bacteriology which he proposed to test by the use of twenty different barrels.

It soon became impossible to keep the expedition a secret. Jean-François told Eléonore in late February; it was still possible to conceal the plans during March, when two ships were allocated, the *Portefaix* and the *Utile*. The first, with its inelegant name (the Porter), was a stolid storeship which needed a complete refit as well as a new name; but neither the port captain of Rochefort, Latouche-Tréville, nor his engineer, was told what she was to be used for. The same applied to the *Utile*, a transport ship of 350 tons. Secrecy could not make for efficiency, and the purpose of this cloak and dagger approach, namely keeping England in the dark, was arguable now that the expedition had grown from a commercially oriented voyage to a major exploration of the entire Pacific.

Once Latouche-Tréville learned the true scope of the expedition, he realized that the *Utile* would not be appropriate. There was nothing better in the port of Rochefort, so eventually Brest, where the *Portefaix* was moored for a more thorough refit, provided a storeship of the same class which was just as inelegantly named — the *Autruche* (the Ostrich).

Once again, Cook's example was being followed. He had chosen solid, heavy vessels like the dependable *Endeavour*, a collier. The storeships selected for La Pérouse were sound ships of 450 tons, with 'tween-decks which provided a more comfortable larger area for the crew and space for the stores. They were 127 feet in length, and 27 in width. And just as Lieutenant James Cook R.N. could not have sailed in command of a coalship, so Captain de La Pérouse could not sail in charge of a storeship. The *Endeavour* was registered on the list of the Royal Navy as a bark, La Pérouse's two ships were listed as frigates. And more appropriate names were found: the

Portefaix now became the *Boussole* and the *Autruche* the *Astrolabe*. That at least was the final renaming, since through some unexplained oddity the new names were first given the other way round.[7]

For a voyage of such length in tropical waters, the ships needed protection from the fearsome worm, the *teredo navalis*, that could reduce their wooden hull to a honeycombed shell. La Pérouse had had unhappy experiences in Hudson Bay with copper sheathing, when the ice floes had ripped back the copper. Accordingly the hulls were nailed with hexagonal flat nails approximately four centimetres across. It was a slow, costly operation, and it encouraged the growth of weeds and barnacles which would have to be scraped off whenever the ships were in port, but in the long term it paid dividends.

The port of Brest was in the care of the Comte d'Hector, an able man sympathetic to La Pérouse and to the planned campaign. Even more advantageous, he was related to Fleuriot de Langle who was to sail with La Pérouse and could tell him in confidence far more than had been told to the bemused Latouche-Tréville. Hector was instrumental in obtaining good supplies promptly and in getting built some additional boats and yawls, and an 18-ton decked vessel to be assembled when required – each piece was numbered and the design followed 'that of boats seen in Hudson's Bay and known as Bermudans'. Having presided over the court-martial that followed Kerguelen's disastrous expedition of 1774, he knew what was required for a major voyage of exploration.

The cloak and dagger approach of the first few weeks of planning is nowhere better exemplified than in Monneron's voyage to England. In March 1785, La Pérouse suggested that Paul Monneron, appointed 'ingenieur-en-chef', should travel to London to obtain up-to-date information on Cook's method of preventing scurvy, and also to 'find a quite minor official of the [Hudson Bay] Company who speaks Eskimo'.[8]

There was to be no Eskimo interpreter, but Monneron's stay in London was highly productive. Unfortunately, his secrecy means that we cannot trace his moves with any precision. He made up the character of a certain Don Inigo Alvarez, reputedly a wealthy Spanish trader who intended to send ships to the Pacific coast.

Acting in his name, he sought out men connected with Cook, but of minor rank. His best connection was John Webber who had sailed in the *Resolution* and had painted a celebrated full-length portrait of Cook. Better still, Webber had made a number of drawings of the North-West Coast. Monneron found Webber amiable and talkative. There can be no easier way of gaining an artist's confidence and establishing a footing of intimacy than having one's portrait painted:

> In order to see him more often, without interfering with my own affairs, I have decided to get myself painted, for the first time in my life.[9]

Monneron's other activities consisted in the purchase of stores, still in the name of the mysterious Alvarez. Cook had used malt, he was told, to prevent scurvy, so Monneron had barrels of it sent to France. Webber took him to the British Museum, showed him what artefacts might be encountered and urged him not to overlook the kind of goods natives would look for in barter deals — not merely nails, but axes, fish hooks, pins, knives, beads and feathers. He gave him addresses in Fleet Street where books and scientific instruments might be found, such as Nairne and Blunt, instrument makers. In all, Monneron spent 8,000 *livres*.

How long Monneron was able to keep up the pretence of acting for Alvarez is not clear. Webber probably guessed what was afoot fairly early; if not he, then the instrument makers would have realized that more than trade was involved. And very little escaped the attention of Sir Joseph Banks, who intervened so that the Royal Society lent Monneron two dipping needles which had been used by James Cook himself — something he would not have done for some obscure Spanish trader.

Britain anyhow knew about the expedition. The government may in fact have been less concerned with a major voyage of exploration than with one aimed at developing trade on the North-West Coast. Once William Pitt and Lord Howe were officially told of the proposed expedition, they could show sympathy and understanding: La Pérouse, in particular, had proved a gallant and humane enemy. They probably learned of the plans through spies in April, and there is every likelihood that Monneron's activities in London were being watched. It was, however, on 5 May that the British ambassador in

Paris, Lord Dorset,[10] formally advised the Foreign Secretary:

> I have the honour to inform your Lordship that Mons. de la Pérouse will shortly sail from Brest, and it is reported, with some degree of authority, that he has orders to visit New Zealand, with a view to examine into the quality of the timber of that country, which it is supposed, by the account given of it in Captain Cook's voyage, may be an object worthy of attention.
>
> This plan is recommended by Mons. de Suffrein, who says that ships may with little difficulty go from Mauritius to that country. It is believed that the French have a design of establishing some kind of settlement there; if it shall be found practicable, as it will be necessary to tap the trees at least six months before they fell them, in order to lighten the wood, which has no other defect, as is said, than that of being too heavy to use in its natural state.[11]

By now preparations were in full swing. Eléonore received letters and gifts from Paris and Brest, but her entreaties were ignored — she had hoped for a short expedition, not one that was expected to last for years. Jean-François had promised . . . Had he not said that his dearest wish was to settle down among his family? Alas, it was something he often said when promotion dragged or time hung heavy with indecision. He barely had time for a last hurried visit to Albi. She would never see him again.

Everything had to be attended to at the same time: the plans, the supplies, the ships, the men. Charts were prepared — with an extra copy for Louis XVI on which he was to trace the route of the expedition as reports came in. There were discussions with scientists and visits from cranks and from parents seeking the inclusion of their son among the officers. The instructions were drawn up, amended by the king, redrafted. The memoirs came in from the *Académie des sciences* and from Buache, 26 pages of them, with questions on geometry, astronomy, mechanics, physics, chemistry, anatomy, zoology, botany, mineralogy, each section the painstaking work of a sub-committee. The *Société de médecine* drew up its list of questions to be investigated, 23 pages long. The instructions with the notes, memoirs and associated papers made up a document of more than 200 foolscap pages.

In their final version, dated 25 June 1785, the instructions outlined a complex voyage across the south and north Pacific. From

Brest, La Pérouse was to go to Funchal and across to South America, continuing south in the hope of finding the Ile Grande, supposedly discovered by a Frenchman named La Roche in the South Atlantic, thence to South Georgia Island and on to Sandwich Land, Staten Land, and Cape Horn. Alternatively, he could touch at the Falkland Islands for refreshments and go through Le Maire's Strait to Christmas Sound in Tierra del Fuego. Indeed, La Pérouse was given the greatest freedom to diverge from his instructions if he so wished. One might have expected, after the unhappy experiences the government had had with the Kerguelen expedition, that it would seek to control the new commander, but so high was the esteem in which Castries, Fleurieu and Louis XVI all held him that they were quite prepared to leave the execution of their plans to his discretion. The instructions, detailed and exhaustive though they were, could be viewed as mere guidelines:

> His Majesty does not intend that M. de La Pérouse should submit completely to this plan . . . The aim of the present instructions is simply to indicate to M. de La Pérouse the discoveries that remain to be carried out or perfected in various parts of the globe, and the route that is considered appropriate to carry out this work.[12]

There were various questions to settle in the south-west Pacific once La Pérouse had entered the ocean, such as the existence of Drake's Land and a supposed discovery made in 1714 by a Spanish captain, which was now believed to be unsubstantiated. A call at Easter Island would enable the French to rest their crews and prepare them for an exploration of the south Pacific, the two ships separating, one to run along the sixteenth parallel, the other along the twenty-fifth, and both to meet up in Tahiti. Louis XVI intervened quite late to oppose this separation which he felt was 'too dangerous in unknown seas' — this comment appears as a marginal note.

After a month in Tahiti, La Pérouse was to visit the neighbouring islands, leaving seeds and shrubs which might later be of value to Europeans navigating in those distant seas, and follow Bougainville's tracks through the Navigators (the Samoas) and the Friendly Islands

The port of Brest in the early 1790s, by J.F. Hué.
(Musée de la Marine.)

(the Tongas), but then veer slightly north of west to survey the western coast of New Caledonia. The next stage would take him to Vanuatu and the Solomons, to the Louisiades, to Cook's Endeavour Strait, north of Cape York Peninsula, into the Gulf of Carpentaria, to begin an anti-clockwise circumnavigation of the Australian continent, ending at Van Diemen's Land (Tasmania) and finally across the Tasman Sea to New Zealand for refreshment and repairs. This, it was calculated, would take twenty months — he was to leave Queen Charlotte Sound, New Zealand, in March 1787.

This part of his instructions La Pérouse almost completely ignored. It was a gigantic undertaking which, if it was carried out in accordance with the wishes of the government and the learned societies, would require far more time than was estimated. He was expected to carry out surveys of coastlines, to report on any European establishments he found, on prospects for trade, on the natives. Precise longitudes and latitudes were to be calculated, climatic conditions analysed, plants and animals collected, artifacts bought and labelled. Even the natives encountered were to have their features, dwellings, settlements and weapons drawn and described. If this was not done and La Pérouse allowed himself to be dominated by a timetable, the voyage would not achieve a great deal. The route to Tahiti could almost be said to be well travelled by then, and even further west he would only be following the tracks of Bougainville and Cook.

Aware that the great plan was merely a detailed outline, he would decide to invert it, and begin with the second part. This suggested that he follow a route from New Zealand to the Marquesas Islands, to Hawaii and California, then along the North-West Coast to seek a passage, if there was one, from the Pacific to Hudson Bay. If he found none, he was to continue north to within sight of the St Elias Mountains, and along the Aleutian chain across to Kamchatka. He could then explore the Kuriles, the east coast of Japan, the Ryukyus and Formosa before putting in at Canton, Macao or Manila as circumstances dictated. This section of the voyage, it was optimistically predicted, would be completed in nine months — by the end of 1787.

The third section would take the expedition north again, to Korea, the Sea of Japan, along the west coast of Hokkaido and back to Kamchatka for a period of rest and refitting before sailing south to the Mariana Islands, to Mindanao, the Moluccas and through the Indonesian group to the Indian Ocean and the Ile de France. The homeward journey would take the ships into the Atlantic where there was an opportunity to avoid boredom by checking the positions of a number of islands — Gough, Diego Alvarez, Tristan de Cunha, Saxemberg, Dos Picos — which would add zest to the final stages of the expedition since it was doubtful that they all actually existed and only a thorough search could settle the issue.

It was anticipated that the ships would be back in Brest in the late summer of 1789, four years after their departure. What we will never know is what was said during the long discussions between La Pérouse and Fleurieu, between Fleurieu and Castries, and with Louis XVI. The expedition could no longer be seen as a voyage aimed at developing the fur trade and forestalling English moves. It was a voyage of exploration, cast in the traditional mould, a grandiose version of all that had gone before. The dignity of the French royal family could be preserved. And La Pérouse could make his own decisions in line with what was logical and possible.

The investment was proportional to the scale of the undertaking. Including the cost of the two ships, refitted and equipped with sufficient spare sails and cables for the first six months, the government spent over a million *livres*. The cost of supplies to be bought at ports of call, and the pay of the officers and men, apart from advances made to them in Brest, were additional to this total. The cargo included nearly one hundred bushels of seeds, 59 trees and shrubs to be given or planted in countries the French would visit and a great mass of gifts for native peoples: bars of iron, buttons of coloured glass, 100 medals with the King's effigy, 52 plumed dragons' helmets, 9,000 fish-hooks, 16 organs, 2,000 hatchets, 1,000 pairs of scissors, 24 sets of ringing bells, 2,000 combs and a million pins. The King's gardener, André Thouin, had selected the seeds and the plants as well as the young man, Jean-Nicolas Collignon, who would be going on the voyage; he had given him two books on agriculture 'for his recreation'.

Books were an important part of the supplies provided, not for the crew, who were probably all illiterate, but for the scientists and officers. They were to read them time and again during the long months at sea. There were 28 volumes on travel, 23 on astronomy and navigation, 8 on physics and 64 on natural history. They included books by de Brosses, Cook, Bougainville, Hawkesworth, Feuillet and Buffon. Some of these books had been bought at the request of the scientists or by them. The physicist, Lamanon, spent 6,000 *livres* on books. All this can be compared with the current cost of living: bed and breakfast at an average inn could be obtained for one *livre* a day; a merchant vessel captain would not earn much more than 3,000 *livres* annually. [13]

An expedition as wide-ranging as this one needed men of an appropriate calibre. The mix was a judicious one of sailors and scientists, but it went even further: many of the officers had a sound knowledge of the sciences, many of the crew were also tradesmen of some kind — carpenters, tailors, shoemakers — and even the two chaplains were qualified naturalists. La Pérouse found no difficulty with recruiting: employment was at a low ebb in the Navy after the war, and he was a highly popular commander.

He wasted no time in recommending Fleuriot de Langle to command the second ship. They were friends. Paul-Antoine-Marie Fleuriot, chevalier de Langle, was 40 years of age. He had concentrated on scientific studies in his early years and had worked for the *Académie de marine*, of which he was now a member. This scientific background led some like Bachaumont, the gossip writer, author of the famous *Mémoires secrètes*, to speculate that de Langle had been in the running to command the entire expedition. A letter by the botanist Lamartinière and a similar comment in the *Mémoires du Chevalier de Cotignon* [14] at first sight appear to add a little substance to the gossip — but gossip twice repeated is still rumour. Admittedly, de Langle came from a family with better connections than La Pérouse; born in the château of Kerloët, in Brittany, he had married Georgette de Kerouatz, [15] the niece of Comte d'Hector, lieutenant-general of the *armées navales* and commander of the port of Brest. But La Pérouse was his senior and had a solid reputation. And if speculation was based on the idea that better connections lead to preferment, it should be remembered that La Pérouse was the close collaborator of Fleurieu in Paris where the expedition was being planned, and that the Minister of the Navy, Castries, was a man of Albi.

De Langle had already served under La Pérouse. During the American War, he had held a number of commands — the *Aigrette*, the *Résolue*, the *Expériment* and finally the *Astrée*, in which he had sailed with La Pérouse to Hudson Bay. Both men were friends and to some extent complementary to each other. De Langle had scientific training which La Pérouse lacked; he was serious, sometimes to the point of melancholy, something of an introvert, often obstinate. La Pérouse was more of an extrovert, a man of the south, determined, at times given to ebullience and anger. Physically they differed. La Pérouse who had always been plump was now indisputably fat, with a pronounced double chin and a stomach which rebelled against the constriction of a buttoned waistcoat. A miniature portrait of de Langle, on the other hand, shows rather slender prim features.

As first officer in his own *Boussole*, La Pérouse picked Robert Sutton de Clonard, a member of a distinguished family of sailors and naval administrators. He had served in ships of the *Compagnie des Indes*, had been wounded at the Battle of Mahé and returned to France in the *Belle-Poule* in 1777 and had received the Cross of Saint-Louis just after La Pérouse. During the American War he had been taken prisoner in October 1779; freed, he had served in the *Glorieux* at the capture of Tobago, commanded the *Diligente* and the *Guyane*, and more recently the *Lourdes*. Now aged 33 he had met La Pérouse on many occasions and in fact had been his first officer in the *Serin* back in 1778.

Charles-Gabriel d'Escures, appointed as second officer, had had a similar career. He had first served in India, and fought gallantly during the War of American Independence, being present at the capture of Grenada and the siege of Savannah; he was Kergariou's first officer in the *Sibylle* and when the captain was too severely wounded to carry on he took over, was finally defeated by the *Centurion* and was taken prisoner. He too was a *chevalier* of the Order of Saint-Louis.

Among the second-lieutenants, or ensigns, were other veterans of the recent war: Charles Boutin, the son of a powerful *Intendant des finances*, had been in the *Magnifique* and taken part in the capture of Grenada and the battle of Savannah; he too had been taken prisoner — he was aboard the ill-fated *Cérès* — two minor commands had come to him in 1784 and 1785 and, just prior to joining the *Boussole* he received the Cross of Saint-Louis. Ferdinand de Pierrevert had fought at Grenada and Savannah in the *Fantasque*, and in three engagements in 1780 while in the *Solitaire*; he was a nephew of the great admiral Suffren Saint-Tropez. The third ensign, Colinet, had been in the *Boussole* in 1784 when she was still only the *Portefaix*.

There were two *gardes de la marine*: one was Henri Mel de Saint-Céran, the son of a *Receveur-général des finances* at Montauban, a town less than 80 kilometres from Albi; his health was delicate, he had been given three months' special leave from the *Médée* at the end of 1784 and he was to be left behind at Manila in 1786 to be re-patriated and to be promoted to ensign on his arrival in France; the other was Pierre de Montarnal, who had entered the *Gardes* at the same time as Saint-Céran; he was related to the La Pérouse family on the Rességuier side. La Pérouse wrote on his death that he was 'the only relative I had in the Navy, to whom I was as tenderly attached as if he were my own son'.

Thus the *Boussole* would contain men with whom La Pérouse would feel comfortable, people he knew or who knew that part of France he came from. Nothing is more important than compatibility when men are to be confined in a small space — a vessel of 127 feet long — for months at a time. La Pérouse took on two *volontaires* — young men with no official status in the Navy who served in order to gain experience. One was Frederic Broudou, his own brother-in-law. Frederic had been troublesome for years. In March 1782 he was arrested for threatening his sister Elzire with a pistol; in April 1784 his mother had requested his incarceration in the Mont-Saint-Michel island prison; the intervening period he had spent in a privateer. Sending him to sea under La Pérouse was one way of keeping him under control and out of harm's way. And indeed there appears to have been no complaints about him during the voyage, although it cannot have been easy for him to maintain a balance between being a largely supernumerary officer of middle-class origin and the commander's brother-in-law. He eventually proved himself worthy of a junior lieutenant's commission. The other *volontaire* was Roux d'Arbaud, a student at the *Ecole militaire*, of whom it is recorded that he was 'a prodigy when it comes to astronomy'. He was appointed *garde de la marine* from 1786.

D'Arbaud's inclusion brings up the fascinating question of whether Napoleon Bonaparte narrowly missed out on being appointed to the *Boussole*. A mention of this occurs in a book published in Paris in 1954[16] in which reference is made to a passage in the *Cahiers* of Alexandre-Jean des Mazis who was at the *Ecole militaire* with Napoleon:

> Buonaparte was in the mathematics class . . . Messrs Dagelet and Monge, two men of distinction, were our teachers . . . During 1784 the question arose of the voyage of M. de la Pérouse. Messrs Dagelet and Monge sought and were granted the favour of joining as astronomers . . . Buonaparte would have liked this opportunity of displaying his energy in such a fine enterprise, but Darbaud was the only one selected: they could not accept a greater number of pupils, and so Darbaud sailed with Messrs Dagelet and Monge in 1784.

The comment is not invalidated by Mazis' getting the date wrong. It is by no means unlikely that the future emperor expressed the wish that he might be allowed to sail with such an expedition as La Pérouse's, but a decision against a naval career had been made by his mother at least two years earlier. Before going on to Paris for further study, Napoleon had been a pupil at the military school at Brienne where training was provided for both services. There he was placed in the so-called naval class and a report to his mother stated him to be 'highly suitable to become a naval officer'. The formidable Letizia Bonaparte saw greater prospects for her son in the army and firmly informed the Brienne authorities that her son was to be regarded as destined for the army and that she wanted no further reports on his suitability for the navy.[17]

Some yearning for the sea, certainly ambition and his sense of adventure, may have led Napoleon to express envy at D'Arbaud's appointment and the wish that he might be chosen as well. Those who like to speculate on quirks of fate can conjure up a vision of what the history of Europe might have been in the 1790s and the 1800s without Napoleon, had he sailed with La Pérouse's expedition and been lost in the Pacific in 1788.

For the *Astrolabe*, Fleuriot de Langle selected Anne-Georges-Augustin, chevalier de Monti, recently appointed *lieutenant de vaisseau*, a man in his thirties who had sailed with Du Chaffault and La Motte-Picquet. Here again was a veteran of Grenada and Savannah; here again was a commander who was selecting a man he knew personally. Monti had sailed in the *Saint-Esprit*, the *Annibal*, the *Indien*, the *Bretagne*, the *Protecteur* and more recently the *Venus*; he had received his Cross of Saint-Louis the previous October. He proved to be a valuable first officer to de Langle, painstaking, tireless, patient, dependable.

There were four ensigns. Prosper-Philippe d'Aigremont was 24, with a fine career behind him. A *garde* in 1778, he had specialized in gunnery and been promoted to *enseigne* in 1780. He had served in the *Neptune* and the *Duc de Bourgogne* before transferring to the *Glorieux* in which he took part in four battles during 1782, including the Battle of the Saintes when La Pérouse had unsuccessfully attempted to recapture her from the English. Taken to England, Aigremont was freed in September and received a grant of 1,000 *livres* to compensate for the belongings he had lost with the *Glorieux*. He later was given a further 800 *livres* in consideration of his actions during the war. At the time of his appointment to the *Astrolabe* he was serving in the *Desirée*. A little more shadowy is Blondelas, a *lieutenant de frégate* serving in the *Levrette* which was then in the port of Brest. His file in the naval archives refers to him as 'an excellent officer with a modesty which makes him very interesting', a somewhat cryptic comment which may indicate that he had been a 'blue' officer who kept at a deferential distance from his aristocratic fellow officers. His war record certainly did not require him to be over-modest: he had taken part in nine naval combats.

Edouard de Laborde de Marchainville was the son of the Marquis de Laborde, a prominent financier linked with the Court who was to end on the scaffold during the Revolution. Laborde-Marchainville was in his mid-20s, tall, slender with fair hair, described as 'gentle and highly knowledgeable in naval science'. Like so many others he had been present at the capture of Grenada and the siege of Savannah and served under Du Chaffault. Then in August 1780 he had been posted to the *Aigrette* which was being taken over by de Langle, and with whom he had transferred to the *Résolue*. He had not gone on the Hudson Bay raid, but he had achieved his own command, of a small corvette, the *Fauvette*, on a voyage to America in November 1783. During the early part of 1785 he had spent three months in Holland and England to further his education. This seems to have been a genuine case of a wealthy young man travelling overseas for his own account, and there is no indication that he was making enquiries on behalf of Fleurieu.

Jérome Freton de Vaujuas had served in various ships before joining the *Amphion* which formed part of the La Motte Picquet squadron at Grenada and Savannah. Monti knew him well for they had sailed together in the *Protecteur* in 1782-83. And Vaujuas knew the *Astrolabe* as he had served in her from July 1783 to March 1784, when she was known as the *Autruche*.

Among the *gardes de la marine* was Laborde de Boutervilliers, Marchainville's younger brother, who had earlier sailed in the *Iphigénie* and the *Séduisant*; and Jean-Guillaume Law de Lauriston, the 20-year-old son of the Governor of Pondicherry whom La Pérouse had known in his voyages to India. He had sailed firstly in the *Solitaire* but had been taken prisoner in December 1783. Freed, he had seen service in the *Téméraire* where he met Le Gobien, then in the *Guyane* under Clonart and the *Séduisant* with Laborde de Boutervilliers. What we know about him as he prepared to join La Pérouse gives an interesting picture of how a well-to-do young officer readied himself for the rigours of a long voyage. His father sent him a stock of books, including the voyages of Cook, Byron, Wallis and Carteret, plus 40 lbs of chocolate, 102 tablets of concentrated broth (believed to be effective in countering scurvy), 21 lbs of lemon concentrate, 17 shirts, 12 pairs of cotton socks, one pair of black silk stockings, six cravats, 11 pairs of shoes, a set of mathematical instruments and a medical kit. He was a very able youth who learnt quickly, and proved a useful officer on board. He had four brothers, one of whom became a general and aide-de-camp to Napoleon. The third *garde* on board the *Astrolabe* was Joseph Raxi de Flassan who came over from the *Levrette* with Blondelas.

Such were the officers. Most of the men came from Brittany, a number of them from de Langle's own district. However, this was a scientific expedition and the results it would achieve beyond the field of hydrography depended on the calibre of the scientists. We have seen that one young officer, d'Arbaud, came from the *Ecole militaire*. Two of its teaching staff, the astronomers and mathematicians Monge and Dagelet, were also appointed. Louis Monge's role was restricted by poor health. He joined the *Astrolabe* at a salary of 2,400 *livres*, but he was unable to proceed beyond Tenerife.

Joseph Lepaute Dagelet consequently assumed greater prominence in the expedition. He was as yet only 33, but he had already sailed on a major expedition – Kerguelen's of 1773. He belonged to a family of clockmakers and had been sent to Paris by his uncles to study under the mathematician Lalande. In 1778 he was appointed to a position at the Paris military school and was now approached for the La Pérouse expedition. Des Mazis' claim, mentioned earlier, that he sought this appointment has doubtful validity. Lepaute seems to have shown considerable reluctance. His parents were elderly and he was about to marry his cousin Henriette Lepaute. It was admittedly the usual arranged marriage, not an all-consuming passion. He was a serious, hard-working man, a little straightlaced:

> In our sailor's world, one sings, swears, smokes, drinks and talks of women all in the space of a half-hour . . . . For my part, as you know, I know love only when it is veiled by modesty, I constantly suffer in these conversations.[18]

He postponed the wedding, but obtained a promise that, if he should die, his parents would receive an annuity of 750 *livres*: and when his death was confirmed, the French parliament honoured the

debt. His own salary was to be 3,000 *livres*. He fulfilled all the expect-
ations people had of him and got on well with La Pérouse, keeping
out of cabals and taking no sides in personal rivalries. His discretion
had already served him well during Kerguelen's quarrel-filled voyage,
and Kerguelen, who fell out with most of his officers, had written
him a glowing testimonial. La Pérouse referred to him as 'a charming
man'.

Lamanon, who sailed in the *Boussole*, was a different proposition.
For one thing, he came from a family that was higher on the social
scale. Jean-Honoré-Robert de Paul, Chevalier de Lamanon, was no
clockmaker's son. He was a man of the South, and at 32 was more
lively by far than the scholarly Dagelet who came from the Ar-
dennes, not far from what is now the Belgian frontier. With his
brother Auguste, he had travelled through much of Europe on
natural history treks. They had met most of the *philosophes* and the
encyclopédistes of the age. He was a friend of Condorcet, the mathematician whose *salon* at the Mint, of which he was inspector-general,
was one of the most famous of the day. Lamanon began to specialize
in geology as his brother's health failed and the travels had to end.
He wrote articles, including an 'Origin of Mountains and Valleys' for
a massive *Nouvelle théorie de la terre* which he did not live to complete. He was imbued with the philosophical spirit of his century
and certainly an enthusiastic supporter of the ideas of Jean-Jacques
Rousseau.

But energetic and widely read though he might be, he was still
only an enlightened amateur. His approaches to join the expedition
were met with coolness. This was an undertaking suitable only for
professionals. As early as April 1785 he had pressured Condorcet to
write to Fleurieu. When this did not produce a speedy response, he
got the Duc de La Rochefoucault to write. Fleurieu was an administrator who respected only efficiency, but a duke's recommendation
could not be overlooked. Fleurieu agreed to meet Lamanon and was
forced to agree that the man had talents which would be useful to
the expedition. The study of rocks and land formations, to which
Lamanon could add meteorology, was an essential part of the voyage.
The only sticking point was salary: if Dagelet was getting 3,000

livres, then the Chevalier de Lamanon could not accept less! Yet an astronomer's position, especially with Monge's obvious poor health, was a key one; furthermore there could be relativity problems with the other scientists. Fleurieu skilfully used Lamanon's own snobbishness as a weapon: 'A man of his status should not be paid on an annual basis', he wrote to Castries and offered 12,000 *livres* flat, which Lamanon accepted.

Joseph Boissieu de Lamartinière was another difficult character. Hard-working but dominating by nature, he wanted to be regarded as Collignon's superior. Nicolas Collignon, aged 24, was the expedition's gardener, a protégé of Thouin who had taught him and guided him and who was obviously fond of him. Collignon was in fact to produce more lasting results than most of the scientists through his detailed reports to Thouin and the packets of specimens he sent him at every opportunity, whereas much of the other men's work was lost when the ships disappeared without trace. But Collignon was a mere gardener, whereas Lamartinière was a doctor, a graduate of famed Montpellier University, a noted botanist, and a friend of such scientists as Lamarch, Bosc d'Antic, Broussemont and Thouin himself. La Pérouse rejected his claim, however, and avoided friction by allocating the two men to different ships.

If Lamanon was a gifted amateur, Jean-André Mongez (or Monges) was certainly a professional. He was the editor of the *Journal de Physique*, a member of numerous learned societies, including the *Société d'histoire naturelle,* and possessed of a wide knowledge of ornithology, entomology, and chemistry, on all of which he had written scientific papers. He was furthermore a priest, a canon regular of the church of Ste Geneviève, with friends among several Spanish orders. Thus he could double up as chaplain and La Pérouse appointed him to the *Boussole* where he would complement, with due humility, the ebullient Lamanon.

The *Astrolabe* became the home of another priest, a Claude-François-Joseph Receveur who was to have the dubious honour of being the first known Frenchman to be buried on the Australian continent and certainly the first to be buried in the new colony of Australia. He was the son of a farm labourer from the village of

Noel-Carneux, close to the Swiss frontier, an austere place clinging to the shoulder of a mountain range. His was a pious family — one of his brothers also became a priest, vicar of Clerval — and by no means inconsiderable — another brother became mayor of the village, and a great-uncle was the Jesuit missionary, Fr Parrenin, who went to China in 1698, became an adviser to the Emperor Kang-Si and died in Peking in 1741. After a brief spell in the army, Joseph Receveur entered the Franciscan Order, later joining the Grey Friars Convent in Paris under the name of Brother Laurent. He studied natural history, presented a number of papers to the *Académie des sciences* and acquired a reputation as a sound researcher. Between 1776 and 1780 he had been sent on a number of 'missions' for which he received a substantial grant of 1,500 *livres*. Now still only 28 he was selected for the La Pérouse voyage of exploration. And at the same time he would act as chaplain. He was a gentle soul, charitable towards the Easter Islanders who stole 'a few little things' which he could hardly spare, and minimizing the wounds he suffered in Samoa. 'Whatever you may be told about me', he wrote to his brother from Botany Bay in 1788, 'you can rest quite reassured. My wounds, which were very unimportant, have healed'. Ten days later, he was dead.

Among the technicians, Pierre Guéry, clockmaker taken on at 60 *livres* a month, was a modest, quiet man, moderately educated, but good at his trade and curious about the strange world about him. Four letters to his wife, in the *Archives Nationales,* reveal his character and above all his homesickness. There were few men of his rank aboard the *Boussole* he could confide in. Monneron, the *ingénieur en chef* and his assistant, the *ingénieur-géographe* Sebastien Bernizet, a man from Pézenas, little more than a hundred kilometres from Albi, had little in common with Guéry — indeed, few people aboard had, for he was a man of the Beauce, the great fertile plain south-west of Paris, which had little to do with sailors, ships or the mysteries of foreign oceans.

Paul Monneron was 37, the brother of Pierre Monneron who had sailed across the Pacific with Surville in 1769-70. The Monnerons were a large family, with connections in banking and the India trade.

Paul had studied at the *Ecole du génie* at Mézières and worked in France until 1778 when the Comte d'Arbaud, Governor of the West Indian island of Guadeloupe, had appointed him his military engineer. He got excellent reports — 'an officier full of spirit and talent for an occupation he carries out with zeal and incredible willpower.'[19] The War Minister, Ségur, seconded him to the Navy in 1782 for the Hudson Bay raid. La Pérouse was as impressed by him as others had been and had no hesitation in selecting his as engineer in chief for his expedition. His military experience would be valuable when it came to assess the defences of the foreign ports visited. As we have seen, he was employed at an early stage to assist with the preparations.

Artists had a significant role to play in such an expedition. Today there would be photographers, but in those days men who could draw with a high degree of accuracy newly discovered flora and fauna were essential. If they could also depict scenery and natives, so much the better, even though they might embellish their drawings in accordance with what they had been taught, and engravers after them might reproduce their work at one more remove from reality.

The expedition's leading artist was Gaspard Duché de Vancy, a student of the famous Joseph Vien, the pioneer of the classical reaction who also taught the great J.L. David. Duché de Vancy may well have known David, who went to Rome with Vien, and whose famous 'Oath of the Horatii' had just been completed. Duché de Vancy had certainly been to Italy — he left a number of drawings and architectural studies of Naples and Rome — and he had also travelled to London. How his experiences in the Pacific might have affected his style at a time when Roman models and classical composition were gaining favour is a matter for conjecture, since most of his work was eventually lost with him. It is certain that La Pérouse had a high opinion of him, as he recorded his view that Vancy's salary of 1,500 *livres* a year was not commensurate with his talent.

Guillaume Prévost was paid 1,200 *livres*, his task being to paint the botanical specimens gathered by the expedition, especially by Lamartinière. He was a man of moods, melancholic for much of the time, with occasional bursts of enthusiasm followed by equally sudden fits of despondency. He irritated Lamartinière by refusing to draw insects, birds or fishes. A man should stick to his last: Prévost was a botanical draughtsman. Let others draw the fauna. He was accompanied, in de Langle's ship, by his young nephew, Jean-Louis-Robert, who was more amenable. La Pérouse had a good opinion of both of them and lumped them together in his comments as 'Prévost, uncle and nephew'. They might have their firm views on an artist's lines of demarcation, but they continued to work within them.

This motley collection of scientists and technicians had little of the similarity of interests and overlap of careers which integrated the officers and men. They were skilled, intelligent, and able, but they were all individuals and few of them had ever had any experience of life on board. Nevertheless La Pérouse might have fared worse: among those whose requests to join him had been declined was the Marquis Abel de Vichy, who sought to come along 'with his servant, his clothes, some books and a few scientific instruments necessary to complete by some practical work twenty-two years devoted to the study of natural history'. La Pérouse may have remembered Sir Joseph Banks who had been something of a burden on Cook's first voyage and threatened to be such a real one on his second voyage that he had to be turned away. In some cases, the applicants could be rejected on the grounds that they were too late. Thus, in June, La Pérouse could express his regrets in polite terms to the Baron de Servières, to the Abbé Georgio Sommazzi of Lugano, and to a few others who felt that the expedition was just what they required to perfect a set of experiments or to see the world. The Abbé Soulavie thought to apply, but decided not to 'because of the pressure of personal business'. It seemed at times as if the Parisians looked on the expedition as a fashionable novelty, like Montgolfier's strange air balloons.

One latecomer, accepted on 18 June after the lists had already closed was the naturalist Dufresne. He is something of a shadowy figure, somewhat reluctant to go at all and not obviously qualified for the position. However, he was strongly protected by Calonne, the *Contrôleur-général des finances,* and his brother Bertrand was a member of the *Conseil d'Etat* and a treasurer of the Navy. He may have been included in order to obtain detailed information on the fur trade, about which he seemed to have some knowledge. La Pérouse wrote to Calonne that his budget would not allow him to pay Dufresne's salary and warned that life aboard a ship would be hard. But the Ministry of Finance provided the additional funds and Dufresne sailed, quiet and unhappy in the background. So unhappy did he become that he asked La Pérouse to leave him behind in Chile. La Pérouse gave him some work to do — supervising the trade in furs with the Indians of the North-West Coast, and finally let him quit in Macao.

Monneron had sought in vain an 'Eskimo interpreter' for the north-west coast of America. Fleurieu and La Pérouse had also looked for a Russian interpreter for the north-east coast of Asia. In April they thought of 'advertising for a servant who spoke Russian to accompany a nobleman on his travels to Russia'. Le Noir, who was in charge of the Paris police, was asked to help, but found no one. By May, this cloak and dagger approach had crumbled and a diplomat, Pierre Hennin, told Castries of a young man who would do very well. He was Barthélémy de Lesseps, whose father had served as Consul-General in St Petersburg; Barthélémy was at Court at that very moment, having arrived from Moscow with despatches from the French Ambassador. He was 19.

Castries interviewed him and Louis XVI approved. He would travel with the rank of *enseigne* at 1,500 *livres*, and be entitled to the status of vice-consul in his dealings with the Russians. He was firstly assigned to the *Boussole* but soon after he transferred to the *Astrolabe* where de Langle instructed him in the art of navigation. Another epic journey awaited him, for he would be sent from Kamchatka across Siberia and Europe with La Pérouse's report. Indeed there would be other epics lying in wait, including retreating from Moscow with Napoleon's troops in 1812, and one day, as one of the very few survivors, he would be called upon to identify relics of the La Pérouse expedition.

Finally, La Pérouse needed two ship's surgeons. Although there was a naval school of medicine at Brest, the number of surgeons available was never adequate and wars inevitably caused further depletions. La Pérouse could nevertheless have obtained a fully qualified registered surgeon from the hundred or so based on Brest; but registration is not everything. On a long hazardous voyage, when medical treatment could depend on initiative and a flair for botany rather than formal training, he wanted someone he knew and could trust. Rollin, whom he had met in the recent war when serving in the *Robuste*, was officially an 'auxiliary surgeon', but worthy of promotion. So too was Lavaux who was appointed to the *Astrolabe*: he had served in the *Nymphe* in 1780, been taken prisoner, been freed and finished the war in the *Héros*. As assistant, the *Boussole* was given Le Cor who had been in the Navy since 1773 and who took over from Rollin when the latter's health deteriorated. Lavaux's assistant was Jean Guillou who was similarly a man of experience. They were provided with the latest information about scurvy, that scourge of seamen which was slowly being defeated, and they received additional training at the School of Medicine. Monneron's anti-scurvy broth tablets were added to some 150 remedies of all kinds and the usual paraphernalia of the eighteenth-century doctor. The training and their skill paid off; there were surprisingly few cases of sickness during the arduous three years of the voyage.

Notes

1. *Bulletin de la Société de Géographie, Edition du Centenaire*, p. 259.
2. 'Mémoire sur la réorganisation de la marine, ibid., pp. 246-54.
3. May 1784. Quoted in Brossard, *Lapérouse*, p. 475.
4. Girault de Coursac, *L'Education d'un roi: Louis XVI*, p. 200.
5. The question has been studied by Mrs C. Eustache (*née* Gaziello) in a thesis on the genesis of the voyage, (Paris, 1977) and in her recent book on La Pérouse.
6. Even Cook had his secret instructions, which did not see the light of day until 1927. See W.G. Perrin, 'Instructions to Captain Cook', *Navy Records Society Publications*, lxiii (1927), pp. 341-364.
7. An order allocating the names is dated 26 June 1785. The possibility of the King having mixed up the names, and that this had to be accepted since the King could not err is an interesting and not invalid conjecture.

8. Letter to Fleurieu, 15 March, A.N.M., 3JJ, 386:2.

9. Monneron to La Pérouse, 11 April, A.N.M., 102:9. The portrait, sadly, has not surfaced.

10. 'He had no great reputation for industry or ability', has commented Wickham Legg, in *British Diplomatic Instructions: France 1745-1789*, so one may assume his despatch embodied information that had come to him some time earlier.

11. *Despatches from Paris 1784-1790*, ed. O. Browing, pp. 52-3. The instructions in fact required La Pérouse to check out the possibility of a British settlement in New Zealand.

12. Instructions, quoted by Milet-Mureau in the official account of the voyage, vol. i, p. 29.

13. The English translator of the account of the voyage, published in 1799, estimated the rate of exchange with London at 24 *livres* to 1 pound sterling.

14. Printed in 1974. The reference is on p. 389.

15. Interestingly enough this marriage took place in December 1783, six months after La Pérouse's own.

16. Bartel, *La Jeunesse inédite de Napoléon*, p. 257.

17. Williams, *The Women Bonapartes*, i, p. 52.

18. Letter of 5 April 1787 to Prévost, reprinted in the 1888 *Bulletin du centenaire*, p. 298.

19. Archives Nationales, Colonies, E 314 bis.

14
South and North to Alaska

APART FROM Dufresne, the scientists had received their orders by 28 May 1785. For the previous week and until mid-June, Monneron's purchases had been arriving from England. Lord Dorset thought it was time for another report to Lord Carmathen:

> Monsieur de la Pérouse will sail from Brest the latter end of this month with only two ships. The King had formed great expectations from the intended voyage of that able officer, but M. de la Pérouse himself is less sanguine, and even despairs of succeeding in the search of new discoveries, after the attempts that have already been made by Captain Cooke [sic].

The end of May came and went, but La Pérouse had not sailed. However Dorset picked up some fascinating rumours which he transmitted to the Foreign Secretary on 9 June:

> I had particularly mentioned the orders [La Pérouse] had received to touch at New Zealand, with a design of examining into the nature of the timber there, which . . . is of an excellent quality for repairing ships, but more particularly for masts. I can now inform your Lordship, from good authority, that 60 criminals, from the prison of Bicêtre, were last Monday conveyed under a strong guard and with great secrecy to Brest where they are to be embarked on board M. de la Pérouse's ships, and it is imagined that they are to be left to take possession of this lately discovered Country.[1]

The British government, which knew a great deal more about New Zealand than Lord Dorset, were unmoved. Two days after the date of this despatch, the Maréchal de Castries gave the scientists a farewell dinner at Versailles. Shortly after, they left for Brest. On the 28th, La Pérouse underwent his final meeting with Louis XVI. It is the subject of a famous formal painting by Monsiau now in the

Versailles collection (see p. 219). On the 30th, Castries took La Pérouse to the Trianon Palace to meet Marie-Antoinette, and the next day Jean-François left for Brest. There was no time for any farewells to Eléonore.

De Langle was waiting for him for a few final decisions. Should barter goods be left behind, or food? There was not room for everything. La Pérouse chose to leave 100 sacks of flour and some crates of biscuit, because he could always buy food with the trade goods. Chaos and crowding were inevitable when a ship was on the point of sailing. For the scientists, this new world was well-nigh unbelievable. Not only were the ships crammed below, but the decks looked like a farmyard: there were five cows tied around the mainmast, 30 sheep in the longboat, 20 pigs along the gangways, 200 hens in cages along the poop deck. Perishable food was secured in every corner — sacks of potatoes, beans, fruit, salads, cabbages. Fish hung down from the shrouds, slowly drying in nets. The cabins were small and cramped, and the very presence of the *savants* ensured that normal accommodation would be even more restricted. The main council room in each ship had been partitioned into small cabins; one or two areas separated by lengths of sailcloth were designated studies.

Thus in the *Astrolabe*, de Langle had a cabin on the poop deck, Flassan, Boutervilliers, Law and Lesseps shared the council room, Monti had a cabin on one side of it, Blondelas on the other, Vaujuas and Marchainville had a cupboard-like cabin near them, while D'Aigremont, La Martinière, Prévost and Dufresne were given a partitioned space christened for the occasion *Chambre des Savants*. There would be only minor changes possible to this arrangement for the next two-and-a-half years.

On 11 July 1785 the two ships, with their total complement of 225 men were hauled by boats out into the stream. But the winds were unfavourable, and with steady westerlies blowing there was no chance of making their way out to the open sea. A week went by, then another. The Count d'Hector sent a spare storeship to anchor between the two frigates; it served as a dormitory for the men, reducing the overcrowding while they waited for the wind to change.

It was just as well — another week went by before the voyage could begin.

Finally, on 1 August 1785, to shouts of 'Long Live the King', the *Boussole* and the *Astrolabe* sailed out into the Atlantic.

They had assembled during the summer, prepared their ships and travelled the long twisting roads from Paris in the warm days of June and July. Now again the sun smiled on the men of the expedition. The skies had cleared to a steady blue, the sea moderated to a regular swell, the Atlantic Ocean's breathing. Nothing of note happened on the run south to Madeira, La Pérouse reported, which meant nothing untoward, no blustering gales, no angry rain squalls. There was still congestion on deck and below; the settling into the unfamiliar world of the sea for some, the establishment of a routine for all. They eyed each other as polite strangers, officers who shared memories of past campaigns, scientists for whom the vessels were merely means by which they could set up experiments and seek new specimens. By their very functions they were at odds: for some the time spent at anchor would always be too short, for others the time at sea was the purpose of their lives. There would be clashes at times, inevitably, but the real wonder of it all is how few these were.

The first occurred not at Madeira, but at Tenerife where Lamanon, anxious to climb the Peak and carry out his observations, had to be told that the expedition could not pay for the number of mules the scientist had ordered. Grumbling, Lamanon cut back on the cost and paid it out of his own pocket. The incident revealed to all a split between the two men which La Pérouse outlined in greater detail in a letter to Fleurieu:

> [Lamanon is] a man who is full of zeal but as ignorant as a monk on everything other than systematic physics. He thinks he knows better than M. Buffon how the world was formed: I am convinced neither of them has any idea of it, but there isn't a fifteen-year-old girl in Paris who doesn't know more about the globe than this doctor who has been aiming his spyglass at the tropic ever since the apprentice pilots told him one could see it from a hundred leagues off . . . [he is] a hot head and displays a

meanness which hardly fits the disinterested portrait the Baron de Choiseul drew of him . . . [2]

But excursions ashore were a form of release for the scientists cooped up on board with no real work to do. La Martinière wrote to Thouin that on landing in Madeira his first feeling was a mad desire to run up the mountains. The days must have seemed long between the morning meal, at 9 a.m., when cold meat or soup was served with whatever vegetables were available, and 4 p.m. when the main meal was laid out, consisting of soup, meat, bread, wine and coffee. There were private stores, but they had to be eked out for a voyage of such indeterminate length. And it was not easy to read or work in narrow cabins occupied by two or three men.

Thus Madeira on 13 August and Tenerife on the 19th were memorable ports of call. Crossing to South America was a different matter — six weeks before any land was sighted, and even so it was only the small island of Trinity where the Governor was so frightened of possible designs on the wretched island in his charge that he offered no assistance and prevented the naturalists from examining the flora. It was not until 6 November that the two vessels anchored off the island of Santa Catarina, Brazil.

After nearly a hundred days at sea, La Pérouse had no cases of sickness to report:

> I had neglected none of the precautions experience and caution advised: and in addition we had taken the greatest care to ensure that spirits remained high by making the crew dance every evening, weather permitting, between eight and ten.[3]

Hornpipes and plentiful food had paid handsome dividends.

After a brief stay, La Pérouse set out for Cape Horn. 'We were about to sail through fogs, in seas reputed to be stormy. The two ships could easily become separated'. He told de Langle that, should this happen, they would meet in Le Maire's Strait, and failing that, in Tahiti. At this point, therefore, La Pérouse still intended to follow his original instructions — across the southern Pacific, practically following the tracks of Bougainville as far as the New Hebrides and on to Australia. But there was to be no separation. By Christmas the

Obverse and reverse of the
medal struck for the expedition.

Louis XVI discussing the plan of the voyage with La Pérouse, by
N.A. Monsiau.   (Musée de la Marine.)

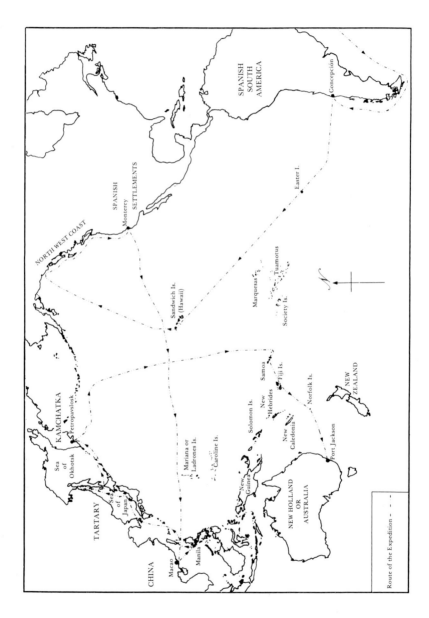

Voyage of La Pérouse 1785-1788

Route of the Expedition – – –

ships were sailing together with a good south-westerly breeze and the southern summer was beginning. In blue skies and calm sea, the officers were even able to lower boats and go shooting for birds. Albatross and petrel, served with a piquant sauce, provided a nice change of diet. 'The sailors preferred them to salted meat, and I think they helped a great deal to keep them in good health'.

By mid-January La Pérouse was sailing south between the coast of South America and the Falkland Islands. A week later he was within sight of the Strait of Magellan, and making speedily for Le Maire's. There was no problem, apart from occasional fog. He veered south-west towards the Horn. 'I turned Cape Horn with far more ease than I had dared to hope'. It made him a little disdainful of its dangers. 'The difficulties one expects to find there are the consequence of an old prejudice that should disappear.'

And now came the change of plan. He had been given discretion and he used it drastically. Instead of sailing west into the South Pacific, he would go north. 'I knew that, if I had not been given such an order, it was only because it was feared I might not have enough time to make such a long voyage before the onset of winter'. But it was only early February. He could easily reach the North-West Coast in time to spend the summer months surveying its innumerable islands and inlets.

Thus he sailed north, along the coast of Chile to the port of Concepción. It was the main town of the southern strip of this long, meandering country squeezed out between the Pacific Ocean and the Andes. It was a strange, closed world, held back by the Spanish policy of exclusiveness which banned all foreign shipping and controlled every facet of its trade. The women's garments belonged to a bygone age — 'made with that old gold or silver cloth we used to manufacture in Lyons' — the manners were redolent of ancient Spain; the district, where barely ten thousand people resided, was filled with convents and monasteries, but there was more superstition about than devotion.

Nothing illustrates more dramatically the remoteness and enforced isolation of Concepción than the fact that La Pérouse could not find it where his charts showed it to be. More than 30 years earlier, an earthquake had so devastated the town that it was decided to rebuild it on a new site eight miles away, but no one in Paris, neither Fleurieu nor his colleagues at the *Dépôt des Cartes et Plans* had been able to inform La Pérouse about it.

It mattered little, for pilots came out to assist him, bringing messages of welcome from the Governor. The Spanish government had passed on news of the French expedition to their South American possessions, and the ships were expected. Fruit, vegetables and fresh meat were brought out in small boats. The Spaniards could not withhold their astonishment: not one of La Pérouse's men was ill, an unheard of situation for vessels arriving from Europe.

The stay lasted three weeks — from 24 February to 17 March 1786 — and it left the most pleasant memories on all sides. For the people of Concepción, it was a welcome relief from crushing boredom; for the French it was a respite from the long months spent at sea. There was a series of receptions, balls and dinners. La Pérouse was able to meet the military commander of the district, 'Monsieur Higuins', who hastened back from one of his endless campaigns against the restive Araucanian Indians. It was Ambrosio O'Higgins, soon to become Governor of Chile, and the father of Bernardo O'Higgins, 'The Liberator'.

Concepción transformed by all the excitement of the daily *fiestas* looked charming and tempting. Two men deserted, whom La Pérouse did not bother to get back. He did not want any reluctant sailors with him. If the country appealed to them so much, let them stay. He noted wryly that in the fishing village of Talcahuano 'every house is a tavern, and the women of the lower classes are as obliging as those of Tahiti'. But he hung on to Dufresne. The unfortunate man was bored, and no one, including himself, seemed too sure why he had joined the expedition; but he did know about trade and the fur market, so that a deal was struck between the two men — Dufresne would report on the fur trade, buy furs from the natives of the North-West Coast and sell them in China. After that, he would be put ashore.

The humanitarian aims of the expedition cannot be overlooked. The exploration of little known areas, hydrographical research, natural history, cartography, ethnography, the assessment of the political balance in the Pacific, the potential for trade, all these had their place in the plan, but there was another aspect:

> Of all the benefits which the King's generosity can bestow on the inhabitants of newly discovered countries, plants that can help feed mankind are without doubt those which will bring them the most lasting benefits and can best increase their happiness.

This was no mere platitude. The ships were packed with seeds, grains, plants, potatoes; and there were still live animals aboard. The inhabitants of Chile had a surplus of crops. The expedition loaded more grains, fruits, fresh meat for its own use. But Concepción hardly qualified as newly discovered, since the settlement dated back to the early sixteenth century.

So La Pérouse, instead of making for Valparaiso or Monterey, sailed west to Easter Island. It enabled him to play his part in eliminating from the charts the Land of Davis, a mythical island which many navigators and geographers had speculated about.

He stayed less than a day at Easter Island. 'We brought them goats, sheep, pigs; we had seeds of orange trees, of lemon trees, of maize, and generally of every species that can succeed in their island'. The French did more. They travelled inland and Collignon sowed cabbages, carrots, pumpkins, maize, beet in soil he considered appropriate, with trees in other places. Was all this owed to the generosity of the King? So ran the fiction, because it was traditional to do everything in the King's name. It may well have been Louis XVI's wish, but this was the age of the *philosophes* and above all of the Noble Savage. For the first time, the two ships had anchored among a primitive people. And Jean-Jacques Rousseau had speculated, in writings which had become enormously popular, that if civilized Europe contained so much that was corrupt and oppressive, civilization itself and not man was the corrupting factor; consequently primitive man, still unaffected by the social and economic evils of civilization, should be happy and indeed noble. It was not his own way of life that European man should bring to the natives, but simply new crops that could raise their standards of life without developing greed and ambition.

Jean-François was no Rousseauite. He was down-to-earth, clear-eyed; a practical man, a sailor with no time for theories evolved by philosophers, academics or drawing-room geographers. Again and again, he would inveigh against those who pontificated without any first-hand experience. Man was man wherever he lived. Kindness need not be blind.

> La Pérouse had already taken a dim view of the goodness of primitive people when, towards the end of the American War, after destroying some British forts on Hudson Bay, he left food and arms for the defeated enemy lest they fall defenceless into the hands of the Indians.[4]

At Easter Island, he found the islanders such shameless thieves that he laughed at their impudence. He took no punitive action. Indeed, seeing them stealing hats from the sailors, he told his men he would replace their losses, so that they would not get angry and start fights to get their property back.

This view of natives was not born of bitterness but of realism. Why should he be led into a false attitude towards human nature by theories evolved in fashionable salons? He had read all the accounts of voyagers who had sailed before him. Marion du Fresne had been through it all, had been attacked in Tasmania and killed in New Zealand; Wallis had been attacked in that paradise of Rousseau's philosophers, Tahiti; Cook had been murdered in Hawaii. What reason could there be for assuming that native people in distant lands were any different from his own men, rogues and drunkards many of them, kept under control only by a stern but paternal discipline, simple, credulous sailors from Brittany or Provence, praying to saints no one else knew much about, or rascals who had fled their homes in search of adventure, quick to wench and quick to brawl?

Although he was a product of the Jesuits, La Pérouse verged on the agnostic, but he was more tempted to believe in original sin than in natural goodness. Above all, he responded to what he saw, laughing with the good humour of the southerner, while shaking his head at human behaviour. The Easter Islanders were not thieves because of their innocence, unaware of any difference between the 'thine' and the 'mine'; no, they were merely bold pickpockets

The French on Easter Island. The composition shows wit, but the figures are heavily romanticized.
(Engraving from the *Voyage*, 1797)

who knew what they were about. 'I esteem them far less because they seemed capable of reflection', he wrote — but this is merely realism and far from Rousseau's extreme view that 'the state of reflection goes against nature and a man who ponders is a depraved being'. He would be equally clear-eyed and unsentimental on the North-West Coast; he would be unimpressionable in Kamchatka; and he would note in the Samoan Islands that Lamanon who had remarked 'these men are worth more than us' was killed by the islanders the next day.

La Pérouse's view is not that of a *philosophe* in the Age of Enlightenment, nor of a traditionalist. It is pragmatic, closer to the physiocrats who were at that very moment attempting to reform the economic structure of France, and who were motivated by the belief in 'progress' that was to be the hallmark of the nineteenth century bourgeois. He had criticized both the policy of Spanish exclusiveness and the number of religious establishments in Chile because they stood in the way of economic progress. In California, he would criticize the missionaries because they were not civilizing the local Indians quickly enough into active Europeans. He was against religion where it preached inaction; he disliked the monks because they were contemplative, but praised them when they acted like missionaries of progress. One is tempted to point out in this context how firmly he had insisted on his ship's chaplains being useful crew members as well as pious men.

So he took his precautions, landed on Easter Island with armed men, guffawed at the antics of the thieves, dispensed gifts and forgiveness in equal doses, but harboured no illusions. He sailed away during the night. This was all the punishment he wished to inflict:

> I flattered myself that when, at dawn, they saw our ships had gone, they would attribute our prompt departure to our just displeasure with their activities, and that this thought might make them better men.

Precautions were also needed in the next island group which the two ships called at — the Hawaiian Islands, then known as the Sandwich Islands from the name James Cook had given them. It was here that the famous English navigator had been killed, for reasons Europeans could only ascribe to perfidiousness, since only days earlier the islanders had feted him. So on 30 May 1786, La Pérouse landed on Maui, protected by 40 armed soldiers. He need not have worried. The reception the islanders gave him was as friendly as anyone could wish. They brought him pigs; he gave them axes, lengths of iron, and some of the commemorative medals that had been specially struck for the expedition. This was barter, not theft:

> My imagination was attracted by the thought of comparing them to the Indians of Easter Island . . . every advantage was on the side of those men of the Sandwich Islands, even though I was wholly prejudiced against them on account of the death of Captain Cook. It is more natural for navigators to regret so great a man than to examine coolly whether some incautious action on his part might not have, in some way, forced the inhabitants of Oahu to resort to justified self-defence.

As far as he knew, no other Europeans had landed on Maui. Strictly, he could have laid claim to the island in the name of Louis XVI, but he considered such a practice ridiculous and immoral. What right have Europeans, he wrote, to lands their inhabitants have worked with the sweat of their brow and which for centuries have been the burial place of their ancestors?

> Modern navigators have no other purpose than to complete the history of man; their navigation must complete the survey of the globe, and the light they try to shed have no other aim than making happier the people they visit and add to their means of subsistence.

After 48 hours, sailing along the west coast of the islands, La Pérouse passed through Kauai Channel, north of Oahu, towards the more austere Alaskan coast.

⊛

By 6 June, the weather was becoming colder, the sky whiteish and dull. Soon fog appeared, damp and clinging. The sailors' clothes were cold and wet, 'with never a ray of sunshine to dry them'. The surgeon suggested adding quinquina to the morning grog, but it had to be done secretly, 'otherwise the men would certainly have refused to drink it'. Whales 'of the largest species', loons and ducks showed that land was not far. On the 23rd, at 4 a.m., the fog parted and suddenly a long chain of snow-covered mountains stretched out ahead. The ships had reached Mt St Elias.

It was here that Vitus Bering had sailed in the *St Peter* in 1741. What he had seen at the height of the northern summer was what La Pérouse now saw in the same season: 'a sterile treeless land . . . a black plateau, as though burnt out by some fire, devoid of any greenery, a striking contrast with the whiteness of the snow we could make out through the clouds'. But this was the world of the sea otter, the Alaskan seal, the blue and the Arctic foxes. It was the heart of the fur trade. Bering had died miserably on his way home, the coastline barely charted, but enough of his crew had returned to Kamchatka with tales of a dense population of fur-bearing animals for the fur rush to begin. Although until 1775 only Russians sailed the Alaskan coast, the numbers of the fur animals and indeed of the Aleut Islanders dropped dramatically. But there was still a great deal of money to be made. The Spanish, anxious to preserve their claims to the entire Pacific seaboard, sent Juan Perez in 1774 to Queen Charlotte Islands. In 1775 Juan Francisco Bodega reached the site of modern Sitka in southern Alaska. All this was claimed for Spain, but in 1778 James Cook staked a claim for England and charted the coastline with his usual precision.

In 1781 the Russians formed a trading company under Gregor Shelikov and the first European settlement was implanted, not on the continent, but on Kokiak Island, strategically situated in the western part of the Gulf of Alaska. Now the French had come, with Dufresne assiduously writing notes for a report on the fur trade and France's chances of joining in the bonanza. For La Pérouse, hydrography was more important. However careful Cook's surveys may have been, there were innumerable inlets and bays in this deeply indented coast, and many of them were still very imperfectly known. There was also the tantalizing possibility of a North-West Passage, from the Atlantic to the Pacific, the northern pendant to Magellan's Strait in the south. People had sought it in vain from the Atlantic side: it might be possible to discover it from the Pacific coast.

In fog which parted at times only to reform, the two ships sailed slowly down the coast. On the 26th, La Pérouse sent three boats to reconnoitre a bay which might be a useful inlet. It led nowhere, but as Monti had led the survey La Pérouse gave it his name. It was in all probability Yakutat Bay, no mean bay, but no passage to the interior either. The fog closed in again. To ensure he could chart the coast without a break, he tacked out to sea, then back again. It was slow, bone-chilling work off a coast that remained bleak and inhospitable. Cook had found the same difficulties.

'The confounded fog . . . a thick fog and a foul wind are rather disagreeable intruders, to people engaged in surveying and tracing a coast', wrote Charles Clerke, during Cook's last voyage when many blank and ill-defined spaces had to be left on the charts. La Pérouse was determined to fill them in.

By 1 July 1786 the ships were just west of Mount Fairweather. Time and again, the boats were lowered to examine the coast. Along it there were now men waving and canoes manoeuvring between the rocks. The next day a bay appeared, shown on no chart and, La Pérouse assumed, never before sighted. It was wide, its waters still and calm. 'If the French government had any plans for a trading post in this part of the American coast, no nation could claim any right to oppose it'. He called it Port des Français — and sailed into it. It is now known as Lituya Bay.

Excellent though it proved as an anchorage, sailing in presented some problems. The wind changed, there were rocks not far below the surface. 'Never in the thirty years that I have spent at sea have I seen two ships so near destruction'.

The danger once behind him, La Pérouse could settle in for a stay of almost a month. A camp was set up on a small island, and the scientists began their observations, while the men collected firewood and fresh water and La Pérouse organized the exploration of this tortuous inlet. The bay seemed to be closed by great glaciers, five of them, grinding their way slowly from steep bare mountains, the silence broken only by the cries of lonely wild birds and the occasional fall of enormous blocks of ice:

> It was at the back of this bay that we hoped to find channels by which we could enter into the interior of America. We supposed that it might

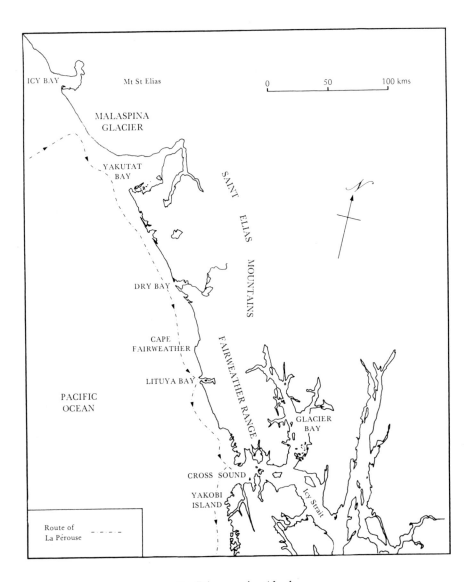

ICY BAY

Mt St Elias

0   50   100 kms

MALASPINA
GLACIER

YAKUTAT
BAY

SAINT ELIAS MOUNTAINS

N

DRY BAY

CAPE
FAIRWEATHER

FAIRWEATHER RANGE

LITUYA BAY

PACIFIC
OCEAN

GLACIER
BAY

CROSS SOUND

YAKOBI
ISLAND

Icy Strait

Route of
La Pérouse

La Pérouse in Alaska

lead to some great river running between two mountains, and that this river might have its source in one of the great lakes of northern Canada.

But there was no way through. The fiords were closed off by waterfalls, ice, or sheer rock faces, so that 'in a few hours we completed our trip into the interior of America'. If this was summer, how dismal a place would Lituya Bay be in winter? Could anyone really contemplate a settlement in such a spot, even with the rewards to be gained from the fur trade? The natives were unprepossessing, willing to trade fish and furs for clothing, nails and implements, but even more willing to steal. Law and d'Arbaud, on duty at the observatory, were robbed of a musket, their spare clothes and a notebook in which the astronomical observations had been entered. 'I am willing', wrote La Pérouse, 'to admit that it is impossible for a society to exist without some virtues, but I am forced to state that I did not have the wisdom to notice any'. As for the women, he dismissed them as 'repulsive'.

Nevertheless, and without much faith in the transaction, he agreed to buy the island from the man he took to be the local chief, but without the Eskimo interpreter which Monneron had hoped to recruit in London it was not easy to communicate with him. It is unlikely in any case that an interpreter could have been found who understood the particular language of these people. For their part, the Tlingit people had taken the French at first for the servants of Yehlh, their bird creator, who had returned to earth in the form of a raven. It was only after an elderly warrior had ventured on board the vessels that they realized these were men in some gigantic form of canoe, and not spirits. From that moment, the French became fair game for thieves — strangers towards whom no hospitality was due.[5]

While La Pérouse was readying the ships for departure, Monneron and Bernizet completed their charting of the bay. Then disaster struck — 'disaster more cruel than sickness and the thousand other happenings of the longest voyages'. D'Escures was sent to sound the bay, so that Monneron could show the various depths on his chart. La Pérouse cautioned him not to venture too close to the rocks near the pass which had proved so dangerous when the expedition had first entered the bay. Apart from that, they could go hunting ashore and picnic. 'It was as much an outing as it was useful'. But d'Escures went too close, the tide was racing madly, and first his boat then the *Astrolabe's* pinnace were carried away and capsized. It was all over in less than 10 minutes.

Six officers and 15 men were drowned, including d'Escures, Pierrevert, La Pérouse's young cousin Montarnal, Flassan and both Labordes. There were no bodies washed ashore, merely the implacable sea breaking on the black rocks. La Pérouse erected a small cairn on the island, which he named Cenotaph Island, placing underneath a bottle with a message setting out the tragedy and giving the names of the dead. Lamanon composed the message:

> At the entrance to this port twenty-one brave sailors perished. Whoever you are, mix your tears with ours.

The tragedy affected La Pérouse for a long time. The blame lay with d'Escures, he had no doubt of that, but as if he felt the need to justify his own actions beyond argument he copied at length the instructions he had given him in writing, including the warnings about the pass, and indeed the admonishment he gave d'Escures after his second-in-command 'asked me if I took him for a child'. A man of 33, who had already commanded warships! he added. What more could he have done?

The death of the two Laborde brothers was particularly tragic. On 3 May 1787 Lord Dorset reported the tragedy to London:

> Two sons of Mons. de la Borde [formerly the Court Banker] were unfortunately drowned on this occasion, to the great grief of their family who are inconsolable at the loss of two very promising young men.[6]

Tragedy was to continue to pursue the family: their father would be guillotined in 1794.

Unfavourable winds, the hope that some survivors might yet be found, and the need to make a number of changes on board the ships kept the expedition in Port des Français until 30 July. The deaths eased the pressure on space; it was melancholy work, but the belongings of the dead men had to be moved, some to be stored,

Lituya Bay. The boats are lost on the bar.
(Engraving from the *Voyage*, 1797)

some to be auctioned, and their cabins altered to provide greater comfort for the living. And there were promotions: d'Arbaud to *enseigne*, and Broudou to *lieutenant de frégate*.

La Pérouse by now realized how impossible was the task he had been set. The innumerable inlets of the coast would require months of painstaking exploration if the ridddle of the North-West Passage was ever to be solved, but he had to keep his sense of proportion. His voyage was one of general Pacific exploration. He had been delayed for three weeks in Lituya Bay, and less than three months had been allowed to survey the entire coastline, largely because he would have to devote the following summer months to exploring the colder regions of the Asiatic coast:

> All my plans had to be subordinated to the imperious need to reach Manila by the end of January and China in February in order to spend the next summer surveying the coasts of Tartary, Japan, Kamchatka and the Aleutian Islands.

The result was an extraordinary period of activity, in which all on board were mobilized, charting, surveying, checking, sacrificing only the time-consuming reconnaissance of minor bays and inlets. In effect, he was compelled to drop the search for a North-West Passage. He was gradually coming to the belief that it was a chimera, a theory evolved with no backing evidence by those who believed that somehow the world had to be a symmetrical concept and that a southern strait must be balanced by a northern passage.

On 4 August 1786, the fog cleared to reveal Cross Sound, marking the beginning of the Alexander Archipelago. If the sea was fair, the winds were contrary. In 24 hours the French covered less than 10 leagues. The coast was wooded, the snow-covered ranges had fallen away to the north or lay hidden behind the persistent low cloud. 'Here, I am convinced, we could find twenty different harbours'. The fog, swirling in each evening, parted reluctantly when the sun rose again. Sitka Sound opened out, then the protean inlets of Baranof Island with so many headlands and hills 'that it is enough to change one's position a little to change their appearance'.

Christian Sound, 'a great opening', marked the beginning of the southern part of the archipelago and the many islands that lie off-shore from Prince of Wales Island like retainers protecting their master. The westerly breeze was more favourable, but the currents drove the ships towards the open sea. The Spanish charts were of little help. 'Maurelle's Bucarelli harbour is in this part: I have found nothing in his map or in his account that could enlighten me'.

By the 9th La Pérouse was crossing Dixon Entrance towards Queen Charlotte Islands. A strong north-westerly breeze helped, but the fog was closing in. 'By seven thirty in the evening we were less than a league from the coast but we could hardly see it'. There was a brief glimpse of land on the 10th, but the wind increased to a fresh gale and the ships veered away. On the 11th, not far from Cape Knox on Graham Island, the fog was so thick that the *Astrolabe* could not be seen from the *Boussole*, even though shouted orders could be heard. Four days went by, frustrating and filled with danger, for the winds had dropped. On the 17th the fog cleared and careful observations were possible. The French were in latitude 53° 12', within sight of Moresby Island, a lonely world of deep inlets and tall dark trees, filled with the cries of seabirds.

Suddenly, 'the coast of America' seemed to end. It was the southern tip of the Queen Charlotte Islands to which La Pérouse gave the name of the man who had done so much to help with the preparations in Brest, Count D'Hector; today, Cap Hector has assumed the name of Cape St James. Fleurieu, whose name went to grace the northern point of Vancouver Island has fared no better.

Thus, the expedition was passing Queen Charlotte Sound and starting its survey of the west coast of Vancouver Island. It was a matter of completing Cook's work. Ideas about discovering a north-west passage had gone. So La Pérouse avoided Queen Charlotte Sound and, later, Juan de Fuca Strait; this decision lost him the opportunity of making his mark on the hydrography of the region, but it saved him from becoming bottled up in the narrowing straits behind Vancouver Island, and from the disappointment of having to turn back from one of the inlets of the coast; Vancouver Island is far too large a land mass for anyone to guess it does not form part of the continent itself.

Clearer weather would have helped, but fogs remained his persistent companions. August was running out, an early autumn was pursuing him down the coast. He had difficulty even in identifying points visited by the Spaniards — which was not surprising since so many of the reports were vague and the old charts fanciful. Even Cook's Nootka Sound was hard to find: on 25 August, 'a very thick fog, rising up at about five in the afternoon hid the land altogether'. It lasted five days, making a sighting of Juan de Fuca Strait impossible. And now the coastline changed. There were few bays, but violent coastal currents. This was Oregon. There was work to be done from 47° to 45° north, since Cook had not charted this coast in detail, but fogs, currents and calms hampered the French survey. It was slow, dangerous, irritating work.

The first half of September was spent on this. The scientists welcomed the fog, which gave them a chance to rest, the sailors found it increasingly exhausting, as the two ships had to change course, alter sails, and manoeuvre close together. The decks were constantly wet, the rigging ever cold and clammy. Each headland was like another prayer for deliverance along a string of beads: Cape Flattery, Cape Lookout, Cape Blanco, Cape Mendocino, Point Arena, Point Reyes, and at last the wide expanse of Monterey Bay.

On 15 September 1786, the *Boussole* and the *Astrolabe* dropped anchor, two cable lengths from land. The Spanish sent pilots on board, and the fort of Monterey fired its gun salute in welcome.

Notes

1. Browning, O. (ed.), *Despatches from Paris*, p. 58.
2. La Pérouse to Fleurieu, 28 August 1785, A.N.M. 3JJ 386: 2-19.
3. Quotations on the voyage are mostly taken from La Pérouse's manuscript in Archives Nationales, Paris, 3JJ: 386-389, and specific source references will be omitted in this and subsequent chapters. The text has now been published by the Imprimerie nationale, Paris, *Le Voyage de Lapérouse 1785-1788* (Dunmore, J. & Brossard, M. de, eds) 2 vols, Paris. 1985.
4. McKenna, 'The Noble Savage in the *Voyage* of La Pérouse', *Kentucky Foreign Language Quarterly*, 1965, No. 1, p. 29.

5. See Emmons, 'Native account of the Meeting between La Pérouse and the Tlingit' *American Anthropologist*, 1911, pp. 294-8.
6. *Despatches from Paris 1784-1790*, p. 188.

15
California to China

MONTEREY was a mere 15 years old when La Pérouse arrived. The bay had been discovered in 1602 by Sebastian Vizcaino who over-praised it, so that when the Spanish decided to establish a settlement there in 1770 they had difficulty in even recognizing it and over-looked the far superior harbour of San Francisco, a mere 40 miles further north.

At first, the Spanish found conditions so harsh that they con-templated abandoning the place altogether — a familiar pattern in the story of colonization. An overland route from Mexico to Cali-fornia was essential. The trail was blazed in 1773 from the Sonora, thus linking Monterey with the rest of Spanish America. There were problems, uprisings by Indians, unruly soldiers, erratic supplies, but gradually a chain of mission stations was established. Most were still miserable establishments, poorly kept, unprosperous. The San Carlos mission at Monterey, soon moved to the Carmel River further south, outshone the rest. Recruiting settlers was more difficult than finding Franciscans willing to run the missions; most of those who came were soldiers, glad enough to marry and farm a small strip of land in this fertile district. Apart from the squabbles of petty officials, the religious festivals and the occasional threat of an Indian raid, Alta California slumbered quietly in pastoral simplicity.

The arrival of the *Astrolabe* and the *Boussole* was a welcome break in the sleepy routine of Monterey. News had already travelled from Concepción that the French were likely to come and should be received as guests of the King. Here were the first foreign vessels to enter the bay, the first Frenchmen to visit Spanish California, men of education and talent, and moreover men who brought news of the distant north coast where, before long, Spain would clash with Russia and Britain. The Governor — of the two Californias, as his grandiose title put it — was a pioneering figure in his own right.

Pedro Fages had left Sonora as a mere lieutenant in charge of a couple of dozen soldiers back in 1769; he had served under Galvez and Portola, and worked tirelessly and efficiently to build up the settlement:

> His government covers an area more than eight hundred leagues in circumference; but his real subordinates are two hundred and ninety-two cavalrymen who have to supply garrisons for five small forts and squads of five or six men to each of the twenty-five missions established in the old and the new California. Such small means are enough to contain approximately fifty thousand Indians who roam this vast part of America, of whom about ten thousand have embraced Christianity.

Coping with the demands of the Franciscans required all of Fages' skills. The viceroy in Mexico usually gave him a free hand, although occasionally forced to arbitrate between his secular representative and the spiritual powers of the missionaries, currently represented by Fermin Francisco de Lasuen, another great figure of early California. On the whole, they coexisted satisfactorily. Lasuen was in the process of transforming the economy of the country. Mission industries were being set up to diversify the agriculturally-based mission stations. Artisans were being brought from Mexico, the Indians were being taught carpentry, house building and a wide range of new trades. It was the organization and aims of the missions which most impressed La Pérouse. These were no obscurantist priests living on tithes and benefices, but pioneers developing for their flock a new social and economic structure. The enterprise was based on paternalism, but to a Galaup this was a sound and sensible basis for a society, far better than the romantic sentimentality of the Noble Savage supporters.

Consequently, much of La Pérouse's journal of his 10-day stay consists of detailed comments on the administration of the missions. They provide an invaluable outsider's report on the early days of California, punctuated by notes of appreciation for the kindness shown to him by the people, who pressed gifts on him, sent supplies of all kinds on board and had to be forced to accept anything in return:

> It is with the happiest satisfaction that I can make known the pious and

La Pérouse memorial at San Carlos Mission, Carmel, California.

The old mission church, San Carlos Mission, Carmel, California.

wise behaviour of these priests who are carrying out so perfectly the aims of their order: I will not conceal what I considered reprehensible in their internal practices; but I will say that, being individually good and humane, they temper the austerity of the rules drawn up by their superiors with their gentleness and their charity . . . . The monks, in answering our questions, kept nothing from us about this kind of religious community; for one can give no other name to the legislation they have set up: they are its superiors in the temporal as well as in the spiritual sense; the products of the land are entrusted to their administration. There are seven hours of work each day, two hours of prayer and four or five on Sundays and feast days which are entirely devoted to rest and worship.

Life was organized communally, with food cooked centrally and distributed to each family, and with the tribal structure and customs retained to the extent that this was compatible with Christianity. It was, in its way, a strangely medieval world, as with serfs attached to a monastery, but without the abbot having the temporal power of a feudal lord. The missionaries had so far succeeded in keeping its lay equivalent — the Governor of Monterey — at bay, but their theocracy, which had arrested time in a world of its own, could not forever resist the growth of secularism. Eventually, the very prosperity and fertility of California would overwhelm it.

La Pérouse's no-nonsense approach to native peoples saved him from viewing the Indians romantically; it made him equally cleareyed about the Spanish. Here was a land of 'inexpressible fertility' in which progress was held back by an economic and political structure that belonged to another age. There was no trade, no enterprise, no ambition. The missionaries impeded the Indian's intellectual development: the Spanish policy of exclusiveness isolated California from the rest of the world and even from other Spanish territories.

There were signs that this would not last. The key was the fur trade which had already attracted Spanish attention:

We found at Monterey a Spanish official named Vincent Vassadre y Vega; he had brought instructions for the Governor to gather all the otter skins of his four *presidios* and ten missions . . . M. Fages assured me he could supply ten thousand of them; and as he knew the country he added that if the China trade involved a turnover of thirty thousand skins, two or three establishments north of San Francisco would soon provide them.

La Pérouse's arrival confirmed Spain's fears that other European nations were beginning to take more than a passing interest in the fur trade. Cook was being followed by La Pérouse, just as Dixon would follow the French, and over the entire North-West Coast there loomed the threat of a Russian advance. The Spanish would shortly send Martinez in the *Princesa* and Haro in the *San Carlos* to check on all these reports — and the stage would then be set for the Nootka crisis which almost led to a major war.

On 23 September 1786, the French sailed from Monterey Bay, assisted by Martinez's sailors. 'I can only inadequately express my gratitude', wrote Jean-François. It was not only Martinez and other naval officers, but Fages, Lasuen and his missionaries, the soldiers even 'who had rendered a thousand services'. In return, Collignon had planted potatoes and other seeds, but California was a real paradise — 'the gardens of the Governor and the missions were filled with an infinity of vegetables' — and the ships were laden with supplies in preparation for the crossing of the Pacific.

La Pérouse had obtained an old Spanish chart of the central Pacific. It did not seem to be very different from one he had found in Anson's *Voyage*. Not a great deal had been discovered in 150 years. La Pérouse's first task was to look for the island of Nostra Señora de la Gorta: its existence was doubtful and he eliminated it finally from the map. On the other hand, he discovered an island far to the north-west of Hawaii, which he named Necker Island in honour of the famous Minister of Finance who had recently attempted, and failed to reform France's chaotic tax system. The island was as austere as his opponents accused Necker's policy of being: 'it is really only a rock about a thousand yards long . . . there is no tree visible . . . the rock is bare . . . the sides were steep, like a well, and the sea broke wildly everywhere'.

It was a danger later navigators needed to be aware of. How little known these seas were was shown a few evenings later. It was the finest night and the calmest seas the French had seen since they had left Monterey: this made the dangers ahead all the more vicious, since the waves were scarcely breaking on the rocks that waited silently ahead. When the lookout sighted them they were a mere 350 yards away. The ships veered just in time. By then the depth had fallen to nine fathoms. The frigates sailed to the south, no more than a couple of hundred yards away. It had been so sudden, so eerie, that La Pérouse began to wonder whether it had not been a mere illusion.

Too many navigators have left a mirage on the charts. He needed to be sure. He sailed back in the morning and there it was — a rocky islet surrounded by reefs and sandbanks 'like a circle of diamonds surrounding a medallion'. He named it French Frigates Shoals, a name it has retained.

His route now took him towards the Mariana Islands. Asunción Island, in the north of the group, was reached on 14 December 1786. It was a bitter disappointment:

> The most vivid imagination could scarcely create a more horrible place. The most ordinary sight would, after such a long crossing, have appeared a delight to us — but a perfect cone with a surrounding area, up to eighty yards above sea level, which was as black as coal, could only cause despondency by disappointing our hopes, because for the last few weeks, we had been talking of the turtles and coconuts we believed we would find in the Marianas.

There were in fact some coconut trees on the island. The French obtained about a hundred nuts, although with some difficulty; but they were suffering from the strain of a long voyage which often causes sailors to over-estimate, or in this case under-estimate, an eventual landfall. Thus Tahiti had looked like a paradise associated with all the lyrical legends of Ancient Greece when Bougainville reached it in 1768 — and so Tahiti had received extravagant praise as the abode of virtues and the home of the Noble Savage.

Strain was appearing in other directions. The French had been at sea for nearly three months. All they had seen apart from the endless sea was Necker Island, French Frigates Shoal and now Asunción — a bleak trio indeed. The sailors and the officers had their daily routine to occupy them: the scientists had very little to do. Once they had written their reports, sorted their specimens, checked over their meagre library, what remained to be done during the long hot days and the equally long hot nights? It was easier for the astronomers who could work with the officers, but the naturalists were frankly bored. Lamanon, ever proud and rebellious to discipline, clashed with La Pérouse and became the leader of a cabal. When the *Boussole* and the *Astrolabe* arrived in Macao on 1 January 1787, La Pérouse naturally stayed aboard, but the scientists took quarters ashore: he was neither consulted nor told where. Receptions were held in the normal course of events, to which they were not invited. Lamanon, Lamartinière, Monges and Father Receveur wrote him a letter of complaint, but how could he invite them, came the reply, when he did not know where they lived? They answered that it would not have been difficult for him to find out if he had really bothered to make the effort. Angered by this insolence, La Pérouse had them brought to the ships and kept under arrest for 24 hours. They had to learn who was in charge and what naval discipline meant.

Letters went off to Paris, each side putting its case to the Minister. La Pérouse unburdened himself in a letter to Fleurieu: 'I must admit that these Lamanons and Monges have tired me of all these learned makers of systems'. Dagelet he could stand, but these others 'above all Lamanon' were 'devilish fellows who try my patience beyond endurance'. Dagelet, the mild hardworking astronomer, had written a letter to his cousin Sully on arrival in Macao which gave in simple terms the background of the quarrel: 'We have just completed a voyage of over a hundred days, it has seemed like a thousand to everyone, and like most on board I needed a landfall. But everything is over. I will settle on land amongst the Chinese and there I hope get back to normal in a few days'. Wisely, the Minister had the letters filed away and the argument, which was months old by the time he learnt of it, was forgotten.

Macao was a world apart, a strange, irrational European toehold on the great inimical land of China, surviving on sufferance, the target of contempt and fear. It dated back to 1557, and was in fact not a Portuguese colony but still a Chinese possession leased to Portugal. It was less a gateway to Canton than a foreign settlement tolerated by the Chinese to contain foreigners and limit their influence. Beyond Macao, China remained a dangerous closed world, eternal and enigmatic.

It was above all a source of great wealth. There were 41 foreign ships at anchor, including 29 flying the English flag, five the Dutch, but only two from France. It illustrated with vivid accuracy the relative positions of the European powers in Canton.

One of the French ships was the *Marquis-de-Castries* newly arrived from Manila, part of a small force commanded by Bruny d'Entrecastreaux and intended to protect French traders in Eastern waters. It was no easy task, with constant vexations by Chinese administrators and the haughty jealousy of the English India Company. In fact, d'Entrecastreaux was to be surprisingly effective in countering this combined opposition. In another context, his link with La Pérouse was a sad one: when the expedition disappeared, d'Entrecastreaux was to be sent on a long and, unhappily, fruitless search.

However pleasant it was to meet French officers again, La Pérouse and all on board were bitterly disappointed by the absence of letters from home. The ship that was expected to bring them from the Ile de France had been held up. It was little consolation to hear general news about the situation in Europe 'which was absolutely the same as when we had left it'. The Portuguese Governor tried to make La Pérouse as welcome as he could: he had been in Goa 12 years earlier when Jean-François was in command of the *Seine*, and there he had married. Now Dona Maria entertained him surrounded by her children. 'Nowhere in the world could anyone find a more delightful picture: the most beautiful of children surrounded the loveliest of mothers'. Jean-François' thoughts would have gone back to Eléonore. The lack of mail meant there was no letter from her. She had thought herself pregnant for a while, but it had been a false alarm. Would she have a second chance?

His thoughts turned to other problems. The furs had to be sold, but prices had plummeted since the days of Gore and King. Furs that would have fetched 100 *piastres* in 1780 now fetched less than 15. The best were set aside to be forwarded to Queen Marie-Antoinette. Dufresne, who was to be left behind, much to his relief, would take them back to France, but as it turned out his help was needed in another direction. La Pérouse had contracted to sell a thousand furs to a Portuguese dealer. The price, an average of nine and a half *piastres*, was low enough, but the cash was not forthcoming and the time of sailing was approaching. Chinese merchants were brought in, but knowing the position the French were in made an offer that was even lower. There was nothing for it but to store the furs and let Dufresne continue the negotiations. The French Vice-consul, Philippe Vieillard, did his best to help. It was little enough, for the consulate was hardly influential, but it helped save the French from being cheated.

The stay in Macao proved to be a mixed bag. It might be fine for the scientists who wanted a break from the strains of shipboard life, but it was fraught with danger for the men for whom the town had little to offer but taverns and brothels. Macao, with an overwhelmingly Chinese population, was surrounded by a wall beyond which no foreigner could go. The teeming world of China was not a place a Frenchman could venture in: if he got into a scrape, he could not be helped; if he were robbed or beaten, there would be little chance of redress.

On 5 February 1787, the *Boussole* and the *Astrolabe* sailed out, taking six Chinese sailors aboard each frigate to make up for the losses sustained in Lituya Bay.

16
From China to Russia

AT MOST, the French would have been non-committal about their stay in Macao. It was a new experience, different from anything they had met with previously, but they could hardly have left with regrets or looked back with nostalgia. Macao was a claustrophobic world. There had been a chance to rest during those four weeks, some pleasant interludes, a few receptions, but no strolls in a pleasant countryside, no excursions along a quiet seashore.

Instead, there had been vexations and arguments both among themselves and with the town's traders. Even the climate had not smiled on them: 'most of us had a temperature and heavy colds which disappeared when we reached the more pleasant climate of Luzon'.

This was three weeks later, on 28 February 1787, when the two ships dropped anchor in Cavite, the port of Manila Bay. Before that, they had stopped at a small island to buy wood which was believed to be more expensive in Manila. It provided at last an opportunity to walk ashore amid peaceful surroundings:

> I went down to the village at around midday. It consists of some forty houses built of bamboo, covered with leaves, and raised about four feet above the ground. These houses have a floor of small bamboo, not joined together, which give these huts the appearance of bird cages; one climbs up by a ladder and I doubt that the materials used for such a house, roofing included, weigh more than two hundred pounds.

The Spanish authorities were a little surprised that the French should prefer the dull neighbourhood of Cavite to the colour and social life of Manila where the population was close to 40,000. News of the expedition had been received from Spain months earlier and the Governor was eager to welcome La Pérouse, but Cavite was where the shipyards were situated and the ships could be repaired easily and more cheaply.

There were opportunities for visits to Manila, in spite of a mediocre road and the great heat. The Spanish very sensibly disappeared for a lengthy midday siesta, but the French found it hard to accustom themselves to the practice. However early they left the ships in the morning they could hardly pay their calls and return to Cavite before late afternoon. La Pérouse had all the time he needed to appraise the state of the colony and pass his usual down-to-earth judgement on its administration and prospects. The beauty of the scenery, the blue expanse of Manila Bay, the colourfulness of its busy streets, the exotic blend of races, might enthuse the romantics among his officers: his own objectiveness was never impaired.

For one thing, the Philippines were not a colony in the true sense of the word, a place like California where colonists were encouraged to settle. Luzon was more a feudal dependency of the King of Spain who had divided most of it into large estates, a number of them allocated to religious orders. Consequently the Philippines were 'still like the landed estates of great noblemen that remain fallow but could make a fortune for several families'.

Manila was excellently situated to become a great trading centre. That it was not, was due to a number of reasons. Basic was the Spanish policy of exclusiveness which protected their American possessions at the expense of the Philippines. The Edict of 1593 had banned direct trade between the Philippines and Spain; goods, in theory at least, had to be shipped to Europe by way of Spanish America, which was absurdly uneconomic. Gold and other precious goods could be sent by only one ship a year — the famous Manila Galleon which even then was limited to a cargo value of three quarters of a million *pesos*. Contraband and false declarations helped to raise this total — the *San Jose* in 1784 had taken almost three million *pesos'* worth — but it still throttled the economy of the Philippines.

In addition, Spain lacked the foothold in China which Macao represented for Portugal, and consequently the geographical advantage which Manila possessed could not be exploited. Indeed the reverse occurred: junks from China came each June for the Manila Fair, bringing silks, tea, jade and porcelain. To benefit from this, Spain would have needed a strong merchant navy and Manila the right to send ships by the Cape of Good Hope route. Instead, only luxury goods were traded, to fill the Manila Galleon, and the great opportunities offered by the eastern trade fell to the English, the Dutch and the French.

The Governor who welcomed La Pérouse was Don Basco y Vargas, an enlightened man who had been struggling since 1778 to change the centuries-old policy of Madrid. He was on the verge of success. A Company of the Philippines had been set up, to trade in competition with the monopolistic annual galleon. In 1789, Madrid would finally decide to turn Manila into a free port. It could have become the emporium of the East had this move been made earlier. As it was, although Manila's trade boomed — there would be 50 trading vessels in Manila by 1795 — it was too late. The influence of Great Britain would soon become overwhelming.

The climate had it drawbacks, particularly at the beginning of the hot season, which normally lasts from April to July. The French spent March and early April in Manila Bay, and they found what often happens at this time of year: the temperature rising into the nineties. The colds and fevers were replaced by stomach cramps. In the case of Lamanon and d'Aigremont, these developed into dysentery. Local remedies were of little avail. The stifling heat made the narrow cabins unbearable. On 25 March, d'Aigremont died. Apart from a servant who had died of tuberculosis during the crossing to Easter Island, this was the first case of death by illness the expedition had to record.

In the meantime, Bruny d'Entrecasteaux himself had reached Canton on his flag-showing mission, found La Pérouse gone and sent the frigate *Subtile* to bring him news and an offer of help. The news was stale — over 10 months old — but the help was welcome. La Pérouse took one officer and four men for each of his ships. Pierre Le Gobien, an officer in his early twenties, joined the *Astrolabe*; Pierre-Louis Guillet de La Villeneuve, a couple of years older, joined the *Boussole*; but young Mel de Saint-Céran's health was giving concern, and rather than risk a second death in Manila Bay, La Pérouse sent him home. The *Boussole* had gained Gabriel de Bellegarde, a young man from the storeship *Maréchal-de-*

Castries, while in Macao, so numbers were adequately balanced. Nothing, however, could be done to compensate for the losses sustained in North America.

Although the Spanish warned La Pérouse that the north-east monsoon would continue for another month, he decided to take a chance and sail for Formosa (as Taiwan was then known) and Japan on 9 April 1787. To begin with, luck favoured him. Within a few days he had sailed up the coast of Luzon to Cape Bojador. Then the monsoon blew so steadily that it seemed determined to show how wrong the French had been and how right the Spanish. Formosa was not sighted until the 21st. The winds remained implacable.

Hoping that the north-easterly might be less strong and regular in Formosa Strait, the French sailed up along the west coast of the island. It was a dangerous decision. Formosa had rebelled against her Chinese overlords and a Chinese fleet was somewhere to the north, landing troops to put down the rebellion. La Pérouse thought it wiser to stay some distance from the coast of China which was closed to all foreigners. This meant sailing past the Pescadores Islands which were only roughly shown on his charts. Almost everything went wrong. The winds did not abate — the weather was 'frightful' — the boats had to be lowered to check the depths along the little-known Penghu Channel, and the Chinese fleet was straight ahead. Uncharted rocks appeared, seemingly closing the channel. The sea was so wild it was not possible to tell whether the waves were breaking against rocks or were merely whipped up by the gale. 'Never in my life have I seen heavier seas'. La Pérouse turned back. He would have to sail up the east coast of Formosa.

By the time he reached that conclusion it was May. He might as well have stayed in Manila waiting for the monsoon to change. But all had not been wasted. The astronomers had been able to survey part of the coast and clarify some points on the rough charts. And now the winds generously turned to speed them on their way north.

From China to Russia

Passing through the Sakishima group, La Pérouse entered the East China Sea, sailing almost due north until 21 May when he sighted Cheju-do which guards the entrance to the Korea Strait and thus to the Sea of Japan. No other expedition had ventured into these little-known waters and none was welcome. Korea was a land forbidden to foreigners: anyone shipwrecked on this coast could expect to spend the rest of his life as a slave. The Japanese, on the eastern side, were scarcely more welcoming. Foreigners were likely to face death or imprisonment, unless the head of the Dutch trading post at Nagasaki, itself kept under strict control, could intervene.

La Pérouse preferred to sail close to the Korean coast which offered better opportunities for hydrographic work. No boats came near, even though the ships were within two leagues of the shore, but they were shadowed by two small vessels that hugged the coast behind them. 'It is more than likely that we have aroused concern on the coast of Korea because, during the afternoon, we saw fires lit on every headland'.

Having sailed along the south coast and finding the coast beginning to trend north and west, La Pérouse veered east towards Japan. It was 27 May. A small island hove into sight which was not shown on any of the charts. He named it Dagelet Island 'after our astronomer who saw it first'. It is modern Ullung-do, a distant possession of South Korea. He sent Boutin in a boat to seek an anchorage, but the few inhabitants there fled into the hills.

It was important to fix the position of some feature of the coast of Japan so as to have some reference point for further hydrographic work, but the French were plagued by recurring fog patches. Closeness to the shore spelt danger not merely because of rocks and islands not shown on the charts, but also because of the presence of other vessels. On 2 June, two Japanese ships were in sight, one so close that they could hail her — but since neither side could understand the other's language the encounter was more comic than useful:

> There were twenty men in the crew, all dressed in blue cassocks, similar to our priests' . . . They had a small white Japanese flag on which some words were written vertically. The name of the vessel was on a kind of drum placed by the mast from which the flag was flying. The *Astrolabe*

hailed her when she went past; we could no more understand their reply
than they had understood our question.

On 4 June, the French saw seven ships; on the 5th they saw 10.
Then they sighted Cape Noto, the prominent headland of central
Honshu. Ten days spent fixing its longitude and latitude with great
care enabled them to assess with final accuracy the width of the Sea
of Japan and, by using Captain King's position for the eastern coast,
the width of Honshu. Although bothered by the fog, La Pérouse was
able to get close enough to the coast of Japan to see 'the trees, the
rivers, the landslips' and a little further on houses and 'a kind of
castle'.

As for landing, that was out of the question. After early missionary successes, Christianity had been banned by a series of edicts
issued between 1633 and 1636, enforced with great brutality.
Effectively, Japan had closed its doors against the world. Even trade
with China was cut back drastically — by the time La Pérouse reached
Japanese waters no more than 10 Chinese junks a year were entering
a major port such as Nagasaki. A few trading vessels were sent out
from Japan to Manila, Cochinchina or Siam, but under such strict
control that in practice no Japanese were allowed out of the country.
And if any subject of the Empire took it into his head to escape, he
could only expect death or slavery in the most accessible country,
Korea: further north the cold bare lands of Sakhalin and the Kurile
Islands constituted an inhospitable and uneasy no man's land between Japan and Russia. The Dutch, being protestants and traders
rather than missionaries, had been allowed a small foothold through
Deshima, in Nagasaki. It was no more than a hatchway through the
cultural wall that defended Japan from the influences and the am-
bitions of the outside world. Through it passed small quantities of
cloth, spices, sugar, ivory, in exchange for Japanese porcelain, silks,
laquer boxes, copper and camphor. Any deviation from this strictly
regulated pattern could mean death. At best, shipwrecked adventurers
such as Benyowski could, with the help of a glib tongue and a good
story, receive some help before the inevitable expulsion. Benyowski
had told the Japanese that Russia was moving south into territory

nominally claimed by Japan. The Minister, Tanuma Okitsuga, was persuaded enough to send an expedition which returned shortly before La Pérouse's appearance off the coast. It had found nothing to substantiate Benyowski's tale.

The French veered back to the Asian continent. 'Our landfall was precisely the point that separates Korea from the Tartary of the Manchus'. This is where present-day Vladivostok is situated. Tartary held a host of romantic and less romantic associations for eighteenth century Westerners. It was the end of the enormous Eurasian landmass which begins on the Atlantic with the Breton peninsula and dies away in the mysterious Sea of Japan. Little was known about it, so that imagination had free reign. The name raised visions of a world of darkness — for was not Tartarus the lowest hell of antiquity, far below Hades itself? What was known of its people was unflattering — the naturalist Buffon made allowance for the harshness of the climate 'unhabitable for any other nation', and Voltaire wrote them off as 'rough, stupid and brutal'. Missionaries had sent back reports usually based on vague rumours, infrequent Russian travellers brought back information that was a little more reliable, but essentially it was a mysterious land, ill-traced on the maps, unappealing to the imagination.

Entering Tartary opened up for the expedition an illusion of suitably theatrical dimensions. The vessels sailed towards the land:

> We could see the mountains, the ravines, in a word all the details of the terrain . . . but soon these bluffs, these gullies vanished. The most extraordinary fog bank I have ever seen had caused this error: we saw it dissolve: its shapes, its colours rose and lost themselves among the clouds, and we still had enough light left to ensure that no doubt remained about the non-existence of this fantastic land . . . the most complete illusion that I have ever witnessed in all my sailing days.

Fogs swirled in like a curtain, then parted to reveal a steep coastline on which no landing was possible. The scientists were impatient to go ashore and the officers to complete their survey. 'This was the only part of the globe that has escaped the attention of the tireless Captain Cook'. They had to wait until 23 June, when they dropped anchor in a small bay which Jean-François named Ternay Bay after his great mentor and friend. One can still find Ternei Bay on most modern maps.

There were animals about — deer and bears — but no inhabitants. At least none that were alive: a tomb on the edge of a brook contained two bodies, wrapped in bear skins and wearing small skull caps, surrounded by small artifacts, a few tools and a bag of rice to see them on their journey to the other world.

Four days later, the two ships sailed north, hugging the coast, surveying the headlands and coves, plotting the small rivermouths, but still seeing no inhabitants. On 4 July, a bay was explored and named, ephemerally, Suffren Bay. The Sea of Japan was being left behind. They were sailing into the Tartar Strait. On the starboard side, the coast of Sakhalin was moving closer. La Pérouse edged towards it and on the 12th he dropped anchor in a bay which he named after de Langle but which is probably modern Tomari. And at last he met the natives.

A sketch by Duché de Vancy recorded this meeting, on 13 July 1787. From it, a famous engraving was made, quite faithful to the original, with only a slight overlay of romantic exoticism and the inevitable addition of artistic balance and perspective. In both, La Pérouse is shown with the middle three buttons of his uniform undone and the lower ones struggling to hold back his paunch. The long months of arduous navigation had done nothing to reduce his weight. The poverty of the natives is transformed by the engraver who embellished their clothing and gave several bystanders the appearance of Romans in a classical tragedy. But La Pérouse's pleasure at the meeting cannot be exaggerated. Poor though they might be, they were not thieves and had to be pressured into accepting gifts. Their leaders, venerable elders with long white beards like Chinese sages, told them how they traded with the mainland and with other tribes who lived further north on their own island — for an island it was, with a navigable strait into the Sea of Okhotsk:

> One of the elders rose and, with the tip of his pipe, he drew the coast of Tartary, to the west, trending approximately north and south. On the east, on the opposite side and in the same direction he drew his island . . . he had left a strait between Tartary and his island and turning towards

Lavaux questioning Sakhalin natives to compile his vocabulary.
La Pérouse, identifiable by his girth, looks on. (Engraving from the *Voyage*, 1797)

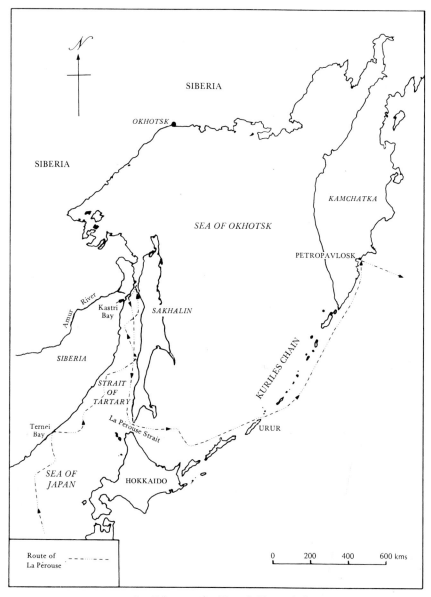

La Pérouse in North-East Asia

our ships, which we could see from the shore, he showed by a line that one could sail through.

Navigability was all-important, since shallow straits would endanger the frigates. As it eventually turned out, the old man had underestimated the draught of the heavy French ships. La Pérouse decided to proceed with caution. It was the anniversary, to the very day, of the Lituya Bay tragedy and no one on board could have failed to remember that on 13 July 1786, in a treacherous pass, 21 of their number had perished.

The expedition sailed north, slowly because of frequent fog and changeable depths, until 19 July when it dropped anchor in a bay close to modern Uglegorsk. La Pérouse called it D'Estaing Bay. Once again, the natives confirmed that Sakhalin was an island. They themselves were from the mainland, having crossed over for fish. Sakhalin appeared to be less and less populated as the French sailed north, but fish were astonishingly plentiful. Clonard, sent to survey a small rivermouth, came back with 1,200 salmon 'although his men had neither nets nor lines' — they had simply killed them with sticks.

On the 23rd, another bay appeared, and now La Jonquière could be given his memorial on the charts. There were a few huts scattered along the shore of Jonquière Bay — the site of modern Aleksandrovsk — but no inhabitants. The coast was becoming more sandy, the depths were gradually dropping with each sounding, and Jean-François began to worry that the strait that lay ahead might be no more than a jumble of sandbanks and shallows. For every league that he sailed north, the depth dropped by three feet. Three more days went by. The shores on both sides, when not obscured by fog, looked barren and uninhabited. There was no current to indicate the existence of a central channel. He lowered two boats, with Boutin and Vaujuas, and sent them to sound not just ahead of the ships but to the side as well: a sudden gust of wind could drive either frigate onto a sandbank. The crew had fallen silent. There was only the low whistle of the wind, now rising through the rigging, and the screams of sea birds.

Vaujuas pulled ahead into the growing gloom. By eight o'clock, those on board could no longer distinguish his boat, although the regular calls of the sailor shouting the depths were faintly audible. Darkness fell. Vaujuas returned at midnight. He had gone a league ahead, into the strait, and had not found more than six fathoms anywhere. There is in fact a navigable channel, as the Russian Nevelskoi was to discover in 1849, but Vaujuas missed it.

The weather was worsening. 'We spent four hours raising anchor; the capstan had broken and this accident seriously wounded three men.' The frigate turned back south, towards the Tartary coast. When the fog cleared, they discovered a bay 'which seemed very deep and offered a commodious and safe anchorage'. It was the evening of 28 July 1787. La Pérouse named the bay after the Marquis de Castries. It is still known as De-Kastri today.

Anxious to reach Kamchatka before the end of the short summer, La Pérouse cut his stay in Castries Bay to five days. The anchorage was safe, the inhabitants courteous and generous, the surroundings attractive at least to the scientists. Lamanon who had been in poor health for some time could not be kept on board. He joined Fathers Monges and Receveur on their walks along the shore and inland. Martinière marched indefatigably along the river shore and into deep gullies in search of plants. The officers went hunting. But, midsummer or not, it was no primitive paradise:

> The cormorant and the gull who gather in groups under happier skies lead a solitary life here on top of rocks. A sorrowful sense of mourning seems to brood over the shore and the woods where only a few ravens, crows and white-crested eagles and other birds of prey seek refuge . . . Although I did not dig the ground, I believe it to be frozen throughout the summer at a certain depth, for the water from our creek was a mere degree and a half above freezing point, and the temperature of flowing water measured with a thermometer never exceeding four degrees: the mercury held itself at 15 degrees in the full light. This brief warmth does not penetrate, it simply hastens the growth of vegetation which must complete its cycle of birth and death within three months, and it quickly multiplies to infinity the number of flies, mosquitoes, sandflies and other troublesome insects.

Collignon, the gardener, went around sowing seeds, as his instructions required him to do. Caught in a sudden freezing shower, he tried to light a fire by using some gunpowder. It blew up in his hands, breaking his thumb, and 'only the skill of Mr Rollin, our chief surgeon, enabled him to save his arm'. Rollin had other worries: several of the men reported swellings of the gums and legs. Scurvy was making its appearance. It was time to leave.

The expedition sailed back the way it had come, hugging the coast of Sakhalin to find the southern straits that would lead into the open sea. Strong gales blowing up from the south did nothing to help. It took a week to reach Langle Bay which they had left on 14 July. Two days later, a gap appeared, but it was merely a channel between the coast and an uncharted island. It was Monneron's turn to gain immortality: La Pérouse named the discovery Monneron Island and it appears as Ostrov Moneron on the present-day charts. Soon came better news: the appearance of a cape that marked the southern extremity of Sakhalin.

Cape Crillon, like the other geographical features named by La Pérouse, has retained its name, somewhat Russianized as Mys Kriljon. The strait that opened out for him the way to the Sea of Okhotsk and enabled him to make for Kamchatka without delay remains La Pérouse Strait to this day.

It marked the end of weeks of slow and dangerous navigation, but also of an invaluable survey of unknown waters. It was one of the most rewarding parts of the entire voyage. The east coast of Sakhalin and the chain of the Kuriles islands they had now reached were better known. The Dutchman Martin de Vries in the *Kastricum* had sailed in this area in 1643, as had King in the *Resolution* in 1784. There was still much that was uncertain, points that should be clarified, positions to be calculated with greater precision, observations to be made, but the tension and excitement of sailing into the unknown had gone. The Kuriles stretch away like a set of links binding Japan to the Kamchatka peninsula. La Pérouse passed through it between the central islands of Urup and Simusir — through what is known as Boussole Strait — back into the Pacific and along the eastern coast. 'I believe this channel to be the finest of all those that can be found among the Kuriles.' It was the kind of praise that reflects a sailor's relief at nearing a long-hoped-for haven. The date was 30 August 1787.

On 6 September, the expedition anchored at Petropavlovsk in Avacha Bay, the main — indeed, the only — town of Kamchatka.

Kamchatka was the edge of Asia and only recently had become the furthest end of the Russian Empire. The empty wastes of Siberia had grown to include the Kamchatkan peninsula which in 1760 had been placed under the control of the military governor of Okhotsk, 700 miles to the west across the sea. There was little to govern; there were no roads, few tracks, inhabitants surviving on fishing and hunting. Only Petropavlosk, with a hundred or so people had any value — it was strategically situated in the northern Pacific and although icebound for several months of the year was at the time the only port Russia could use in the east. The Russian view of Kamchatka, at least from the impression their hosts were anxious to give him, was rosier than La Pérouse's own:

> As the winter is generally less harsh in Kamchatka than in St Petersburg and in several provinces of the Russian empire, the Russians speak of it as the French do of the winter in Provence; but the snows that surrounded us as early as 20 September, the white frost we found covering the ground every morning and the vegetation as yellowed as it is around Paris in January, all tended to convince us that winter here must be unbearable for the people of southern Europe.

That impression was one the French had gained as soon as they sighted the coast:

> all this coastline was hideous in appearance. The eye rested uneasily, almost fearfully, on those enormous rocky masses covered in snow in early September and where no vegetation ever seems to have grown.

The people, however, were hospitable. They saw few visitors, they knew La Pérouse was due to call, and they granted him every facility. There were hunting and fishing expeditions and even what passed for a grand ball in this lost outpost where Russian formality merged oddly with local customs:

> The assembly was not large, but extraordinary to say the least: thirteen women, dressed in silks, ten of whom were Kamchatkans with heavy

faces, narrow eyes and flat noses . . . We began with Russian dances; the tunes are most agreeable and resemble the cossack dance that was known in Paris a few years ago. Kamchatkan dances followed: they can only be compared to the convulsionaries of the famous tomb of St Medard. Dancers in this part of Asia need only arms and shoulders. They scarcely use their legs . . . Their exhaustion is such, during this exercise, that they drip with perspiration and drop to the ground without the strength to rise again. The abundant exhalations which emanate from their bodies perfume the room with a smell of oil and fish to which European noses are insufficiently accustomed to appreciate.

The local garrison consisted of 40 soldiers under a lieutenant. The rest of the population was made up of a few sailors and traders, some local Kamchatkans, and a handful of Russians serving out a term of exile. Siberia was used as a depository for the unwanted or the unlucky. In 1760 landowners had been granted the right to exile to Siberia lazy or rebellious serfs; it is estimated that by the 1780s there were over 20,000 peasants in eastern Siberia who had been sent there by their masters. Few could have been so desperate as to seek out this desolate land's end. One famous exile, mentioned also in the accounts of James Cook's third voyage, was Ivashkin, exiled to Kamchatka, after being flogged and having his nostrils split, for incautious comments made about the Empress Elizabeth. He was then 20. Elizabeth had been dead for 25 years, but he was still in far-eastern Siberia, now working for Kassloff, the Governor of Okhotsk.

Ivashkin showed La Pérouse the tomb of Louis de La Croyère who had died in 1741. He described the funeral he had witnessed almost 50 years earlier. La Pérouse affixed a copper commemorative plaque to the austere monument. La Croyère belonged to a famous family, the De l'Isle or Delisle. His father was the author of numerous learned works, including a history of Siam and a 'Summary of Universal History' in seven volumes. His brother was Guillaume, the first Royal Geographer. Another brother had been commissioned to set up a school of astronomy in St Petersburg and he himself had travelled across Siberia to Kamchatka, had joined Behring's expedition of 1741 and, worn out by his travels, died in Avatcha.

There was another tomb to be visited. Charles Clerke, the commander of the *Resolution* with Cook's last voyage, had died just before the expedition dropped anchor in Avatcha on 22 August 1779. Once again, a copper plaque was engraved and Kasloff promised that a monument would be erected before long to both men.

One great disappointment on arrival in Petropavlosk had been the absence of mail from France. How could they have been forgotten? The Minister knew the *Astrolabe* and the *Boussole* were bound for Kamchatka, and they had in fact reached it a little later than planned. Already, in Macao, the French had suffered the same blow. It was now more than two years since their departure from Brest. Being forgotten and cut off from all news added greatly to the hardships they had to endure.

Bitterness was short-lived. A courier arrived with the mail packets from Okhotsk. With an unbeatable sense of drama, he burst in during the ball, just as the Kamchatkan ladies in a sweaty swoon had concluded their dances. The ball ended, the dancers being dismissed with glasses of brandy. Let the mail be opened now, urged Kassloff. There were letters from families, despatches from Versailles. There was no bad news for anyone, but several were to receive promotions. La Pérouse was promoted to the rank of *chef d'escadre* — commodore and Clonard to post-captain. Kassloff brought out more vodka and ordered all the guns of the port to fire a salute. It was a long and memorable night.

Among the despatches was a significant letter from the Minister of Marine. The English were apparently planning a settlement in New South Wales. La Pérouse was asked to discover the extent of these plans. There was no better way for France to obtain a first-hand report; the political aims of the voyage, never paramount, never obtrusive, were always to be borne in mind.

On 21 September, La Pérouse had written to Castries that he would continue his voyage by sailing to Guam, then down to the Solomons and across to New Zealand. This was consistent with the original plan which, although it envisaged La Pérouse as sailing west from Tahiti, laid down a route which would have taken him to the Solomons, the New Hebrides, New Caledonia and to Queen Charlotte Sound in New Zealand.

A change of route was now forced on him. He advised Castries on the 28th that he would make for Botany Bay at once. He would avoid the dangerous waters around the Solomons and New Hebrides — there was no point in running risks since he would not have time for any useful survey work there. Instead he would sail almost due south to the Samoa group and sweep back west to Botany Bay. All being well, he should be there within three months.

Preparations for a prompt departure began. There had never been any intention to remain in Petropavlosk for more than a few weeks. The brief summer was ending. Early flurries of snow gave warning of that to anyone who might have been lulled into overconfidence by the Russians' boast that a Kamchatkan winter could equal one in southern France. But there was one important matter to be arranged: the despatch of reports and journals to Paris. La Pérouse had been cautious in what he had sent home from Monterey: the Spanish were not always dependable and communication with the rest of the Spanish world was slow and irregular. The presence of French officers in Manila and Macao had made things easier there. But Petropavlosk was a lonely port, soon to be further isolated by snow and ice. No ship could call here for months. The only route for the expedition's mail was overland to Moscow — and for this La Pérouse had the services of young Lesseps who spoke Russian, knew the people, and held the rank of vice-consul.

Lesseps' voyage across Asia and Europe is an epic in itself. Eastern Siberia was little known, even to the Russians; there were few roads, few river crossings, a mere sprinkling of inhabitants. Distances were immense. And he was expected to travel during the winter months when snow obliterated the tracks, made rivers hazardous to cross, and the bitter cold killed off both men and animals. The spring would not make matters any easier, since the thaw rendered roads impassable and the break-up of the ice swept away bridges.

The two frigates sailed from Avatcha Bay on 30 September 1787. Lesseps left with Kassloff a week later. His plan was to cross the peninsula to the west shore and either sail to Okhotsk or follow the coast which ran north and south in a thousand-mile arc.

Merely crossing the peninsula to Bolsheretsk, less than a hundred miles as the crow flies, took a fortnight and involved building a raft to cross the Bolchaiareka River. Bolsheretsk was a dismal place, with fewer than 300 inhabitants. Lesseps stayed there until late January while a caravan of 35 sleighs was assembled. It snowed most days. The tracks to the next village were obscured by snow or blocked entirely by drifts. Not only the weather but Kassloff's official duties slowed the travellers down. Eventually Lesseps chose to separate from the official party. It was now February and he was still travelling north. In March he was following the shores of the northernmost bays of the Sea of Okhotsk. The grey skies merged with the grey horizon, hiding the coastal ranges. It was an alien silent world, save when a sudden blizzard screamed down from the unseen mountains. At the end of April he reached Yamsk, a desolate outpost in a frozen inlet, but at least there was a road of sorts to speed him down to Okhotsk itself which he reached on 8 May.

Eager to leave, he made his way inland along the route to Yakutsk, 800 miles away, but his six sleighs, essential in winter, were useless in the thaw. Spring had come, turning the tracks into quagmires in which the sleighs bogged down. He dragged them back to Okhotsk, bought what horses the township could spare him, 'frightful, half-starved beasts', and on 6 June left again for Yakutsk. After that, it was a matter of sailing on the Lena River, not downstream unhappily, because, easier though this would have been, the Lena flows north towards the mysterious frozen expanse of the Laptev Sea. He sailed upstream in a primitive river boat on 5 July towards Lensk and Kirensk, mere huddles of log houses, tiny lonely military posts scattered in the empty wilderness of central Siberia. Who but an exile or a discarded serf would wish to settle in such a hostile environment? At Kirensk, his boats broke up among the rapids. It was mid-summer and the water was better than freezing, but great clouds of black midges danced a welcome on the banks. He completed the journey to Irkutsk on horseback. In spite of all his misfortunes, he could not fail to be moved by the silent beauty of Lake Baikal brooding in the August sun. But a hundred miles to the south lay the secret world of Mongolia, ruled by no one, the home of roaming tribesmen who had once terrorized Asia and even Europe.

It was time to turn north-west, in a carriage this time, bumping over the hardback ruts of the road to Krasnoyarsk, and then west, clear of the great marshlands, towards the north-south wall of the Urals, through staging posts and settlements that have now grown into cities or whose names have been swept away by the storms of history — Achinsk, Tomsk, Tobolsk, Tumen, Katerinburg, over the ranges to Kongur, and on to Kazan and Nijni Novgorod. He was hurt in an accident after leaving Kazan but he pressed on, driven by the need to avoid the early onset of a second winter. It was September by the time he crossed the Volga, with the first warnings of the coming cold sweeping over the plains, but he was now travelling north towards Novgorod and St Petersburg where he arrived on 22 September 1788. He had been nearly a year on the way and although he did not know it — nor did anyone else — La Pérouse and his friends were long since dead.

He handed all his despatches to the French Ambassador, the Comte de Ségur 'as instructed to do by the Count de La Pérouse', but he was wanted in Paris. He pressed on by way of Riga, Königsberg and Berlin to Paris where he arrived on 17 October. The new Secretary of State for the Navy, Luzerne, was waiting for him at Versailles. As soon as his carriage rumbled over the cobblestones of the great courtyard, Luzerne stepped forward and took him to Louis XVI. He was the hero of the moment. The King ordered that the account of his travel should be printed as soon as he had finished writing it. Then he was appointed consul at Cronstad — thus missing the storm of the French Revolution, just as he missed the cyclone that destroyed the *Astrolabe* and the *Boussole*. Lesseps still had his share of adventures ahead of him: imprisonment in Turkey when he was serving there as First Secretary, and the retreat from Moscow in 1812 with Napoleon's defeated army. Kind fate allowed him to spend the last 20 years of his life as Chargé d'Affaires in the warm, mild backwater of Lisbon.

17

South to Botany Bay

'SEEK THESE ISLANDS in the northern Pacific', they had told Jean-François. 'The Spanish think they exist. We have our doubts'. Once again, it was a question of sweeping from the charts islands and rocks which someone had once seen or imagined, but no one had ever found again. La Roche's Isle Grande, Davis Land, and now 'a great island rich, discovered, so it is said, by Spaniards in 1620', lying somewhere along the parallel of 37° 30' north.

Whoever was the first to sight it could have it named after him, but in case such immortality was too intangible a reward, the captain promised a golden *louis* as well to the sharp-eyed sailor.

There were flights of birds around 14th October, ducks or cormorants, useful signs of nearby land, but nothing was seen of the island which now finally vanished from the charts. The search cost a young sailor's life; he fell from the yards and disappeared in the waves, drowned or killed by the fall.

'Birds that do not stray far from land' were seen time and again during these October days, but the land they were believed to announce never appeared. The winds were strong and favourable, the seas heavy. Creaking, straining, lumbering, the two frigates ploughed their way south, and the cold of the northern autumn gave way to the heat of the tropics — so soon in fact that the abrupt change affected the health of crew and particularly of the scientists, but 'no one stayed in bed' or, to be more realistic, could find any comfort in the cramped cabins or the rope hammocks. La Pérouse ordered frequent rations of coffee to restore waning energy. It was better than nothing. Kamchatka had provided almost no fresh food, what little he had been able to buy had quickly gone, and everyone, the officers included, was living on tough dried meat and ship's biscuits. On 6 November, eight bonitos were caught, providing a welcome feast for all on board. The fact that it was mentioned in Jean-François' journal shows the dire straits to which they were reduced – for the eight fish had to be shared between 200 people.

On 21 November, the expedition crossed the Line for the third time since it had sailed from Brest. Two days later, a couple of sharks were hauled aboard and cut up to make a meal for the crew; for the officers there was 'one curlew, very thin, served in a salmi, and it was hardly any better tasting than the sharks'. The weeks were passing. 'Nothing happened to interrupt the monotony of this crossing'. The expedition had left Petropavlosk on 29 September: two months had gone by, and still nothing was in sight. Tempers were strained; a clammy heat filled the 'tween decks; when dawn broke there was only a brief respite before the sun would begin to beat down implacably on the decks – and what was there to see, anyhow, but the endless horizon and the seabirds whirling and shrieking around the vessels? The sails, rotted, split with sudden shifts of wind; the ropes, perished by the long months of use in damp and sun, snapped as the men hauled on them to adjust the canvas.

The route was almost due south. There were islands to be visited somewhere to the south-west. The instructions had mentioned New Caledonia whose western shore was still unknown, Santa Cruz and Surville's Arsacides which Fleurieu was convinced were the lost Solomons, the Louisiades and the many offshore islands of eastern New Guinea, still imperfectly known. But now it was a matter of making for Australia, as quickly and directly as one could, to report on the activities of the English. Australia was a prize that could not be lost by default. It was the continent which the Spanish, the Dutch, the French and the English had sought for so long. It was not the southern Eldorado that imagination had built up over the centuries, but at least it existed, enormous, both inhospitable and promising, a gigantic enigma in a Pacific that was everywhere else so empty. Every one of the leaders of French expeditions, indeed every one of their officers, had fought against England at some time to hold back her tide of conquests. Everywhere, be it India, Canada or the West Indies, the British had made advances. Now the Empire, so obviously inspired by that Roman Empire which had once dominated the entire known world, was spreading to the Australian continent. The English might well sing 'Rule Britannia' at their gatherings, the French had no desire to see them rule the world, and French naval officers most of all had no wish to see them rule even the waves.

But it was no conquering fleet that had sailed from Portsmouth in May 1787 for Botany Bay. As the *Astrolabe* and the *Boussole* struggled on through the vast central Pacific, Captain Phillip and his 11 ships were battling their way through the southern Indian Ocean. He had left England almost six months later than planned, thus giving plenty of time for the French Court to know of the plans. Two naval ships and six transports accompanied by storeships were scarcely concealable. The pressures put on the British authorities to get rid of their convicts had grown too public anyhow. In March 1786, the Mayor and Corporation of London had petitioned the king to do something about the 'rapid and alarming accumulation of convicts within the kingdom'. Until the American War of Independence, felons had been transported to America at the rate of a thousand a year. When this outlet was closed up by the war and then, more finally, by independence, Africa proved a poor substitute because the convicts died off so quickly that public opinion was aroused. Disposal, not death, was what English justice intended, and transportation had shown that convicts, if they were not reformed by being sent out of England, were at least of use in building up a colonial empire. Clearing England's prisons of what was regarded as human refuse could pay dividends. The climate of New South Wales was suitable for Europeans; men like Sir Joseph Banks and James Matra, who had sailed with Cook, were convinced that a successful colony would develop there in much the same way as colonies had spread along the Atlantic seaboard of America. The French government, somewhat fearfully in their case, shared this view.

But the ships were a scratch lot; the fitting out, in spite of all the delays, was rushed; the men chosen to found the settlement, of uneven quality. The primary aim, after all, was to ease the pressure on English prisons by dumping their surplus population half a world away, out of sight and out of mind. It was not something a government bent on balancing the budget wanted to spend money on.

So, as La Pérouse sailed on towards his first landfall, which was to be Samoa, Captain Phillip's fleet was being driven off course by storms in empty southern seas where whales blew and albatrosses swooped, in weather that grew more piercingly cold day by day, until inevitably scurvy began to appear among his wretched crew and his far more wretched human cargo. Jean-François need not have worried about arriving late in Australia. He had time enough for a stay in Samoa.

It was on 6 December 1787 that the lookout sighted the first of the Samoan islands, the easternmost Tau and then Tutuila. At last here, among the islands which Bougainville had called the Navigators, La Pérouse could find the supplies and refreshments his crew so badly needed. He could see numbers of coconut trees, villages set among the greenery on the hill slopes, and the canoes of the islanders, mediocre crafts mostly, but manoeuvred through the waves with the skill which Bougainville had so admired.

Langle was well satisfied, indeed impressed, by the welcome. Admittedly, this was not the golden paradise of Tahiti, as Bougainville himself had remarked nearly 20 years before: 'I do not believe these islanders are as gentle as our Cythereans. Their appearance was more savage and they displayed far more mistrust',[1] but after over two months at sea any landfall had charms. La Pérouse did not share Langle's enthusiasm. He had remained aboard and, although there had been no incidents, he did not find the Samoans attractive. When he did go ashore, he saw nevertheless that fruit and poultry could be obtained once an orderly market was set up. The soldiers were lined up to establish a line of protection and the bartering began. It was brisk and tumultuous.

Jean-François left the market area and hazarded himself a couple of hundred feet into the trees to a village where he was almost effusively greeted. He unbent a little: 'This charming country presented the double advantage of a soil that was fertile without needing cultivation and a climate that required no clothing.' The South Seas were living up to their legend, but for him it was still only a legend, not the abode of the Noble Savage:

> The bodies of these Indians, covered with scars, proved that they were often at war or quarrelling among themselves, and their features betrayed a ferocity we did not see on the faces of the women. Nature had no doubt left this mark on the face of these Indians to warn that Man in a state of near savagery and of anarchy is more harmful than the fiercest beasts.

These were not the words of a follower of Rousseau. La Pérouse trusted only his own eyes. He wished no one any harm, considered reprisals as nothing more than an act of revenge that brought a man down to the level of the savages, but he had no time for romantic notions. His views were confirmed when he learnt on his return that a Samoan had climbed into the longboat and struck a sailor, that stones had been thrown at Rollin, and that Monneron had almost had his sword stolen from its scabbard. These were still only minor incidents and Langle who had found 'a charming village, close to a waterfall of the most limpid water' believed that the French should stay longer. La Pérouse felt there was enough drinking water in the barrels. The two men argued:

> I told him we did not need any, but he had adopted Capain Cook's approach — he believed that fresh water was a hundred times better than what we had in the hold.

The comparison with Cook had an ominous ring about it, for Cook had become over-confident and been killed, but Langle insisted. La Pérouse gave way:

> M. de Langle was a man with such judgment and such qualities that these facts more than anything else caused me to give my consent, or rather to subordinate my wishes to his.

On the morning of 11 December 1787, Langle therefore led a group of 60 men to the shore of his 'charming village'. The tide was out and the shoreline looked less attractive. It was also more difficult to land and to roll the barrels ashore. Worse still, the boats were out of sight of the two frigates. By the time the barrels were full, a crowd of over a thousand had gathered. The tide had still not turned; the

The massacre at Tutuila, Samoa.

(Engraving from the *Voyage*, 1797. Alexander Turnbull Library.)

longboats now heavily laden would not float. Langle was forced to wait. He was vulnerable, stranded on this lonely beach in boats encumbered by heavy barrels. Suddenly, with a great roar, the Samoans attacked.

By the time the boats struggled back to the *Astrolabe* and the *Boussole*, it was after five. Langle was dead, as were Lamanon and 10 of the men. Many others had been wounded. Boutin had five head wounds, Colinet's arm was broken, Fr Receveur had almost lost an eye.

Once the wounded were cared for, the crews readied for reprisals. The ships were still surrounded by canoes trading their fruit and their poultry:

> with a sense of security that proved their innocence — but they were the brothers, the children, the compatriots of these barbarous murderers, and I must admit that I needed all my reasoning power to contain the anger that shook me and to stop our crews from killing them.

All La Pérouse allowed was one blank shot to warn the canoes away. And when the next day they returned, not to trade this time, but to shout challenges and yell their scorn, he ordered a single shot, carefully aimed so that the cannon ball curved over the foremost boats and splashed down in the midst of the crowd. The Samoans fled, saved, although they did not know it, by La Pérouse's sense of justice: ' I could have destroyed or sunk a hundred canoes, with more than five hundred people in them; but I was afraid of striking the wrong victims: the call of my conscience saved their lives'.

The *Astrolabe* and the *Boussole* sailed from Massacre Bay, Tutuila, on 14 December. Whatever illusions Jean-François might have harboured had vanished. His anger was largely directed against those philosophers in their booklined studies who constructed their theories about the nature of man and the evils of Western civilization:

> I am a hundred times more angry against the philosophers who praise them [the Noble Savages] than against the savages themselves. Lamanon whom they massacred was saying the day before that these men are worth more than us.[2]

Poor Lamanon, even in death, had to be proved wrong!

As had happened after the Lituya Bay disaster, shipboard life had to be reorganized. The dead men's belongings had to be sorted through to be packed and eventually sent out to their families, or auctioned among the crew. It was a sad task. Men had gone out in the morning, intending to finish a letter or mend a garment, and their lives had ended as abruptly as a clock that is suddenly stopped. There were pitiful mementoes of the voyage, curios bought in a port, half completed wood carvings, pressed leaves, markers in a half-read book.

Monti took over command of the *Astrolabe* by virtue of his position as first officer; Clonard who was senior to him would take over from him when it was convenient to transfer him from the *Boussole*. Young Lauriston, whom de Langle had trained in the mysteries of astronomy and lunar observations, helped out. Others were compelled to do less: Father Receveur had been more seriously wounded than he cared to admit, and scurvy was making itself felt. Already, on 10 December, David, one of the cooks, had died of 'scorbutic dropsy'.

A pall had fallen over the ships. They sailed west to the other islands of the Samoan group — Upolu and Savai'i — but the sailors who had laughed and catcalled at the girls and waved at the men, remained silent. The sky was still the same tropic blue, the coconut trees still arched their slim trunks and their head of greenery over the golden beaches, the sea still foamed white over the reefs, but they knew these paradise islands hid sudden, inexplicable death. The canoes came out to the ships, filled with islanders offering food, shouting and gesticulating to barter pigs and coconuts for glass beads and cloth, but who could tell what plans they might be hatching against the visitors? La Pérouse reduced canvas so that the ships were slowed down and trading could proceed, but he made no attempt to land, and any signs of challenge or warlike attitudes were met by the display of firearms. The country was breathtakingly beautiful; the people were, because related to those of Tutuila, dangerous savages:

These islands, situated between 14° south and 171° to 175° west make up one of the most beautiful island groups of the South Seas, as interesting for their art, their products and their people as the Society or the Friendly

Islands ... As for the morals of these people, even though we saw them, only briefly, we learnt to understand their character well enough through our misfortunes, and we are not afraid to assert that one would attempt in vain to arouse by gifts the gratitude of these ferocious minds which can only be controlled by fear.

In this mood, the French sailed on to two islands, close together, one very high, the other flat. One was Tafahi and the other Nuiato-putapu, which the Dutchman Schouten had called Traitors Island. The French were not alone in assuming there was treacherous be-haviour in these waters. The books in the ships' libraries told them that. Schouten and Le Maire had passed this way in 1616 and they too had met with a sudden, unprovoked attack. But the islanders were friendly towards the French, who found them more honest in their dealings than the Samoans had been and keener on iron than on the baubles which had proved so popular in Tutuila and Upolu. But everywhere the French remained on their guard. Contacts were limited and carefully supervised. Barter was carried out by lowering baskets overboard. The French did not land and the islanders were not allowed on board.

A storm drove the ships away, while the canoes fled back ashore. 'The night was frightful'. Heavy rain poured down, rapidly finding its way below decks. A clammy damp filled all the cabins; clothes and bedding were wet and uncomfortable; the wind seemed merely to bring hot humid air into the ships which rolled and creaked ceaselessly. Dagelet had managed to complete the observations he needed to determine with finality the position of Schouten's two islands, but he found it impossible to work in the days that followed:

The last months of a voyage are, to be frank, the hardest to bear; the body's resistance has lowered with the passing of time; the food goes bad: yet, if there are limits one cannot go beyond in long voyages of discovery, it is important to know those one can at least reach, and I believe that by the time we get back to Europe our experience in this respect will be complete.

The rains lasted for more than a week. On 27 December the *Boussole* and the *Astrolabe* reached the Vavau group in the northern Tongas, which the Spaniard Francisco Maurelle had visited in 1781.

Bernizet and Dagelet worked to fix the position of the islands which Maurelle had not determined with accuracy:

> he placed these islands some six degrees too far west; this error, copied from one century to the next, and enshrined by geographers, would have given birth to a new archipelago which would have had no reality except on the maps.

One senses in La Pérouse's journal signs of the weariness and the dejection that was affecting both ships. The dig at the geographers, safe in their study, is another instance, although not an isolated one in his writings. The presence of scurvy among the crew depressed him further. He ordered regular issues of brandy and water for the two crews, and the killing of the small pigs he had bought in Tutuila. These measure helped, and the swellings in legs and gums which had worried the surgeons disappeared — 'which shows that sailors have a less pressing need of land air than of good food'.

But what really mattered was reaching Botany Bay. The bad weather, the need to sail cautiously through the Tongas, the small amount of food they managed to obtain from the few islanders who ventured near the ships, determined the French to get away as soon as they could. On the first day of 1788, La Pérouse ordered the expedition to sail west by south-west direct for Australia.

It was a route no one had yet followed. There was little to be found on the way, except Pylstart Island, or Ata, discovered by Abel Tasman nearly 150 years earlier, a lonely island south of the main Tonga group. Even so, La Pérouse would not have gone near it had the winds not driven him south. It gave him the minor satisfaction of correcting the position James Cook had assigned to it — the Englishman had placed it four miles too far south.

But now the winds dropped, the skies cleared, and the expedition found itself becalmed. It remained for three days in view of this bare rocky island, scarcely a mile across. A welcome gale blew up on 6 January, driving the French south-west, through heavy seas admittedly, but this was the kind of progress they had prayed for. On the 13th they were in sight of Norfolk Island. There was little hope of getting supplies since the island was believed to be uninhabited, but La Pérouse took pity on the bored naturalists 'who, since our departure from Kamtchatka, have had very few occasions to consign any observations to their journals'. He sent Clonard to look for a landing place, but everywhere the sea was breaking angrily at the foot of steep cliffs. It was not worth risking any lives for. The expedition sailed on and the scientists went back to their books and their endless card games.

A few days later, they could still make their 'little bets', but in a geographical context. There was something to speculate about: a multitude of seabirds surrounded the ships. How close were they to land? Were the vessels close to rocks or near the shore? Would they see some other part of the Australian coastline than the Botany Bay area? There were no answers, and the birds vanished. Then, on 23 January 1788, the French gathered on deck. There was a low coastline, some 20 or 30 miles away. On the 24th they tacked to turn Cap Solander, a couple of miles distant, to reach Botany Bay.

When they did, they beheld a sight they had not seen since Manila: British ships at anchor.

Captain Arthur Phillip had arrived in the *Supply* a mere six days earlier; the rest of the fleet had joined him two days later. La Pérouse therefore arrived while the English were still surveying the shores of Botany Bay. Phillip had been bitterly disappointed on discovering that, attractive though it might be to a botanist like Sir Joseph Banks, it was quite inadequate as a place for a permanent settlement:

> I began to examine the bay as we anchored, and found that though extensive, it did not afford shelter to ships from the easterly winds; the greater part of the bay being so shallow that ships of even a moderate draught of water are obliged to anchor with the entrance to the bay open, and are exposed to a heavy sea that rolls in when it blows hard from the eastward ... The small creek that is in the northern part of the bay runs a considerable way into the country, but it has only water for a boat. The sides of this creek are frequently overflowed, and the lowlands a swamp... Several good situations offered for a small number of people, but none appeared calculated for our numbers, and where the stores and provisions could be landed without a great loss of time.[3]

Shallows, swamps, sandy shores, midsummer heat, a plague of insects,[4] and a land that seemed incapable of producing crops — this was what they had come to after a voyage lasting more than eight months. Still cooped up in the transports were more than seven hundred convicts, male and female, ill-fed, ill-clothed, guarded by soldiers as surly and as tired of the voyage as the rest. Even the few aborigines Phillip encountered were unfriendly or, at best, indifferent.

Botany Bay would not do. Phillip set out with a small party to seek a more suitable place to found a new colony, not too sure that such a spot existed. James Cook had sighted an inlet further north, which he had named Port Jackson, but he had not explored it and there was no particular reason to expect that it would prove any more attractive. As it turned out, Port Jackson was 'the finest harbour in the world, in which a thousand vessels of the line may ride in the most perfect security'.

Phillip was away three days on this exploration. He was back on the 23rd. The next day, the *Boussole* and the *Astrolabe* arrived.

Rumours raced around the English ships, raising fear in some, hope in others. Was England at war with France, and were these enemy vessels come to destroy the colony before it was established and free the convicts so that they might hold this land against those who had sent them here to rot? Or were they ships bringing supplies? Phillip knew that La Pérouse was in the Pacific with two ships and he quickly realized who the intruders were. But the weather held up contact for two more days. Then Clonard went in the *Boussole's* boat to speak to the English and explain that it was not La Pérouse's intention to remain for any length of time in the bay, but simply to rest his crew, carry out a few repairs, and take on water and firewood.

The English made it clear they could do little to help him. Indeed, surveying the fleet, grimy-looking after months at sea, and its cargo of rotting humanity, the French hardly expected anything:

> An English lieutenant and a midshipman were sent by Captain Hunter, commanding the frigate *Sirius*; they offered on his behalf every service he could render me, adding however that as they were about to sail north, their circumstances would not allow them to give us food, ammunition

or sails, so that their offers of services were reduced to good wishes for the success of our voyage.

The one service the English could provide was to take letters and reports back to Europe. Lieutenant Shortland, who had travelled with the fleet as agent for the transports, was given the final section of La Pérouse's journal, plus his letters and those of the officers and scientists. He would leave on 14 July in the *Alexander* with Phillip's first reports and the French mailbag. Had there been no ships in New South Wales when La Pérouse arrived, we would know nothing of the last long lap of his voyage, not even how Langle died.

The French ships spent more than six weeks in Botany Bay, watching the English move to Port Jackson and begin to set up their struggling settlement. La Pérouse must have reflected that its chances of survival were not great and may have shared the thought Captain Phillip had once expressed in a memorandum to the Home Department that 'he would not wish convicts to lay the foundations of an Empire'. Certainly, during those weeks, escaped convicts caused both of them trouble, as they fled from Port Jackson in the hope of finding asylum in the French vessels. Embarrassed and punctilious, La Pérouse returned them to Phillip who had them flogged. One wonders whether any of them, in later years, learning that the French had all been lost at sea, may have felt some belated gratitude towards Jean-François for having effectively saved their lives.

On 17 February, Father Receveur died. He had made light of his wounds — indeed he did not think them serious as he wrote to his brother: 'We shall be back in France in the spring of 1789 or even earlier. So write to me at Brest or at Rochefort'.[5] But he was worn out by the voyage and the privations he had suffered. Ten days after writing that letter he was dead. He was buried ashore, in what is now the La Pérouse district of southern Sydney, and La Pérouse put up a small memorial over his grave, bearing the Latin inscription: '*Hic jacet L. Receveur E.F. Minoribus Galliae sacerdos, physicus in circumnavigatione mundi, Duce de Lapérouse, obiit 17 februarii Anno 1788*'. The aborigines destroyed it. When he later discovered this had happened, Phillip had a new memorial erected.

It is in fact through Captain Phillip's despatches that we can glean a little of the French's activities in Botany Bay. They built two long-boats, 'the frames of which they had brought from Europe'. Conditions were far from pleasant. Heavy rain fell during February, and scurvy was raging among the convicts. Aborigines roamed around the rough encampments. 'Mons. La Pérouse . . . was obliged to fire on them'. And some sailors ate of 'a large fruit, not unlike a pineapple, but which when eaten by the French seamen occasioned violent retchings'.[6] La Pérouse took the trouble to erect a defensive fence around the longboats he was having built on the shore:

> These precautions were necessary against the Indians of New Holland who, although weak and not numerous, are like all primitive people very mischievous and would burn our boats if they had the means to.[7]

The shock of Tutuila was still affecting him. Illusions had been shattered and the minds of many on board the two frigates had completely swung over to antipathy towards native people. And the long voyage of exploration had taken its toll. In a letter to a friend, La Pérouse expressed his weariness and some disenchantment:

> Whatever professional advantages this expedition may have brought me, you can be certain that few would want them at such cost, and the fatigues of such a voyage cannot be put into words. When I return you will take me for a centenarian, I have no teeth and no hair left and I think it will not be long before I become senile . . . Farewell until June 1789. Tell your wife she will mistake me for my own grandfather.[8]

Among the letters handed to Shortland there must have been some to his wife, but none has survived the troubled times she had to live through. Fortunately for posterity, the letter he wrote to the Minister, outlining his plans reached its destination and was carefully preserved:

> I shall go up to the Friendly Islands and will do exactly what my instructions require me to with respect to the southern part of New Caledonia, the island of Santa Cruz of Mendana, the south coast of Surville's Arsacides [the Solomons], and Bougainville's Louisiades, endeavouring to assess whether the latter form part of New Guinea or not. I shall pass, towards the end of July 1788, between New Guinea and New Holland, by

La Pérouse memorial, erected by Hyacinthe de Bougainville in the La Pérouse district of Sydney. Botany Bay forms the background.

another channel than the Endeavour's, if such exists. In September and part of October I shall visit the Gulf of Carpentaria and the whole of the west coast of New Holland as far as Diemen's Land; but in such a way as to enable me to go back north in good time to reach the Ile de France in December 1788.

For someone as weary as he was claiming to be privately to his friends, this was an ambitious programme. La Pérouse was never a man to shun what he considered to be his duty. And we may also suspect that the private letters he was writing at this time displayed no more than one of the passing moods of despondency and home-sickness he was prone to when promotion was slow or things seemed to be going badly. He shook them off promptly once he was faced with a new challenge.

On 10 March 1788 the *Boussole* and the *Astrolabe* weighed anchor from Botany Bay. The sailors of Captain Phillip's fleet saw them sail past, going north, not far from the coast. They were the last white men ever to see them, for La Pérouse and his ships vanished completely into the Pacific, and 40 years would pass before the first hints of what had happened began to reach Europe.

Notes

1. Bougainville, Journal entry of 4 May 1768, in Taillemitte, E. (ed) *Bougainville et ses compagnons autour du monde*, Paris, 1977.
2. Letter written from Botany Bay, dated 7 February 1788.
3. Phillip's first report to Lord Sydney, 15 May 1788, *Historical Records of Australia*, I, p. 17.
4. In a letter written to the scientist Condorcet from Botany Bay, Dagelet apologized for his bad handwriting, saying, 'I am blinded by the bites of flies that infest my wretched observatory'. Institut de France Library, MS 867-4.
5. Letter dated 7 February 1788, quoted in Gautier, 'Le Père Receveur', in *Courrier des messageries maritimes*, 140, 1974, pp. 24-34.
6. *Historical Records of Australia*, I, p. 28.
7. Letter to Fleurieu, 7 February 1788, A.N.M. 3 JJ 389-22.
8. Letter to Lecoulteux de La Noraye, 7 February 1788, in Bibliothèque nationale, N.A.F., 9424.

18

An Expedition Vanishes

ALLOWING for a month or so in New Caledonia and the New Hebrides and a similar period in the Louisiades and the Solomons, La Pérouse could have completed a partial circumnavigation of Australia as far as the west coast of Tasmania and reached Mauritius by the end of 1788. During that period no news was to be expected from him, since he would not have called at any European-held port and the chances of meeting another European vessel were infinitesimal.

It was therefore not until the middle of 1789, by which time news of his arrival in Port-Louis could have reached Paris, that concern began to be felt in France. As the months went by, concern grew into anxiety. By mid-1790 men like Fleurieu were drawing up plans for a rescue operation. Eléonore moved from Albi to Paris, to be on the spot should news of the expedition reach the Ministry, but also to press for government action.

The times were scarcely propitious. The Revolution had begun, heralded by the calling together of the States-General for the first time in almost 200 years. The Bastille had fallen to the Paris crowds, the privileges of the nobility had been swept away, and Louis XVI, in the process of being reluctantly transformed into a constitutional monarch, was compelled to move from Versailles to Paris. Economic problems were aggravated by civil disorders. Not merely the old social order but an entire administrative structure was collapsing throughout France like buildings in an earthquake.

Claret de Fleurieu had summarized the facts as they were known or could be surmised in a report of 21 April 1790 which he discussed with the King. At the same time, the Academy of Sciences was debating what might be done. The expedition had been no mere aristocrat's whim, but a scientific voyage in keeping with the mood of the time, staffed by scientists — colleagues of the men who were not only ushering a new era of knowledge but who had, by their logical reasoning, contributed to a considerable extent to the new egalitarian society now dawning. But all the Academy could suggest was that Bougainville, who was commanding a squadron at Brest, should sail 'to meet' La Pérouse. It implied that the members were still not sure whether the expedition neeeded help or whether it had been lost.

As an alternative, the French government considered asking the Spanish to help. Two ships under Malaspina and Bustamente had sailed from Cadiz for the Pacific in July 1789. But by mid-1790 they had not even reached Guayaquil, in Ecuador, and they were firstly bound for the North-West Coast. In fact, they would not reach the area where La Pérouse was known to have gone, until 1793.

Fleurieu was appointed Minister of Marine in October 1790. In this position, he could do a great deal more to hasten a search. Unhappily, his ally Louis XVI was losing his remaining grasp on power, even though his popularity was still high — he was now scarcely even a constitutional king: he was in effect a figurehead. Power had moved to Parliament. Fleurieu consequently worked through his scientist friends to have the matter raised in the National Assembly. He could depend on the help of men like Condorcet, the mathematician La Pérouse had written to from Botany Bay, who was now a prominent parliamentarian.

On 22 January 1791 the Academy of Sciences joined with the *Société d'Histoire Naturelle* to deliver a formal appeal to the National Assembly. On 14 February, Fleurieu made the situation official by declaring the expedition to be lost and ordering the navy formally to close their accounts as at 31 December 1788, this being the latest date by which La Pérouse had said he would reach Mauritius.[1]

The Deputies met on 9 February, under the chairmanship of Mirabeau, to debate the issue with the fervour and eloquence that had become typical of those heady days: 'May they return to our shores, even though they die of joy as they kiss this free land!'[2] It was agreed that a rescue expedition would be sent to the Pacific. The problem was the cost. Economic troubles had been the immediate cause of the Revolution, but they had not gone away. Far from it: they were increasing daily. As an interim measure, the Assembly voted a decree on 15 February promising 10,000 francs and a life pension to anyone discovering traces of the two frigates. But a greater effort was needed. On the 25th, a budget was approved of 400,000 francs for the first year of a rescue expedition and 300,000 francs in subsequent years. Fleurieu could now set the machinery in motion. This he did with impressive speed — it would be ready to sail by September. Louis XVI signed the 'Loi relative à la découverte des deux frégates françaises *La Boussole* et *l'Astrolabe*' which was ratified on 7 April.

Eléonore was active in Paris on her own behalf as well. She had little money and like the wives of those who had sailed with her husband, she was faced with the problem of the expedition's accounts and therefore of the men's pay being stopped as at the end of 1788. Fleurieu was successful in getting the Assembly to examine the problem and agreeing to her receiving the balance of any sums due to La Pérouse. This decision, dated 22 April, favoured her, and not surprisingly it led the other wives to protest their own penury. Eléonore was promised 40,000 *livres* — but payment was postponed time and time again. The treasury was empty and the ponderous administrative machine was slowing down day by day.

Mirabeau, who might have worked some form of agreement between the Court and the Assembly and held extremists at bay, died on 2 April. Fleurieu was moved from his post as Minister of Marine on 6 May. On 20 June, Louis XVI tried to flee the country to join the growing number of *émigrés* abroad, but he was arrested as he neared the frontier and brought back to Paris. A republican uprising was nipped in the bud in a bloody clash at the Champs de Mars, but it was obvious that the days of the monarchy were numbered. In Britain, after a wave of enthusiasm — Fox had hailed the fall of the Bastille as 'the greatest and best event in the history of the world' — people began to agree with Burke whose *Reflections on the Revolution in France* caused a sensation at the end of 1790 by predicting war and bloodshed.

The Assembly still had time to discuss La Pérouse. In the wake of its offer of financial grants to anyone discovering traces of the lost ships, it was approached by four merchants from the port of Lorient — Garnier, Torkler, Piron and Dussault — for a permit to trade in furs in Kamchatka and look for remains of La Pérouse.[3] They were probably more interested in furs than in the lost expedition and anyhow La Pérouse had expressed no intention of returning to Kamchatka. The four-man proposal for a ship of 300 tons, the *Flavie*, under Captain Magon de Villaumont, was laid aside. A second proposal came forward soon after from Aristide-Aubert Dupetit-Thouars, a mixture of commerce and altruism which was more worthy of consideration since finding La Pérouse was the primary objective and the itinerary was clearly in line with that aim.

Dupetit-Thouars planned to travel to New Holland and New Guinea, through areas where the frigates could be presumed to have been lost, before proceeding to Nootka Sound on the north-west coast of America where he would buy furs to cover a part of his very considerable costs. Dupetit-Thouars' problem was that the Assembly had already authorized one major expedition which was preparing to sail under Bruny d'Entrecasteaux. He accordingly suggested that he might join the latter with his own ship and abandon the idea of trade. But neither d'Entrecasteaux nor the Ministry would agree — and as it turned out d'Entrecasteaux was going to face enough trouble with his own officers without having another captain tacking along with a status inevitably tainted with ambiguity. Dupetit-Thouars was not discouraged. He launched an appeal for funds for a separate voyage under his own command. Two expeditions must surely be better than one.

Louis XVI headed the subscription list, but money did not come as readily as was hoped. And in the meantime d'Entrecasteaux's expedition sailed from Brest. An appeal to Parliament for funds was made easier by the dissolution of the National Assembly and the elections of a new Legislative Assembly on 1 October. The previous parliamentarians had declared themselves ineligible for re-election and handed over the task of making laws to a brand new House. When Dupetit-Thouars appealed for funds, he was in fact approaching a new audience. He received 10,000 *livres* and the legislators' blessing for an expedition which included once again trade among its aims.[4]

This was still not enough. In April news came of some wreckage in the Admiralty Islands, north of New Guinea, which it was believed came from the frigates. It was certainly along the route La Pérouse was expected to follow. And d'Entrecasteaux's ships were almost there. The Assembly consequently rejected Dupetit-Thouars' second appeal for funds. A wiser man, one less of a romantic, would have taken the Deputies' advice and given up. Instead, Dupetit-Thouars who had already mortgaged his property and borrowed from his relatives mortgaged his future. On 29 May 1792, the Assembly granted his request for a cash advance equal to two years of pay. He sailed finally on 22 August in the *Diligent*.

Doomed he was to fail; even so his downfall came through a gesture of romantic generosity. In Cape Verde he found some 40 marooned Portuguese sailors whom he took aboard. The crowded ship was struck by an epidemic, so that by the time he reached Fernando de Noronha off the coast of Brazil nearly one third of his men had died and all were in poor shape. The French moreover were suspect. The Revolutionary Wars had begun back in April when France declared war on Austria; the French monarchy had been abolished, Louis XVI and Queen Marie-Antoinette were in prison, facing charges of treason and soon to be guillotined. Dupetit-Thouars was arrested and his ship seized. He was not freed until 1796 when he returned to France to serve under Napoleon and die at the Battle of the Nile.

Thus it fell to d'Entrecasteaux alone to sail in search of La Pérouse. He was given two ships — heavy storeships of 500 tons — renamed appropriately the *Recherche* and the *Espérance*. Few men had his experience. He had entered the navy in 1754 at the age of 17 as a *garde de la marine* and had taken part in numerous campaigns. He had commanded the Indian Naval Station and carried out his duties in eastern waters with efficiency, indeed with brilliance. To mark the importance of his new mission he was raised to the rank of rear-admiral, being thus the first French admiral to enter the Pacific.

He carried with him, however, the seeds of the Revolution.

Leaving the troubled shores of France did not mean escaping the virus of unrest and of challenges to the established order and consequently to naval discipline. Some of his officers, like D'Auribeau, Rossel and de Boynes, belonged to the nobility; others belonged to lesser families, were *volontaires* of middle-class descent, or endorsed the egalitarian ideals of the Revolution. But among the scientists, especially the botanist La Billardière, there were open adherents of the republican cause. It was only a matter of time, as the usual tensions developed between officers and *savants*, and sickness, shortages and disappointments arose, before the two ships' complements divided into openly warring camps.

Taking scientists on board, adding to the basic purpose of the expedition a secondary scientific research programme, could only multiply the difficulties. Speed was essential if the Frenchmen presumed wrecked somewhere in the vast ocean were to be rescued. Collecting botanical and zoological specimens, carrying out hydrographical surveys, even though it continued the task undertaken by La Pérouse — as was put forward by way of justification — was bound to cause delays. In times of social unrest, when scientists were particularly conscious of the role they had played and were continuing to play in transforming French society, these problems were inevitably multiplied to danger point.

Progress was irritatingly slow. It took almost four months to reach the Cape of Good Hope where d'Entrecasteaux received the reports about wreckage sighted in the Admiralty Islands. They were third-hand and included the information that La Pérouse had told an English captain in Botany Bay he would sail north of New Guinea rather than south as he had written to Fleurieu. Garbled though the information seemed to be, d'Entrecasteaux felt compelled to sail for the Admiralties. The winds decided otherwise. He gave up and made for Tasmania. His stay there produced important results from the scientific point of view, but was of little use as far as the lost ships were concerned. It was the end of May 1792 before the *Recherche* and the *Espérance* set off for New Caledonia, along the route La Pérouse could reasonably be expected to have taken. Most of June was spent around New Caledonia; then d'Entrecasteaux sailed to the

Solomons, to New Ireland and finally to the Admiralty Islands. It had taken 10 months — but all that could be seen were bleached shapes of great trees washed up on the reefs, which with some effort of the imagination could be claimed to look like wrecked boats.

After a stay in the Dutch Indies, d'Entrecasteaux proceeded to sail around Australia and back to Tasmania. On 21 January 1793 the ships dropped anchor in Recherche Bay, having completed the full circle but found no trace of La Pérouse. A month later, they sailed for New Zealand, then veered north towards Tonga. On 23 March they anchored off Tongatapu. The islanders, friendly and boisterous, had no knowledge of the *Boussole* or the *Astrolabe*. In May, d'Entrecasteaux was back in New Caledonia.

The search seemed hopeless. There were so many islands, so many inlets . . . . Communication with the natives who spoke different languages and dialects was wellnigh impossible. The scientific results of the expedition were impressive, but the strains and hardships were becoming unbearable. Huon de Kermadec, the commander of the *Espérance*, died, and d'Entrecasteaux's own health was getting steadily worse. On 9 May the expedition sailed towards the Santa Cruz group in the northern New Hebrides. On the 19th, while off Utupua, the French sighted Santa Cruz itself and another island to the south-east which was not shown on any chart.

They did not sail close to it, merely recording it on their maps and naming it Recherche Island before sailing away for a second exploration of the Solomon Islands.

The island they had discovered was Vanikoro — where the La Pérouse expedition had met its doom and where, it seems likely, some survivors were still living.

If there were, we can only hope that they never saw the distant sails of d'Entrecasteaux's ships appear on the horizon and then, heartbreakingly, vanish. 'We saw [the island] at such a great distance that we could not determine its bearing with precision', reported the searchers. D'Entrecasteaux's failure to locate the remnants of the 1788 expedition, when he was so tantalizingly close, weighed heavily on his memory, but with two slow ships and a immense expanse of seas to explore, only extreme good fortune could bring him success. He had been almost two years on the way, supplies had run low, his officers and men were split into antagonistical camps, he himself was now seriously ill. He sailed on to the Solomons and the Louisiades. On 20 July 1793 he died and was buried at sea. D'Auribeau took over command and struggled back to Surabaya, in the Dutch Indies, where the expedition finally disintegrated.

Meanwhile in Paris the publication of an official account of La Pérouse's voyage was proceeding slowly. This had been decided by the National Assembly on 4 May 1791, just two days before Fleurieu gave up the Navy portfolio for the rather less stimulating and potentially dangerous post of tutor to Louis XVI's son. Preparing La Pérouse's journals for the press might have been more suitable for a man of his ability, but even that task was fraught with danger. Eléonore herself asked him, but he declined, alleging ill-health. She next suggested Rosily who had sailed with Kerguelen. The government turned instead to an army general, the Baron Milet de Mureau who dropped the nobiliary particle in accordance with the egalitarian mood of the times and became known as Milet-Mureau.

His native town, Toulouse, had sent him to Versailles in 1789 as a member of the States-General. He had worked on numerous committees, displaying a talent for marshalling facts and writing reports. A spell in the artillery with the Army of the Alps sent him to Italy, but his views were suspect, he did not get on with his superiors and he returned to Paris.

Eléonore had still not been paid. Indeed the accounts of the Navy at this stage in France's history when the issue of paper money, the *assignats*, and the cost of the war were causing severe inflation, are far from clear. Notionally, all the families of the men who had disappeared with La Pérouse were to be paid until the d'Entrecasteaux expedition returned. In effect, only occasional grants were made. It was decided that Eléonore would be paid out of the proceeds of the sale of the 1,800 projected copies of the Milet-Mureau book. She was owed 40,000 *livres*: she could receive up to 144,000 if each copy were to be sold at 80 *livres*.

Milet-Mureau's troubles arose from references to the king and to various titles and practices which had vanished when the monarchy was abolished. This was no mere pedantry. Milet-Mureau was worried about his own head. The period later known as the Terror had begun, the guillotine was daily claiming its quota of aristocrats, moderates and out-of-favour politicians, and he had no wish to join them. He wrote to the Navy, which passed the matter on to the Education Committee which referrred it to the Committee for Public Safety whose most prominent member was Robespierre. His punctiliousness was approved, but the Committee had other things on its mind. The months went by; the task was far more time-consuming than he had imagined. Robespierre was overthrown. By 1796 when Milet-Mureau completed his voluminous manuscript, France was being ruled by a Directory, and a young general named Bonaparte was its rising star. The terms which would have angered the more extreme republicans were now acceptable. Milet-Mureau was thanked and went back to the army.

The book appeared in 1797 in three volumes with a great deal of introductory material and a number of notes. It sold poorly and was eventually remaindered.[5] The economic situation was still bad and attention was concentrated on the war. In 1799 Bonaparte overthrew the Directory. Five years later, as Emperor, he signed a decree giving Eléonore a pension of 2,400 francs a month. The relative wealth which the publication of the *Voyage* had intended to provide for her had never materialized. She was granted a grace-and-favour appartment at the château of Vincennes, a bleak place which she disliked, preferring to stay in Paris. She died in genteel poverty on 4 April 1807, at the age of 52.

The La Pérouse expedition was now almost forgotten. There were occasional rumours, garbled reports or straight works of fiction such as the *Découvertes dans la mer du Sud. Nouvelles de M. de la Peyrouse jusqu'en 1794*, published anonymously in Paris in 1795.[6] Those who sailed the Pacific remembered the ships that had vanished, but it was one more mystery of the sea that would probably never be solved.

It fell to an Irishman, Peter Dillon, born in French Martinique of an immigrant from Country Meath, and as Fate would have it in the very year of La Pérouse's disappearance, to discover the vital clue.

After some years in Ireland, Dillon had sailed to India and in time obtained the command of various trading vessels, including the *St Patrick* in which, in 1826, he called at the island of Tikopia, part of the Santa Cruz group. He found a silver sword-guard and learnt from an old sailing companion of his who lived there that the Tikopians knew of other items of European manufacture, such as bolts, axes, knives, spoons and teacups which had come from the neighbouring island of Vanikoro where two large ships had been wrecked 'when the old men now in Tucopia were boys'.[7]

Realizing that here were the first tangible clues to La Pérouse's disappearance, Dillon made for Vanikoro but was prevented from landing by unfavourable winds. He sailed for Calcutta where he called on the British authorities who were sufficiently impressed by his evidence to organize a return voyage. Dillon undertook it in a better ship which was named, appropriately and symbolically, the *Research*. Britain's role in providing help and encouragement was dominant; France was represented on board by Eugène Chaigneau, an unattached French consul; and science by the eccentric Dr Tytler whose manoeuvres during a call in Hobart, Tasmania, almost wrecked the expedition — the experiences of La Pérouse and d'Entrecasteaux with troublesome scientists aboard ship, were once again repeated.

After disengaging himself from Tytler, Dillon sailed to Port Jackson, New Zealand and Tonga. In September 1827 he was back in Tikopia where he bought more relics and obtained from a native he called Rathea the clearest account so far of what had happened in Vanikoro almost 40 years earlier:

> From him I gleaned the following particulars relative to the ships which were wrecked there when he was a boy of about eight or ten years of age. From the natives he learned that the two ships alluded to in his narrative ran on shore in the night on reefs some considerable distance from the land. The one which got on shore near to Whannow was totally lost, and

such of the crew as escaped to land were murdered by the islanders. Their skulls were offered to a deity in a temple where they remained for many years and were seen by many Tucopians. The narrator did not see the skulls himself, but believed they were not mouldered away. The ship which had been wrecked at Paiow, after being on the reef, was driven into a good situation. The crew of these ships consisted of several hundred men. The ship stranded at Paiow was broken up to build a two-masted ship. The people, while employed building the two-masted ship, had a fence built round her of wooden palisading, within which they lived. There were several of the islanders friendly disposed towards them: others were very hostile, and kept up a continual war with the shipwrecked people. When the new vessel was built, all but two of the men embarked in her, and sailed away for their native country, after which they never returned.[8]

Allowance must be made for language difficulties and for faults of memory on the part of Rathea who anyhow had not witnessed these events. In time, divers would help to reconstruct what had happened. For the present, Dillon had enough to confirm that the *Boussole* and the *Astrolabe* had been wrecked on this lonely island and that there were no survivors left alive. He spent a month on Vanikoro, where he bought a ship's bell, part of a plank showing a *fleur-de-lys*, and guns with the maker's identification mark still visible. On 8 October 1827, he sailed for New Zealand and then for Europe.

In Paris the ageing Lesseps tearfully identified the relics. Dillon was the hero of the hour. King Charles X, reminded that his brother Louis XVI had once signed a decree promising 10,000 francs and a pension to whomever discovered the fate of the vanished explorer, gave Peter Dillon the cash grant and an annuity of 4,000 francs, and in addition bestowed on him the rank of *chevalier* of the Legion of Honour.

⊛

Meanwhile, the French captain, Jules-César Dumont d'Urville had also gone to Vanikoro. His voyage of exploration did not have as its central purpose the discovery of his countryman's fate, but like all navigators of the time he had been instructed to keep in mind the possibility of finding clues to the disappearance. When he reached

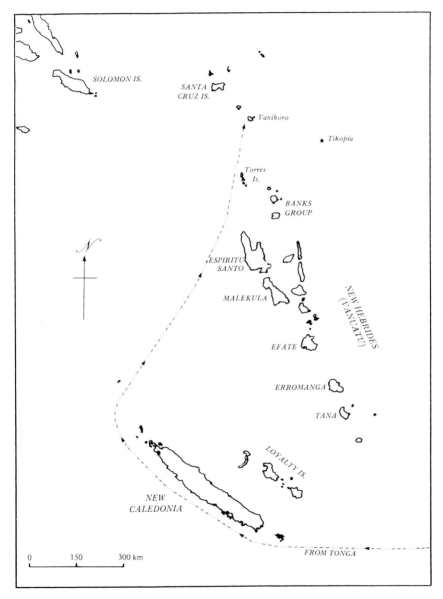

Possible route of the expedition May-June 1788

La Pérouse monument, Albi, showing anchors and guns brought from the wreck site in 1883.

Hobart in December 1827 he learned enough about Dillon's earlier finds to alter his plans and sail without delay for Vanikoro.

D'Urville arrived on 21 February 1928 and remained until 17 March, charting the coastline, questioning the natives as best he could and purchasing more relics. Even more important, he was shown remains of a wreck lying in four metres of water. With great difficulty, since the wreckage was already encrusted in coral growth, the French brought up an anchor of 1,800 lbs, and some guns bearing identification numbers. Unhappily, records of the port of Brest that would enable us to know from which vessel they came are lacking.

And now the first of several memorials was erected on Vanikoro. Using kauri timber from New Zealand, d'Urville built a simple monument with a lead plaque bearing the words: 'To the memory of La Pérouse and his companions in the *Astrolabe* 14 March 1828'.

In June 1828 the ship *Bayonnaise*, commanded by Legoarant de Tromelin, appeared off Vanikoro. She stayed 12 days, collecting little additional information — the islanders could hardly do more than repeat what they had told d'Urville. A few more items were found — a length of chain, a key, a pulley wheel. But Tromelin added a 'medal' to the monument. It was not found again until 1958, by which time the structure d'Urville had erected was smothered by mangroves. It was a bronze ten-centime coin, but not one in current use in Tromelin's day, which was the period of the Restauration when money bore the effigy of Charles X. It was a coin issued some time between 1795 and 1800. Had Tromelin chosen it because it was the oldest he had, the one nearest to La Pérouse's own day, issued at a time when d'Entrecasteaux's companions were still struggling back to France after the collapse of their ill-fated expedition?

Vanikoro fell back into its age-old isolation. No ship, other than infrequent trading schooners called until the centennial of the La Pérouse voyage approached. In 1883, the *Bruat* was sent by the Governor of New Caledonia to look for more remains of the wrecked ships. Three anchors and various guns were brought up after explosives freed them from the growing coral. They were sent to

France and deposited at the foot of the monument which Albi erected to her famous son.

On occasion, a French naval unit called briefly at Vanikoro, but no attempt to recover further relics was made until 1938 when a group of Frenchmen from New Caledonia and the New Hebrides spent a month on the island. The only tangible result was the erection of a metal cross on a part of the reef. In 1959 the ship *Tiaré* set off on a search, but bad weather led to the loss of the diving equipment before any results were achieved.

However, after World War II, the technology of diving operations made great advances. Divers were freed from the need to encase themselves in heavy diving-suits linked with an air tube to the mother ship. With the aqualung they could now swim freely among the reefs and along the sea floor. The expedition of Pierre Anthonioz in 1958 brought to the surface a number of relics, including a large anchor. This again focused attention on the Pacific's most discussed mystery. During 1959 the French sent two ships, the *Rossinante* and the *Tiaré* to Vanikoro with a team of researchers led by the vulcanologist Haroun Tazieff.

The general belief was still that only one wreck had been discovered, that of the *Astrolabe*. It fell to a resident of Port Vila, in the New Hebrides, to discover the site of a second wreck. Reece Discombe, a New Zealander, had made several visits to Vanikoro. In 1962 and 1963 he dived along the reef, exploring the many undersea caverns formed by the coral. A mile along the south wall of the reef he found a trove of objects ranging from guns to small metal weights. The presence of guns ruled out the possibility of the current carrying pieces of wreckage from the site where it was believed the *Astrolabe* had foundered.

France organized three expeditions in 1964 to survey the new site. The first under the Port-Vila Resident Delauney sailed in February in the *Aquitaine*, accompanied by Reece Discombe. In three days, divers brought up a bronze gun, and various small items, the most valuable of which was a metal plaque bearing the name Langlois and the date April 1736. Claude Langlois was more than a noted Paris instrument maker; he was the official supplier of the *Académie des Sciences* and he had provided a quadrant for Lepaute Dagelet who was the *Boussole*'s astronomer.

Unless Dagelet's quadrant had been transferred at some time to the *Astrolabe*, this was evidence that the *Boussole* and the *Astrolabe* had been wrecked close to each other. A later 1964 expedition, under Rear-admiral de Brossard of the *Service historique de la Marine* brought up more evidence that there was a second wreck. A new study of Dillon's reports showed that he had in fact mentioned two sites, but that Dumont d'Urville had overlooked it and created a state of mind in which, for nearly 140 years, people had been allowed to wonder whether the *Boussole* might not have floated off, only to be finally wrecked in some other disaster. The fact is that there are two wrecks and that we cannot be totally certain which is which: allowing for all the elements of uncertainty and the problems of a precise identification of age-old relics, there can today be no doubt that the entire expedition was wrecked during a tropical cyclone on the coral reef of Vanikoro. As if to assist the 1964 searchers to reconstruct the scene, another cyclone struck the island, whipping up the waves into a foaming frenzy, uprooting trees, destroying buildings, and swamping the island with torrential rain.

Notes

1. Letter to Hector and Redon, Brest, in A.N.M., C6 885.
2. M. Delattre, *Rapport sur la recherche à faire de M. de la Pérouse, fait à l'Assemble nationale.*
3. Reported in the 1888 special issue of the *Bulletin de la société de géographie*, pp. 305-6.
4. 'Projet de décret' published in the *Moniteur* of 24 December 1791.
5. 'The edition was handed over at a knock-down price to a bookseller ... Whether it was because the circumstances were unfavourable, or the Voyage itself aroused little interest, or finally that people were generally dissatisfied with the narrative, the fact is that the work did not sell'. Note appended to a report for Napoleon, December 1804. He granted her 2,400 francs a year and she returned 100 unsold copies she had kept. At her death, La Pérouse's

sister, through her husband, tried to get the government to pay the 40,000 *livres*. Sundry letters in A.N.M. C7 165.

6. Plausible enough for an English newspaper to publish a summary of it in 1804 as a factual report.

7. The most complete study on Dillon's career and his role in solving the La Pérouse riddle will be found in J.W. Davidson, *Peter Dillon of Vanikoro*, (1975).

8. Dillon, *Narrative and Successful Result of a Voyage in the South Seas . . . to ascertain the actual fate of La Pérouse's Expedition*, vol. ii, p. 120.

19
Epilogue

'I WILL GO up to the Friendly Islands', La Pérouse had written from Botany Bay in February 1788, 'and I will carefully follow my instructions in respect of New Caledonia, Mendaña's Santa Cruz, the south coast of de Surville's Arsacides, and Bougainville's Louisiades . . . .'

Now that we know he came to grief in the Santa Cruz group, we can reconstruct his route from Botany Bay.

The Friendly Islands are the Tongas to which James Cook had given this name in appreciation of the welcome he received there. The evidence we have that La Pérouse sailed to these islands, presumably in a fairly direct line from Botany Bay, derives from Dumont d'Urville who was in Anamuka, in the Hapai group of the northern Tongas in May 1827. Questioning a local chieftainess:

> I ventured to ask her whether she had seen any vessels between those [of Cook and d'Entrecasteaux]. After some thought she replied none had come to Tongatabu, but shortly before D'Entrecasteaux . . . two ships, similar in appearance and flying a white emblem, had dropped anchor together in Anamuka where she was living with her family. They had stayed ten days and had left one morning, sailing westwards . . . Everything was confirmed by her brother who was present and some five or six years younger than her, and who like her had often visited those vessels.[1]

We can place this stay in early April 1788. La Pérouse's plan was then to sail for New Caledonia; his instructions had suggested that he should follow the latitude of the Isle of Pines.

In 1857, a geologist on a visit to the island learnt of a local tradition concerning two large ships which, some years after James Cook, had stopped off the Isle of Pines and been forced to repel an attack launched against them by the natives:

> Displeased with this savage welcome, the two ships sailed towards the mainland, after firing a gun which the islanders took to be a thunderclap.[2]

This would have taken the two ships along the south coast of New Caledonia. Evidence of their passage remained speculative until recently. The mineralogist Jules Garnier had found an old sword in the hands of a Kanak; the *fleur-de-lys* design showed it to be of the pre-Revolutionary period, but nothing specific linked it to La Pérouse. It could have been stolen from one of the officiers, but there was no local tradition to back this theory. Much the same could be said of a varnished plank found by La Billardière in May 1793. A graphometer found in 1880 near Noumea and manufactured in 1781 was believed to have been lost by D'Entrecasteaux.

However, in 1964, on a further voyage to Vanikoro, divers from the *Dunquerkoise* brought up several rounded green stones which geologists later identified as diabase stones from the Pilou district of northern New Caledonia. They do not exist in other islands visited by La Pérouse. And in 1983, it was ascertained that D'Entrecasteaux had never lost a graphometer, so that the 1781 instrument could only relate to the La Pérouse expedition.

There is thus no reason to doubt that La Pérouse had followed his plan of going to Tonga, thence to southern New Caledonia and on to Santa Cruz, intending after that to veer west for the Solomon Islands and home. Vanikoro, a lonely outpost of the Santa Cruz group, and as yet undiscovered, lay in wait for him. It was probably June 1788 when he reached it.

The location of the wrecks suggests that the *Boussole* and the *Astrolabe* were sailing abreast, a small distance apart, as was their custom. Vanikoro is not a low island — its Mt Kaporo rises to over 900 m. — and the look-outs cannot have failed to see this unknown island rising along the horizon. Here, on the last stage of the voyage, was another discovery. But how could the look-outs fail to see the reef as La Pérouse sailed towards it? He was a seaman of great experience, although we must bear in mind that even James Cook's *Endeavour* had struck on the Great Barrier Reef of Australia. However even at night, reefs issue a warning to approaching sailors, the sound of the breakers clear and unmistakable to seamen's ears. French Frigate Shoals in the mid-Pacific had issued their timely warning. But local traditions, told to Dillon and Dumont d'Urville,

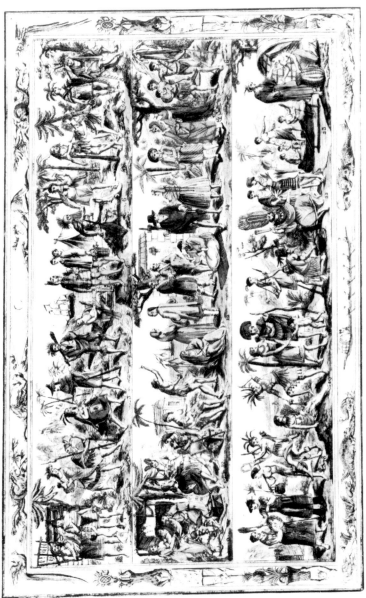

Painting showing the achievements of James Cook and La Pérouse.

(Musée de la Marine.)

From top left:

"1. Habitants de Nootka 2. Habitants de la Zélande 3. Habitants de l'entrée du Prince Guillaume 4. Habitants de l'Ile de Pâques 5. Habitants de la Baye de Norton 6. Habitants des Iles Sandwick 7. Habitants de Tanna 8. Habitants de Sainte Christine 9. Habitants de la Baye de Castries 10. Habitants de la Baye ou Port des Français 11. Habitants de Maouna 12. Habitants de Macao 13. Habitants de la Baye de Langle 14. Habitants de la Conception 15. Habitants de la Baye des Manilles 16. Habitants des Iles Pelew 17. Habitants d'Oonolaska 18. Habitants d'Ulietea 19. Habitants des Iles Marquises 20. Habitants de l'Ile des Amis 21. Habitants de la Nouvelle Calédonie 22. Habitants d'Otaïti 23. Habitants d'Anaamoka 24. Habitants de Hapaée."

all mention a cyclone during the night and are unanimous that the wrecks occurred in the darkness. Tropical cyclones can strike with aweful suddenness and they are rightly feared for their destructiveness.

Some men made it ashore. Much of the wreckage, possibly part of the upper works of one of the broken ships, was washed over the reef into the calmer waters of the lagoon and onto the shore. How soon the islanders attacked the survivors no one can tell; the after-effects of the cyclone were enough to keep both groups busy salvaging their own property for several days. After that, clashes were inevitable. The French established a fortified camp of sorts and started building a boat in which they could sail to safety, probably to the Dutch East Indies. The other possibilities were Guam or the Philippines, or back to New South Wales — a place which, however, they knew offered more risks than the others from the yet untamed Aborigines, to say nothing of the formidable dangers of the Great Barrier Reef.

The task before them was not impossible. A few months after the French attempted to leave Vanikoro — which we can estimate as being December 1788 or early 1789 — William Bligh was set adrift by mutineers in the *Bounty*'s longboat and began an epic journey from near Tonga to Timor, 4,000 miles away.

Although it is clear from native accounts that the French tried to sail away, evidence as to what happened is contradictory. In 1840, the French corvette *Danaide*, visiting Ponape in the eastern Carolines, was told that fifty years earlier a small boat with white men aboard had landed nearby, the men all being killed by the islanders.[3] But Vanikoro traditions, although obscured by the islanders' wish to avoid reprisals or allowing their ancestors to appear in a bad light, suggest that the boat was attacked as it tried to get through the reef and into the open sea. Consistent reports that several survivors were still living on the island in the 1790s, when both D'Entrecasteaux's ships and the British frigate *Pandora* sailed past it, may therefore refer to men who had decided not to risk their lives in the makeshift boat or, more likely, to a handful of survivors from that last attack.

To a considerable extent, the mystery of the lost expedition overshadowed its achievement. A Romantic age seized upon the tragedy, wrote plays, poetry and novels about it — and what had been accomplished was eclipsed. It has been said that the death of James Cook was one of the great dramatic points in Pacific history.[4] Another of these great dramas was the disappearance of La Pérouse and his two frigates with their complements of men, prominent officers and leading scientists, into nothingness. Cook's third voyage was affected in the same way: the events in Hawaii captured the attention of educated Europe and turned people's minds away from what had been achieved during the voyage.

Indeed the parallel between Cook and La Pérouse is worth drawing. France had hoped for someone who could stand close to the man they called 'the incomparable Cook', and in La Pérouse they found their hopes realized even in the tragic end that befell them both. Thus, one can say of La Pérouse, as did Beaglehole of Cook, that:

> he was the genius of the matter of fact. He was profoundly competent in his calling as a seaman. He was absolutely professional in his trade as an explorer. He had, in large part, the sceptical mind: he did not like taking on trust. He was therefore the great dispeller of illusion. He did have imagination, but it was a controlled imagination that could think out a great voyage in terms of what was possible for his own competence. He could think, he could plan, he could reason; he liked to be able to plan clearly for a specific objective. But he liked to be elastic: there was always in his mind, as he planned, the possibility of something more, the parenthesis or addendum, there was also the sense of proportion that made him, more than once, refuse to waste time looking for what he was not sure to find.[5]

There is, of course, the difference of temperament: the man of the warm south and the austere Yorkshireman, the Frenchman who served an absolute king and the Englishman who was guided by the influence wielded by a learned society in a semi-democracy.

The achievements of La Pérouse's expedition are of course diminished by the tragedy of Vanikoro. The vast collections of plants, animals, mineralogical specimens — with a very small exception in the latter group — were destroyed. Many of the charts, of Duché de Vancy's drawings, of the notebooks and diaries, private notes and

Bust of La Pérouse by François Rude (1828).
(Musée de la Marine.)

journals, vanished. The fruit of long months of painstaking work, the collective experiences of a voyage that lasted almost three years, an entire human dimension — all that has been lost.

But at every port of call where the French felt that onward transmission was feasible, they posted letters, reports and journals. These documents lie today in the National Archives in Paris, housed in the former home of the Rohan-Soubise family, a town residence of elegant classical proportions. The most precious of all is La Pérouse's own journal — not his captain's log, admittedly, which vanished with his ship, but his detailed personal narrative, irrational syntax and erratic spelling included.

The expedition swept from the maps rumoured islands which had troubled geographers and sailors alike. It produced a careful survey of the complex North-West Coast of America and the mysterious coasts of distant Tartary. The frigates criss-crossed the Pacific in a breathtaking pattern, verifying latitudes and longitudes, adding their own discoveries — Necker Island, French Frigates Shoals, and in the Samoan group, Savaii, Manono and Apolima — thereby tidying up the map of this vast ocean which was still only emerging from centuries of conjectures and speculation.

The *mémoires* sent back included lengthy reports on Chile, on the fur trade, on the American Indians, the people of Easter Island and of Tartary, on California, Formosa and Manila, taking up over 200 pages of manuscript, plus tables of longitudes and latitudes, bearings and hydrographic information, observations on currents, water temperature and climatic conditions. And there were enough charts and drawings to enable Milet-Mureau to add engravings to the account of the voyage. They enshrine, with the journal, the letters, the scraps of notes and jottings, a world of endeavours, hardships and devotion to the cause of knowledge.

There have been plays and poems, speeches and monuments; there are streets and buildings, mountains, and straits that bear the name of La Pérouse. The real story is written across the great expanse of the Pacific Ocean where, one day in utter loneliness and isolation, it ended.

Notes

1. Dumont d'Urville, *Voyage de la corvette L'Astrolabe*, vol. iv, p. 122.
2. Letter from Bouquet de la Grye in *Bulletin de la société de géographie*, 1858.
3. G. Froment-Guiyesse, *La Pérouse*, p. 154n.
4. J.C. Beaglehole, *The Life of Captain James Cook*, p. 698.
5. Ibid.

Bibliography

ONE can draw on an extensive and growing literature on La Pérouse's 1785-1788 expedition, in addition to the manuscript sources held in the French National Archives in Paris (Marine C165 for his service file and Marine 3JJ 386-390 for the voyage) and in the records of various learned societies and museums. The 1797 account by Milet-Mureau, *Voyage de la Pérouse autour du monde*, has been reprinted in full or abridged versions and in translations through the years. The original documents have now been published in a critical edition, *Le Voyage de Lapérouse 1785-1788* (eds J. Dunmore and M. de Brossard), 2 vols., Paris, 1985. A detailed study of the origins of the expedition will be found in C. Gaziello, *L'Expédition de Lapérouse 1785-1788* (Paris, 1984). Most biographies have tended to concentrate on the voyage and the disappearance of the frigates; broader studies include Brossard, M., *Lapérouse, des combats à la découverte* (Paris, 1978). Allen, E.W. *The Vanishing Frenchman* (New York, 1959), Bellesort, A., *La Pérouse* (Paris, 1926). Froment-Guiyesse, G., *La Pérouse* (Paris, 1947), Maine, R., *Lapérouse* (Paris, 1946), Marcel, G., *La Pérouse* (Paris, 1881), Scott E., *Lapérouse* (Sydney, 1912).

In addition to the foregoing, works consulted and manuscript sources are referred to in the text. The following are either not specifically mentioned or have been of particular or general importance.

CHAPTERS I and II

The occasion of the first centenary produced the invaluable *Bulletin du centenaire* (Paris, 1888), a collection of source material and papers read at the Sorbonne. For the explorer's early life, one is grateful to P.M. Vieules for his *Centenaire de La Pérouse: notice sur la famille et la vie privée du célèbre marin* (Albi, 1888), with a *Supplément* in 1892. On eighteenth century ships and sailors, J. Boudriot's monumental *Le Vaisseau de 74*, (4 vols., Grenoble, 1973-1977) is a unique work of reference. A source additional to those acknowledged in notes is an anonymous *Histoire de l'Ecole navale* (Paris, 1889).

CHAPTERS III and IV

The Seven Years' War has its own literature. I drew on R. Furneaux, *The Seven Years War* (London, 1973), Z.E. Rashed, *The Peace of Paris, 1763* (Liverpool, 1957) and V.T. Harlow, *The Founding of the Second British Empire* (London, 1952) which carries the story of Franco-British rivalry to 1793.

The Battle of Quiberon is examined in Admiral de Brossard's biography of 1978; Montagu Burrows' *Life of Admiral Lord Hawke* (London, 1883), although ageing, gives a different viewpoint. F.P. Renault, *Le Pacte de famille; la politique franco-espagnole de 1760 à 1792* (Paris, 1922) helps one to follow the diplomatic convolutions. On Choiseul, I used E. Daubigny, *Choiseul et la France d'outre-mer après le traité de Paris* (Paris, 1892), and G. Lacour-Gayet, *Choiseul, ministre de la marine* (Paris, 1925). A detailed biography of Ternay, M. Linyer de la Barbée, *Le Chevalier de Ternay*, appeared in Grenoble in 1972.

CHAPTER V

On Franco-English rivalry in the Pacific and the Falklands affair, see J. Dunmore, *French Explorers in the Pacific vol. I* (Oxford, 1965) and J. Goebels, *The Struggle for the Falkland Islands*, (New Haven, 1927). Various works on the French West Indies give a useful picture of a bygone society. F. Girod, *La Vie quotidienne de la société créole: Saint-Dominque au XVIIIe siècle* (Paris, 1972) is full of fascinating sidelights. There are also interesting descriptions in J. Saint-Vil, "Villes et bourges de Saint-Domingue au XVIIIe siècle" in *Cahiers d'outre-mer*, (July-Sept 1978, pp 251-270).

CHAPTER VI

J. Auber, *Histoire de l'océan Indien* (Tananarive, 1955) casts its net wide. For the Ile de France, H.C.M. Austin's resoundingly titled *Sea Fights and Corsairs of the Indian Ocean, being the naval history of Mauritius from 1715 to 1810* (Port-Louis, 1935) is quite useful; A. Toussaint, *Histoire de l'île Maurice* (Paris, 1971) and *Une Cité tropicale: Port-Louis de l'île Maurice* (Paris, 1966) are meticulously researched. C.G. Ducray, *Histoire de la ville de Curepipe* (Port-Louis, 1957) draws one closer into small town life. For visitors and residents such as Commerson, Kerguelen and Marion du Fresne, I have largely relied on my own sources from my *French Explorers in the Pacific vol. I*, (Oxford, 1965). Etienne Taillemitte, *Bougainville et ses compagnons autour du monde 1766-1769* (Paris, 1977) is especially useful on Commerson.

CHAPTER VII

There is an anonymous "La Campagne de Lapérouse dans l'Inde" in *Revue de l'histoire des colonies françaises* (1929, pp. 301-306). Two major studies of French India: G.B. Malleson, *History of the French in India* (2nd ed., Edinburgh, 1909) and S.P. Sen, *The French in India 1763-1816* (Calcutta, 1958) cover the complexities of the period, which were further analysed in a thesis by B.E. Kennedy, "Anglo-French Rivalry in India and the Eastern Seas 1763-1793" (Canberra, 1969).

Bibliography

CHAPTER VIII
The career of Benyowski still awaits treatment by an inspired novelist and an enterprising television-series producer. P.L. Férard, *Benyowski, gentilhomme et roi de fortune* (Paris, 1931) bravely copes with the problem of disentangling fabrication and reality in the life of this extraordinary character.

CHAPTER IX and X
Main sources used were E. Chevalier, *Histoire de la marine française pendant la guerre de l'indépendance américaine* (Paris, 1877) and A.M. de Noailles, *Marines et soldats français pendant la guerre de l'indépendance des Etats-Unis* (Paris, 1903). An extract from La Pérouse's journal of the *Amazone* was published in the *Bulletin du centenaire de la mort de Lapérouse* (Paris, 1888) pp. 238-245. G. Lacour-Gayet, *La Marine militaire de la France sous Louis XVI* (Paris, 1905) deals with changes and problems of the later period. More recent works inspired by the bicentenary pale in readability before Claude Manceron's encylopaedic if anecdotic *Les Hommes de la liberté*, vol. I: *Les Vingt ans du roi 1774-1778*, vol. II: *Le Vent d'Amérique 1778-1782* (Paris, 1972 and 1974).

CHAPTER XI
The earliest English report on the Hudson's Bay raid is the anonymous "Chart of Hudson's Bay, with an Account of the Destruction of the Company's Settlements" which appeared in the *Political Magazine* (London, Nov. 1782) pp. 686-690. An anonymous "Rapport officiel de l'expédition de 1782" was reprinted in the *Revue de Dauphiné et du Vivarais* in 1879 (pp 507ff); Hearne's journals were edited by J.B. Tyrell, *The Journals of Samuel Hearne and Philip Turner* (Toronto, 1934), and another French account, P.B. J. de la Monneraye's "Expedition de la Baie d'Hudson" appeared in the *Bulletin du centenaire* (Paris, 1888) pp. 268-283. More recent sources are R. Glover, "La Pérouse on Hudson Bay" in *The Beaver* (Winnipeg, 1951) pp. 42-46, and "Remarks on the French raids on Churchill and York 1782" in G. Williams (ed.). *Hudson's Bay Miscellany 1670-1870* (Winnipeg, 1975) which contains valuable bibliographical leads. De Langle's role and subsequent association with La Pérouse are detailed in A.A. Kernéis, "Le Chevalier de Langle, ses compagnons de *l'Astrolabe* et de la *Boussole*" in the *Bulletin de la société académique de Brest* (1899-1900) pp. 221-288, and especially in P. Fleuriot de Langle, *La Tragique Expédition de Lapérouse et Langle* (Paris, 1954).

CHAPTER XII
La Pérouse's private life, naturally enough, is touched on indirectly in most studies, but its sad and romantic aspects have been the subject of one book, C. Péru's *Le Mariage de Lapérouse* (Albi, 1947)

CHAPTER XIII

Catherine Gaziello's recent book mentioned earlier deals exhaustively with the preparations for the expedition. Numa Broc, *La Géographie des philosophes, géographes et voyageurs français au XVIIIe siècle* (Lille, 1972) is particularly useful on contemporary attitudes and knowledge. British reactions are contained in O. Browning (ed). *Despatches from Paris 1874-1890*, published by the Royal Historical Society in its Camden series, (III, vol. xvi, London, 1909). For the various participants, I found the following useful: E. Delignières, "Note sur Gaspard Duché de Vancy", *Réunion des sociétés des beaux-arts des départements* (Paris, 1910) pp. 79-90; G. Petit, "Le Chevalier Paul de Lamanon 1752-1787", *Actes du 90e congrès des sociétés savantes* (Nice, 1965) pp. 47-58; Lepaute G.J., *Notice sur la famille Lepaute* (Paris, 1869) and M. Le Paute, "Notice bibliographique sur Le Paute d'Agelet" in the *Bulletin du centenaire*, pp. 293-301; A. Hautier, "Le Père Receveur, aumonier de l'expédition La Pérouse", *Courrier des messageries maritimes* (May-June 1974) pp. 24-34; and, on Monneron, J. Bouchary, *Les Manieurs d'argent à Paris à la fin du XVIIIe siècle* (vol. iii, Paris, 1943) and E. Nicod, "Monneron aîné," *Revue du Vivarais*, (IX, 1896).

CHAPTER XIV

There is a small book by M.M. Dondo on the Hawaiian visit, *La Pérouse in Maui* (Hawaii, 1959) and an unsigned article, "The Alaskan Adventure of Jean Francois Galoup [sic] de La Pérouse" in *Alaska Magazine* (Juneau, 1927) pp. 109-143. The Alaskan episode has been examined from the ethnological side by, among others, E. Gunther, *Indian Life on the Northwest Coast of North America* (Chicago, 1972). G. Chinard's *Le Voyage de Lapérouse sur les côtes de l'Alaska et de la Californie* (Baltimore, 1937) is a valuable early study. H.H. Bancroft's *Alaska 1730-1885* (San Francisco, 1886) is still sound and H.R. Wagner's *The Cartography of the Northwest Coast of America to the year 1800* (Berkeley, 1937) authoritative, but there is now a growing volume of interesting studies about Russian Alaska. Bancroft's *History of California* (San Francisco, 1884) was reprinted in 1963; there are several good studies on the early missions, but C.N. Rudkin, *The First French Expedition to California* (Los Angeles, 1959) is the major local work on La Pérouse.

CHAPTER XV

Two impressive studies on the French in China are H. Cordier, *Le Consulat de France à Canton au XVIIIe siècle* (Leiden, 1908) and L. Dermigny, *La Chine et l'Occident: le commerce à Canton au XVIIIe siècle 1713-1833* (Paris, 1964). On the Russian northern islands, we have J.J. Stephan's excellent *Sakhalin; a history* (Oxford, 1971) and *The Kuril Islands* (Oxford, 1974). Lesseps' *Journal historique* . . . (Paris, 1790) was translated promptly as *Travels in Kamchatka during the years 1787 and 1788* (London, 1790).

Bibliography

CHAPTER XVII

For this section, we have J.F. McKenna, "The Noble Savage in the *Voyage of La Pérouse*", *Kentucky Foreign Language Quarterly* (vol. xii, 1965) pp. 28-37, and R. de Kerallain "La Pérouse à Botany-bay", *La Géographie* (Paris, 1920) pp. 33-48, but more useful are the *Historical Records of Australia*, Series I, and the *Historical Records of New South Wales* vols I (i and ii) and II, as well as the *Voyage of Governor Phillip* (London, 1789), the *Narrative* of W.Tench (London 1789), and his *Complete Account of the Settlement* (London, 1793), White's *Journal of a Voyage* (London, 1790) and Hunter's *Historical Journal* (London, 1793).

CHAPTER XVIII

The disappearance of the ships, the shipwreck and speculation about likely routes after the departure from Botany Bay have attracted a number of authors, many of them adding little to previous ones. For the major expedition sent to search for the frigates, see E.P.E. de Rossel, *Voyage de D'entrecasteaux envoyé à la recherche de La Pérouse* (2 vols, Paris, 1808); for the discovery, see P. Dillon, *Narrative and Successful Result of a Voyage to ascertain the actual fate of La Pérouse's expedition* (2 vols, London, 1829) and J.S.C. Dumont d'Urville, *Voyage de la corvette l'Astrolabe* (5 vols, Paris, 1830-1833); for subsequent investigations, see M. de Brossard, *Rendez-vous avec Lapérouse à Vanikoro* (Paris, 1964), and F. Bellec, "Le Naufrage de l'expédition Lapérouse", *Neptunia* (1983), Nos 149-150 pp. 1-11, 1-14. Admiral de Brossard has concisely summarized the complexities of the Vanikoro affair in 'Disparition et recherche de l'expédition' in our edition of the journals (Paris, 1985). For James Cook, I have used throughout J.C. Beaglehole, *The Life of Captain James Cook* (London, 1974) and his editions of Cook's *Journals*, published by the Hakluyt Society Cambridge, 1955-1969).

Index